12 MILE REMEMBERED
Our Lives Before
They Burned Our Homesteads

~~~~~~

Flooded and Burned Dreams of a
Small Community in British Columbia

ADA DOMKE JARVIS

Order this book online at www.trafford.com
or email orders@trafford.com

Most Trafford titles are also available at major online book retailers.

Designed, Illustrated and Cover Design by Ada Domke Jarvis.

Print information available on the last page.

ISBN: 978-1-4251-6951-0

Trafford rev. 10/22/2018

North America & international
toll-free: 1 888 232 4444 (USA & Canada)
fax: 812 355 4082

DEDICATION

This book is dedicated to loyal family friend,
historian and archiver extraordinaire.
Walter had the foresight to chronicle for posterity
much of Twelve Mile's existence
while others were preoccupied with
meeting life's daily challenges.

Walter Kozek

His input and encouragement kept this project alive.

Ada Domke Jarvis

PREFACE

I took my home in the British Columbia wilderness for granted. But after gaining the perspective that a long life bestows, I came to appreciate the place, people and times that marked my early years. Sadly, the rural community of Twelve Mile ceased to exist in the 1960s when BC Hydro flooded the Columbia Valley south of Revelstoke. The seed of curiosity and nostalgia developed into a full-blown flower of determination to record Twelve Mile's history. The stark contrast between my early pioneer, rural life and the one I now live in Southern California only added to its intrigue.

Uppermost in my "inquiring mind" was, Who were the first settlers and why did they choose Twelve Mile of all places?

Our family and neighbors were poor by today's standards, but were fiercely self-reliant and daring. They survived without electricity or indoor plumbing; and many did not have motor vehicles despite great distances to town and work.

I realized that only one who had lived there during that period of time could adequately portray its spirit and write about it. So began my quest for answers to the many questions.

I feel humbled and privileged to be entrusted with the personal stories and feelings that "co-historians" have shared. Where surviving family members were not located, information was gleaned from friends who remembered them, from archives in Revelstoke and Nakusp, from Internet and from maps. Questionable information was verified or omitted in an attempt to maintain accuracy. *Savoir-faire* prevents me from including certain incidents that happened.

It is human nature to live in the present. Over the years, new experiences and concerns take priority and relegate the past to some remote corner of our minds. Since much of the information provided was from personal memories, the reader must realize that two people recall a shared incident or experience through their individual eyes and interpretation.

Former Twelve Milers with whom I discussed the possibility of writing a history about their home community felt it needed to be done and were excited and supportive of the idea. They have encouraged me with every step of this process and for this I thank each of them.

--Ada Domke Jarvis

INTRODUCTION

This is the place. Stand still, my stead,
Let me review the scene,
And summon from the shadowy Past
The forms that once have been.

Author Unknown

There is a point along Highway 23 between Mulvehill Creek and Blanket Creek where one can view the previous site of the Twelve Mile community. When I go there, the expanse of turquoise water lying below belies Twelve Mile's history, now forever burned, buried and washed away. I try to visualize where my school was, where the ferry was that I crossed every day to get to school, where the road was that I rode my bicycle on past Sutherland Falls to school every day, and where my friends' homes were. It's difficult. My mind wanders.

I envision giant glaciers carving this broad valley in which the Columbia River has flown undisturbed for years, creating a perfect, damp habitat necessary for the growth of huge virgin cedars; its moist western slope climate producing enormous snowfalls in the winter and dependable rainfall the rest of the year; and how it creates rich bottomlands ready for cultivating.

I envision the first wave of pioneers logging off the cedar giants and setting the valley ablaze burning leftover rubbish, and leaving thousands of enormous cedar stumps charred black.

I envision new growth springing up in the burned areas. First fireweed dazzles the landscape with its spiked fuchsia heads. Then raspberries, followed by huckleberries and blueberries in the open spaces. Strawberries follow like strewn rubies, flourishing in the open, sunny patches.

I envision spring carpets of yellow and purple violets, twinberries and Bethlehem stars. At the mountain's edge where springs dribble into rivulets, orange tiger lilies, yellow slide lilies, scarlet Indian paintbrushes, ferns, mosses and grasses take hold.

I envision mountain streams, fed by aquifers from centuries of snow and glacial pack, trickling into creeks that drop into waterfalls on their way to feed the river below. I feel the painful stab of the thorny devil's club with its huge green leaves and cones of showy, red berries that monopolize shady, moist banks. I smell the pungent cow parsnips and smelly skunk cabbage. I wonder how whimsical monkey flowers and elegant lady slippers find places to plant their feet among the rocks and moss.

I envision beaver families building lodges in the backwaters of the river, developing ponds for frogs to gather and fill the evening air with chorus.

I envision stands of cottonwood, birch and aspen in the lower regions protecting tiny cedars, spruce, hemlock and pines taking root. Catching my eye are networks of fragrant, tiny, pink trailing arbutus bells; and blue bells floating at the tops of their thread-like stems.

I envision tasty morels and numerous other mushrooms popping through layers of damp, fallen leaves warmed by spring sun. Later, shaggy manes and meadow mushrooms scatter like golf balls on a fairway.

I envision creatures of all sizes on surrounding slopes and in valleys. Grizzlies, black bears, coyotes, lynx, cougars, deer, elk, moose, porcupines, mink, martens, weasels, skunks, beavers, muskrats, gophers, squirrels, chipmunks, flying squirrels, bats, mice and rats all finding refuge in this place.

I see homesteaders, mostly from central Europe where their families were disrupted by years of war and unrest, also finding a safe, peaceful refuge and final destination here in which to build homes and raise families.

I see my parents, puzzling over where to go, what to take, what to leave, what to sell and what to give away, after over 30 years on their Twelve Mile homestead. I wonder what it was like for all the others who also had to make those decisions. Through two world wars, the Great Depression, relief camps, rationing, prejudice against aliens, and backbreaking land clearing of their homesteads—the hardy, resilient Twelve Milers survived.

I'll find them. I'll get their stories. Their stories deserve to be preserved, albeit their homes are now gone.

The Columbia River Valley at Twelve Mile, looking toward the southwest. (Walter Kozek photo)

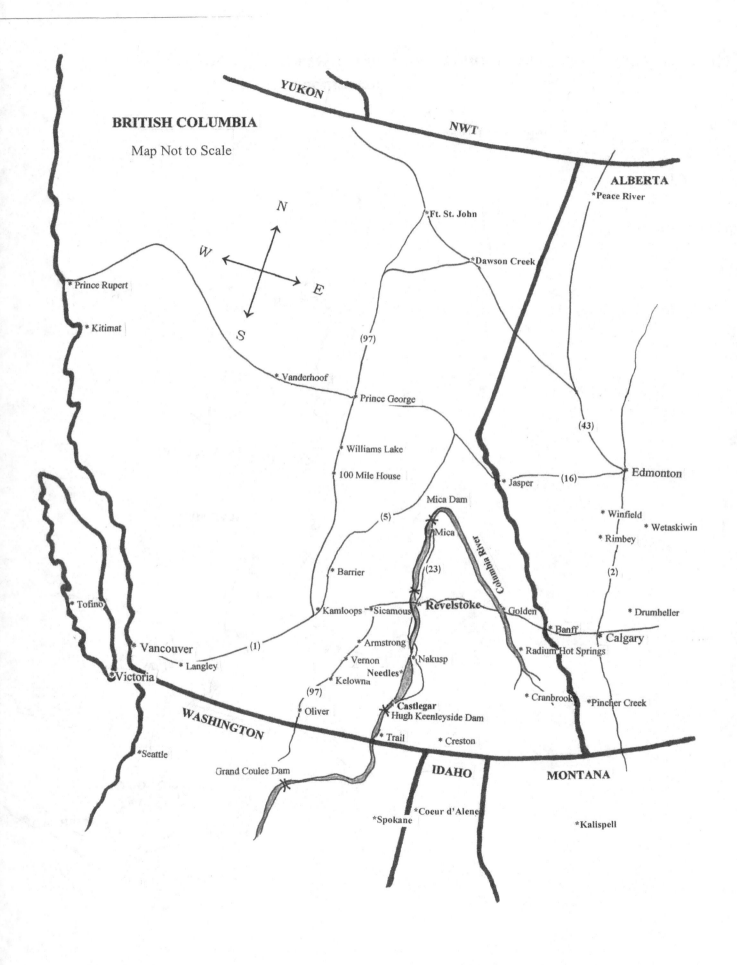

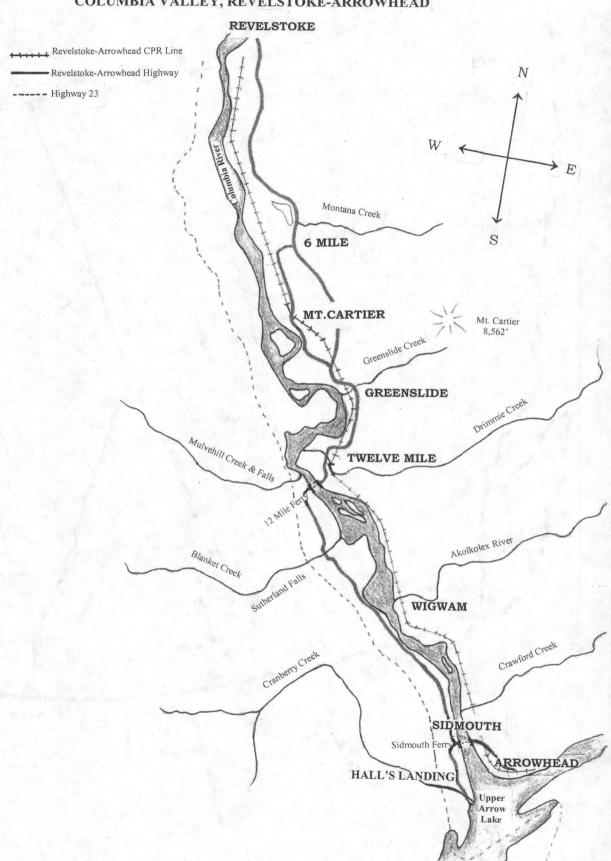

COLUMBIA VALLEY, REVELSTOKE-ARROWHEAD

REVELSTOKE

- ┼┼┼┼┼ Revelstoke-Arrowhead CPR Line
- ───── Revelstoke-Arrowhead Highway
- - - - - Highway 23

N

W ← → E

S

Columbia River

Montana Creek

6 MILE

MT. CARTIER

Mt. Cartier
8,562'

Greenslide Creek

GREENSLIDE

Drimmie Creek

Mulvehill Creek & Falls

TWELVE MILE

12 Mile Ferry

Blanket Creek

Akolkolex River

Sutherland Falls

WIGWAM

Cranberry Creek

Crawford Creek

SIDMOUTH

Sidmouth Ferry

ARROWHEAD

HALL'S LANDING

Upper
Arrow
Lake

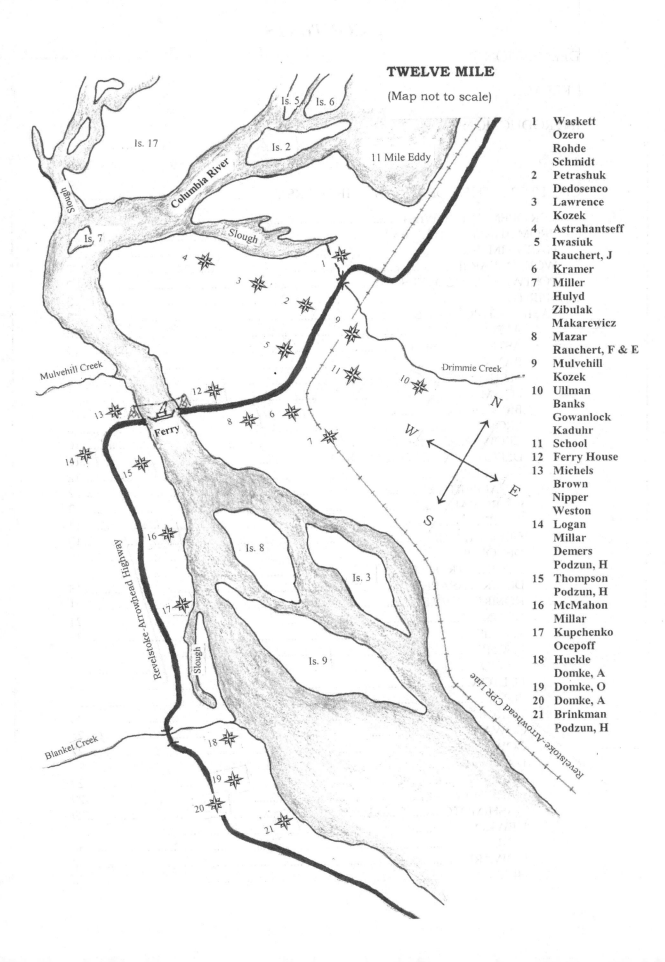

TWELVE MILE

(Map not to scale)

11 Mile Eddy

Columbia River

Is. 17
Is. 5   Is. 6
Is. 2
Slough
Slough
Is. 7
Mulvehill Creek
Drimmie Creek
Ferry
Revelstoke-Arrowhead Highway
Slough
Is. 8
Is. 3
Is. 9
Blanket Creek
Revelstoke-Arrowhead CPR Line

N
W   E
S

1	Waskett
	Ozero
	Rohde
	Schmidt
2	Petrashuk
	Dedosenco
3	Lawrence
	Kozek
4	Astrahantseff
5	Iwasiuk
	Rauchert, J
6	Kramer
7	Miller
	Hulyd
	Zibulak
	Makarewicz
8	Mazar
	Rauchert, F & E
9	Mulvehill
	Kozek
10	Ullman
	Banks
	Gowanlock
	Kaduhr
11	School
12	Ferry House
13	Michels
	Brown
	Nipper
	Weston
14	Logan
	Millar
	Demers
	Podzun, H
15	Thompson
	Podzun, H
16	McMahon
	Millar
17	Kupchenko
	Ocepoff
18	Huckle
	Domke, A
19	Domke, O
20	Domke, A
21	Brinkman
	Podzun, H

CONTENTS

DEDICATION

PREFACE

INTRODUCTION

MAPS

CHAPTER 1: THE COMING OF THE FOLKS 1

   CPR OPENED THE WEST 1
   PROMOTING SETTLEMENT 1
   HARD TIMES 2
   WORLD WAR II 2
   POSTWAR HANGOVERS 2
   SPIRITUAL 3
   FAMILY CHRONICLES 3
      ASTLE 3
      ASTRAHANTSEFF 4
      BANKS 6
      BITTNER 8
      BOHM 8
      BRINKMAN 9
      BROWN 10
      CROWLE 10
      DEDOSENCO (DEDOOSENKO) 11
         HELEN 12
         ALBERT 12
         RONALD 13
      DEMERS 14
      DEVERALL 15
      DEVOLDER 15
      DOMKE, ARTHUR 15
      DOMKE, ASAPH 15
      DOMKE, OSCAR 21
      DUNN 24
      ENGLISH 25
      FISCHER 25
      FLOYD 25
      FULTON 26
      FUNK 26
      GARDINER 26
      GOWAN 26
      GOWANLOCK 27
      HAMPTON 28
      HANSEN 29
      HARRISON 29
      HASHIMOTO 29
      HEWKO 30
      HORSLEY 30
      HOWARD 30
      HUCKLE 30

HULYD 31
IWASIUK 32
JOHNSON 32
JOHNSTONE 32
JONES 32
KADUHR 33
KELLY 36
KERNAGHAN 38
KLAPSTEIN 38
KOZEK 39
   WALTER 41
    STEVE 43
    JOE 44
KRAMER 44
KUPCHENKO (KUPCHANKO) 45
LAMONTAGNE 45
LAWRENCE 45
LINDSAY 46
LOGAN 46
LOZIER 46
LUSCHNAT 46
MACRAE 47
MCINTOSH 47
MCKAY, JACK 47
MCKAY, NELLIE 47
MCKINLEY 48
MCLEOD, CLARENCE 48
MCLEOD, WILLIAM 50
MCMAHON 51
MCQUEEN 51
MAKAREWICZ 51
MANTEI 53
MARAUN 54
MAZAR 55
MICHELS, ALEC 56
MICHELS, HARRY 57
MILLAR 57
MILLER 60
MINION 60
MITCHELL 61
MOBLEY 61
MORGAN 62
MULVEHILL 62
MYERS 63
NASH 63
NELSON 63
NIPPER 63
NORRIS 65
OCEPOFF 66
OZERO 68
PATRIQUIN 68
PETRASHUK (PYTRASHUK) 68
PODZUN, HANS 70
PODZUN, ULLI 73

POFFENBARGER 75
POITRAS 75
RAUCHERT, FERDINAND AND EMIL 75
RAUCHERT, JOHN 78
REVELLE 81
RIBALKIN 81
ROBSON 81
ROHDE 81
ROMANSKY 82
SCHMIDT 83
SHAMON 84
SHEPPARD 85
SHIELL 85
SLYM 86
SMITH 86
STOLLER 86
STORY 86
SUTHERLAND 87
THOMPSON 87
TOWNSEND 89
ULLMAN (ALMEN?) 89
VIGUE 90
WALTERS 91
WESTON 91
WHEATON 92
WHYTE 93
WRAIGHT 93
YINGLING 94
ZIBULAK 94

CHAPTER 2: RAILWAY, HIGHWAY AND FERRY 97

RAILWAY 97
HIGHWAY 97
FERRY 98
FERRY TALES 103

CHAPTER 3: THE LAST COUNTRY SCHOOL OF DISTRICT #19 108

PRE-SCHOOL TIMES 108
SCHOOL ESTABLISHED 108
GETTING TO SCHOOL 110
SCHOOL DAYS 111
HOLIDAY CELEBRATIONS 116
SCHOOL PICNICS AND SPORTS DAYS 116
THE TEACHERS 117
THE TEACHERS 118
THE LAST YEARS 119
HIGH SCHOOL THE HARD WAY 119
REPORT CARDS 121

CHAPTER 4: THE FARMS 123

PRODUCE 123
FARM ANIMALS 123
RAMMED 126
DAIRY FARMING 128

HAYING 129
PRODUCE 131
FORAGING 131
FALL FAIRS 132
SEEDS 132
FARMERS' INSTITUTE 133
COUNTRY BOYS' PRANK 133

CHAPTER 5: LOGGING 135

EARLY LOGGING 135
TWELVE MILE TIMBERMEN 136
TYPES OF TREES LOGGED 139
WEATHER DEPENDENT 142
HAZARDS 142
FINAL DAYS 144

CHAPTER 6: UTILITIES 145

THE MAIL 145
WATER 145
ELECTRICITY 145
RUBBISH 146
RECYCLING 146
TELEPHONE 146
BATHROOM 147
THE HOUSE BEHIND THE HOUSE 148

CHAPTER 7: HOUSEKEEPING 149

LAUNDRY DAY 151
COOKING AND BAKING 153
  DILL PICKLES 153
  SWEET PICKLES 153
  SAUERKRAUT 154
  DILLY GREEN BEANS 154
  POTATO PANCAKES 154
  RUSSIAN BORSCH 155
  VARENIKI 155
  BLINTZES 156
  PADLIFKA 156
  GOLUPTSY (PR. HOLOPSI) CABBAGE ROLLS 156
  HEAD CHEESE (HOLODETS) 157
  CHEESE 157
  POTATO SOUP 157
  EASTER BREAD 158
  LENA'S BREAD 158
  EASTER EGGS 159
  BOOLKA 159
  BLONDE BROWNIES 159
  GERMAN CHEESE CAKE 159
  HUCKLEBERRY BREAKFAST PUFF 160
  HUCKLEBERRY SAUCE 160

CHAPTER 8: WILD ANIMALS 161

TRAPPING AND HUNTING 163

FISHING 165

CHAPTER 9: MOSQUITOES 167

HOW BAD THEY WERE 167

CHAPTER 10: FIRE 169

FOREST FIRES 169
ARSON 170
ACCIDENTS 170
FINAL FIRES 171

CHAPTER 11: PLAY 172

WINTER PLAY 172
THE SNOW TUNNEL 173
INDOOR PLAY 175
SPRING PLAY 175
SUMMER AND FALL PLAY 177

CHAPTER 12: HEALTH AND MEDICAL 180

PUBLIC HEALTH NURSES 180
EPIDEMICS 180
HOME REMEDIES AND BIRTHS 181
DENTAL 182
ACCIDENTS 182
FAMILY ALLOWANCE 182

CHAPTER 13: SPECIAL EVENTS 183

CHRISTMAS CONCERTS 183
OTHER EVENTS 186

CHAPTER 14: BC HYDRO 187

A GRAND PLAN 187
URGENCY 187
SELLING THE PLAN 188
CLEARING THE VALLEY 188
COMPENSATING THOSE DISPLACED 190
UNJUST COMPENSATION FOR THOSE DISPLACED 190
ABOVE THE HIGH WATER MARK 191
THE END OF THE RAILWAY, HIGHWAY AND FERRY 192
REMNANTS STILL VISIBLE 192
OPPORTUNITIES TO RETURN 193
BUY LOW, SELL HIGH 193
MOVING ON 193

SOURCES 194

NOTES 195

NAMES 195

ACKNOWLEDGMENTS 196

ABOUT THE AUTHOR 197

Chapter 1

THE COMING OF THE FOLKS

*The reality of a place lies in
the remembrance of its people.*

Author unknown

Twelve Mile would not have existed without "the folks" who left behind their sweat, and sometimes blood. The first to come to this area along the Columbia River between 12 and 15 miles south of Revelstoke, British Columbia were loggers in the late 1800s. Most left as soon as their jobs were finished, but a few stayed. Next came the homesteaders, most from central Europe. They came to find peaceful, more profitable lives, and property. These folks eagerly accepted Canada's offer of affordable land. For most, it was their first experience of land ownership. Little did they realize they would be caught up in repercussions of WWI and WWII as Canada entered those wars.

CPR OPENED THE WEST

Although the Dominion Lands Act of 1872 was initiated by Canadian parliament to encourage immigration, settlers were unable to take advantage of the free land offered in the west due to lack of transportation. However, when eastern and western Canada were finally linked up in 1885 with the completion of the trans-continental Canadian Pacific Railway (CPR), settlers began pouring in. Its construction required an enormous amount of timber for ties, pilings, bridges, tunnels, trestles, telegraph poles, train stations and hotels which kept loggers, sawmills and pole makers well employed. When the main line was finished, many workers looked elsewhere for jobs. Some used their skills building CPR branch lines being built into mining and logging areas, while others started their own lumber and shingle mills. The CPR line from Revelstoke to Arrowhead was completed in 1895 and opened up the Columbia valley south of Revelstoke for settlement.

PROMOTING SETTLEMENT

After WWI, legislative barriers on immigration were lifted by Canada. A movement began, with the urging of the CPR, to establish an Immigration Policy that would entice a large number of desirable colonists into Canada. Vigorous publicity campaigns followed and Twelve Mile received its first actual settlers. A two-column publicity story appeared in the November 28, 1923 *Revelstoke Review* that read like a pitchman's sales exaggeration under the heading, "Highway to Arrowhead Opens Up Rich Country." It explained that the road being built would soon be completed and surfaced and that hundreds would be enticed to settle on the west side of the river (including Twelve Mile). In addition to the rich alluvial soil which had been logged off and would require minimal clearing, it went on to exaggerate that the district would become "one of the wealthiest and most productive of any in the province," and how valuable and important it would be to the city of Revelstoke. It continued,

At the falls on Gold Creek a beautiful natural camping site is afforded, with fishing and hunting in abundance. In the creek fish up to two feet in length have recently been taken, while up on the hill caribou, deer and bear are plentiful. The falls at

Gold Creek are beyond giving an adequate description of, so magnificent in grandeur are they, and they will become a favorite resort for sightseers and picnickers. On the mountain range at the headwaters of Gold Creek some very rich samples of ore have been found, and in the creek itself rich placer deposits were worked in the early sixties. The new road therefore opens up a new field to the prospector.

The sales pitch must have worked, because people responded.

HARD TIMES

The "Roaring 20s" with its increased economy was shattered by the stock market crash in 1929. The "Hungry 30s" and worldwide depression that followed devastated many a human. The Twelve Milers, whose little farms were already established, were able to grow their own food, but the newcomers had yet to clear land on which to plant gardens. They joined the work forces in the Alberta coal mines or the relief camps building the Big Bend Highway between Golden and Revelstoke. But relief workers were stigmatized by police and upper echelons as being lazy or failures. This ate at their pride and in following years, many men in Twelve Mile refused to use the unemployment system even when logging was slow.

WORLD WAR II

With the Nazi invasion of Poland in 1939 and Canada entering WWII, the depression ended, and industries, mills and mines began operating again to meet the demands for war supplies. Even though they were Canadian citizens, those of German descent were treated with suspect. They were required to give up their rifles and register with the authorities on a weekly basis, which was a great injustice. Twelve Mile youth serving their country included Jack Kelly, Douglas Kelly, Kenneth Kelly, Nordy Kelly, Chris Kelly, Joan Kelly, Sharry Kelly, Pat Kelly, Robyn Kelly, Walter Kozek, Mack Mazar, Pete Ocepoff, Betty Petrashuk and Jack Petrashuk.

This was a time of gasoline rationing for general use, but farmers were allowed more. Foods and liquor were also rationed. Evelyn Domke remembers that "we shared our ration coupons with others because we had our own meat." She also remembers using Fruit Keep instead of rationed sugar to preserve canned fruit. When they used the fruit they sweetened it with what sugar they could spare. Since the war effort needed all the rubber it could get, rubber boots, vehicle and bicycle tires were patched and re-patched, and buttons replaced elastic waists on underwear.

When word came over their battery-operated radios about "blackouts," the children of Twelve Mile asked their parents what that meant? Having no electricity, they were always blacked out. In the summer, it was even darker from the burning mosquito powder indoors and smudge pots outdoors.

Twelve Milers held benefit parties, drawings and dances to help the Red Cross that sent weekly packages to the prisoners in the 28 camps in Germany imprisoning British Columbia soldiers. To supplement the prisoners' meager diets, the packages included "milk, butter, cheese, meats, fish, raisins, dried apples, prunes, sugar, jam, Pilot biscuits, eating chocolate, salt and pepper, tea and soap" according to July 27, 1944 *Revelstoke Review*.

POSTWAR HANGOVERS

In the aftermath of WWII, Twelve Milers along with their countrymen again experienced insecurity. They were warned not to pick up Japanese balloons sent over the Pacific. Families lost track of their loved ones in Europe. The *Revelstoke Review* of July 4, 1946 notified the public that the Canadian Red Cross was "designated by the Canadian government as the National Tracing Bureau for Canada for persons seeking the whereabouts of lost members of their families dispersed during hostilities." The Domkes located many of their family members through the Red Cross and began sponsoring them to Canada in 1949. The Canadian National Committee on Refugees reported in 1947 that there were about a million Displaced Persons living in Germany who survived Hitler's slave labor concentration camps. Canadians were urged to give these people a chance to work and become Canadian citizens. They included Baltics, Poles, Jews and Yugoslavs who did not want to stay in Germany or return to their former places of residence, according to the May 15, 1947 *Revelstoke Review*.

SPIRITUAL

Since Twelve Mile was a community with only the school in common with everyone, there was no store, no post office, and no church. Families practiced their faiths in their homes with friends and relatives, or went to special services in Mt. Cartier or Revelstoke. The school day always began with the reading of Scripture and the recitation of the Lord's Prayer by teacher and students.

Ferdinand, John and Emil Rauchert were the prime movers in reactivating the Lutheran Church of the Resurrection in Revelstoke. When Carolyn Rauchert remembers attending that early church in the 1950s, she smiles as she says, "The congregation was mostly made up of old German people. We always had to be on our best behavior or they would all scowl at us. At Christmas time we learned the hymns in German and that seemed to please them."

Several other families such as the Kaduhrs, Bohms, Schmidts and Rohdes also drove to Revelstoke to attend Lutheran services. In 1963 Walter Kozek joined and served as its treasurer for more than 37 years.

In the summer, the Nipper girls and others of the Catholic faith attended catechism classes in Revelstoke, before being confirmed.

The Domkes studied the Bible with their children at home and attended services in Revelstoke whenever a Seventh-day Adventist minister came to town. Evelyn remembers having "church under the apple trees with mom teaching us from the Bible."

Mike and Nettie Kozek were brought up in the Greek Orthodox Church. They occasionally attended St. Anne's Church at Eight Mile, but none of their children were baptized there.

In 1939 Lois, Audrey and Jim Millar were baptized in the school by the Anglican minister from Revelstoke. "Mom took cookies to quiet Jim during the service so Audrey and I nicknamed them 'holy cookies'," remembers Lois. Their father listened to Catholic midnight mass on the radio

Lois Millar remembered attending Vacation Bible School for two weeks one summer in the schoolhouse, directed by two young missionary ladies. She thought the games and contests were a lot of fun. In the summer of 1948 Miss Phyllis Day of Victoria held Sunday School in the school house.

FAMILY CHRONICLES

Chronicled below are the stories of the folks of Twelve Mile who worked the land, forest and other jobs in order to make a living for themselves and their families. Included also will be those who taught at the school, and those who lived elsewhere but sent their children to Twelve Mile School. Information about some of the families could not be located, and for this the author apologizes.

ASTLE

Three Astle brothers from Winfield, Alberta logged for John Rauchert on Mt. Cartier in 1947. Bill, his wife and son, Wayne, returned to Alberta when logging closed for the winter. They returned in

1948 to continue working for John. Joe and his wife also returned to Alberta during the winter shut down.

ASTRAHANTSEFF

Gregory Astrahantseff, circa 1918. (Astrahantseff family photo)

Gregory Astrahantseff was born and educated in Russia. He worked in civil engineering surveying and building irrigation systems. During the Russian Revolution, he rode with the Cossacks. When the Czar was deposed in the Revolution of 1921, Gregory left for his own safety in 1923. He lived in Kazakstan, then escaped into China and headed for Canada by way of Vladivostok, landing in Vancouver. He farmed for several years in Edgewater, B.C. near Asaph Domke, and then moved to Twelve Mile in the early 1930s. He homesteaded the property between Kozeks and the river and later added 20 more acres to his farm. He built a log house, barn and dug a well—all by hand.

When he started teaching Russian to the children of Russian descent in southern B.C., he met and married Polly Rosinkin of Crestova in 1937. Polly was born in Yorkton, Saskatchewan, to John and Anna Rosinkin. Anna was born in Russia and followed the Doukhobor faith. When they were persecuted by the Soviets, the Canadian government offered the sect freedom and land in Saskatchewan. The Rosinkin family moved on to southern British Columbia's Crescent Valley. Polly's first husbanddied, leaving her with daughter, Marie, who was about eight years old, when Polly and Gregory married. They had two sons: Olympe born in 1938 and Sergei born in 1941.

On their farm, Gregory and Polly had two to three cows, a couple of horses, ducks, geese, rabbits, chickens and hogs. These animals kept them in meat, milk, butter, cheese, and feathers for pillows and comforters. They grew fields of raspberries and hired some of the local young people as pickers. The crates of berries were shipped by rail to Calgary.

Every year they cleared more land. With horse-drawn wagon or sleigh, Gregory picked up from Revelstoke his orders of dynamite used to clear the stumps. Olympe thinks the farmers were given a subsidy by the government of perhaps $2 on each $10 box to encourage land clearing.

Gregory taught his sons how to figure the number of sticks of stumping powder necessary to blast out certain size stumps. They would set it up, light the fuse, run off and hide behind a big tree or stump and wait for the "boom." Olympe recalls "roots and chunks of stumps went flying everywhere." Every year they cleared some new land in this manner to be ready for planting their potato crop at the end of June. Potatoes always grew best on new land and they raised hundreds of sacks full every year. Some they sold in town for about $3 a 100-pound sack and others they shipped in railcars from the Twelve Mile siding.

Astrahantseff's first log house. Note laundry on front porch. (Astrahantseff family photo)

In 1946 the Astrahantseffs took advantage of a government-sponsored program to clear land

Gregory, Polly, Marie, Olympe and Sergei Astrahantseff. (Astrahantseff family photo)

for the farmers. The caterpillar fees charged were: "over 90 DBHP, $9.00/hour; 70-90 DBHP, $7.50/hr; 45-70 DBHP, $6.50/hour; 30-45 DBHP, $5.00/hour." (*Revelstoke Review*, April 4, 1946). But they and other farmers "were not satisfied with the job that was done because the men operating the bulldozers (cats) pushed much of the topsoil into the huge piles of trees, stumps and roots, leaving them impossible to burn until they tediously tore apart the piles to separated out the soil," recounts Olympe. The ladies had to cook the meals for the cat operators, and the men slept in the bunkhouse that they pulled with them. To get their cats to the McLeod farm, they built a road from Banks' place, past Echo Lake, and on to Wigwam. The Astrahantseffs later hired Mr. McKenzie of McKenzie Trucking Co. to clear more land, and were satisfied with his work.

Like so many others in the area, for extra cash income, Gregory logged in various areas including Beaver Mouth, Big Bend, and in the south valley for Columbia River Timbers (CRT). He worked in various sawmills, in maintenance for the Highways Department, and fought forest fires. While with the relief workers during the Depression, his civil engineering experience came in handy building the road and bridges of the Big Bend Highway. Polly worked for several years in Revelstoke including Lena's Café, returning home on her days off. They also sold wagonloads of blackened stumps called "brewery wood" to Revelstoke Enterprise Brewery. The boys also picked up beer bottles along the road and recycled them at the Brewery for two cents each.

Polly and Gregory were both good cooks. He was known for his crescent-shaped vareniki filled with ground beef and boiled in soup. She was known for her raspberry pastries made with fresh cream, and for the special Doukhobor-style borsch, pickles, sauerkraut with pickled apples, and home made bread. They often shared their abundantly-laid table with neighbors from Twelve Mile and Eight Mile.

Being practical in all areas, they rendered down large vats of fat to make their own laundry soap. They also kept their own bees. Carolyn Rauchert remembers the honeycomb frames hanging on the walls in the cool pump house where they sorted the berries they picked for shipping. The scent of the raspberries, beeswax and honey lingered with her through the years. This is also where the big crock of wine was stored and sometimes the older kids would sample it.

Polly, her mother Anna who lived with them part of the time, and Marie all were proficient in handcrafts. Polly spun yarn on her spinning wheel, knitted socks and sweaters for her family and wove rag rugs on her loom. In 1950 she displayed her woven wool cloth at the Revelstoke Hobby Show. Marie displayed her beautiful solid embroidery on a tea cloth, traycloth and cushion top. Anna's many handcrafts included cute, knitted, life-like poodles.

Marie and Bill Popoff, Shoreacres, B.C. (Astrahantseff family photo)

Gregory didn't own a motor vehicle until 1954. For years, he used his horse and wagon for hauling supplies to and from town. At times he and his family would catch rides with neighbors. Their 1948 Jeep came in handy when Olympe and Sergei had to meet the bus at Greenslide in order to go to high school in Revelstoke in the winter. In the summer they rode their bikes to Greenslide to meet the bus.

Marie finished eighth grade at Twelve Mile and went on to work in Revelstoke before moving to Shoreacres, B.C. There she married Bill Popoff. They raised one adopted son. Marie passed away in 1997.

Olympe finished grade 12 at Revelstoke High School and worked for the Highways Department on the Big Bend construction crew, as well as the surveying crews on the Rogers Pass from 1958-62. In addition, he worked with the Federal survey crews on Mount Revelstoke and various highway interchanges. He also started his own business contracting with the City of Revelstoke for garbage pick-up for about seven years, and also contracted earthwork. In 1980 he began working on the Shelter Bay ferry as a deck hand, progressed to oiler and within five years qualified for, and passed the engineer's exam. This was his work until his 2003 retirement.

Olympe married Joan Reedman from Kamloops on July 18, 1959 in the Revelstoke United Church and celebrated their wedding reception in the Twelve Mile School, which by then had been turned into a community hall.

Olympe Astrahantseff on CPR tracks in Twelve Mile. Note siding tracks. (Astrahantseff family photo)

They have eight children including four whom they adopted, plus many other children they fostered through the years from the early 1960s until the present. Being retired gives Olympe time to pursue his hobbies that include acting in plays put on by the drama group in Revelstoke.

Sergei attended Revelstoke High School through grade 10 and then logged in the Revelstoke area. He married Lillian Skiboff from Shoreacres and they have three sons. In 2005 Sergei passed away.

Sergei Astrahantseff, circa 1955. (Astrahantseff family photo)

When BC Hydro bought them out in 1964-65, Gregory and Polly moved to Enderby where they purchased a small, four-acre farm. When Gregory died in 1967, Polly moved to Castlegar and lived out her years with Marie. She passed away in 1976.

BANKS

Cecil Banks moved from Nova Scotia to Alberta around 1935. He worked in logging and farming in the Wainwright, Hoadley, Winfield and Bluffton areas. While in Winfield, he met his future wife, Lucy Glanfield.

Frederick and Isabel Glanfield and their children, Lucy, Ruth, Peggy, and Fred, emigrated from Winmarleigh, Lancashire, England in 1929. They landed in Montreal after a long and tiring ship voyage and then caught the train to Winfield, Alberta. Lucy, who was just nine years old at the time, was the eldest child.

Cecil and Lucy married in 1940 in the new little church in Hoadley, the church's first wedding! In 1941, their baby girl, Dorothy, who was born in Wetaskiwin, had the distinction of being the second baby christened in the Hoadley Church.

The family suffered two tragedies in 1943. Lucy's father, Frederick, became ill and passed away while stationed in the Canadian army in Ontario. Then Lucy delivered stillborn infant, Leona, who is buried in Hoadley.

Dorothy, Lucy and Cecil Banks. (Banks family photo)

Soon after this, they moved to Twelve Mile, B.C. where Lucy's sister and her husband, Ruth and John Rauchert, had moved the previous year. Cecil and Lucy purchased John Ullman's (Almen?) property on Drimmie Creek. They made the little one-room log cabin with an attic into a cozy home. Their son, Douglas, was born in 1944.

Cecil was very much a "mountain man," trapping, hunting and logging. Lucy was left at home with the children much of the time while her husband was working away from home. A story in the December 6, 1945 *Revelstoke Review* assured everyone that Lucy was a typical pioneer woman that could protect her family. It read, "Another cougar was killed in this district by Mrs. Cecil Banks of 12-Mile South."

In 1946 they sold their farm to the Kaduhrs and Gowanlocks and took a three-month holiday to visit Cecil's family still in Nova Scotia. When they returned, they made their home in Salmon Arm, where Cecil was the night watchman at the nearby mill. In 1949-50 Lucy's brother from Alberta, Oliver, lived with them for a year while attending school.

1950 was another year of change for the family. Daughter Penelope Gail (Pennie) was born in April, and in June they moved to another little one-room cabin in Three Valley. Dorothy and Douglas were bussed to school in Malakwa for the next three years. In order to have enough students to warrant the bus picking them up, Douglas had to start school when only four and a half years old.

In 1953, Cecil and Lucy moved back to the Revelstoke area where they purchased a home four miles south of town. The three children all attended school in Revelstoke with Dorothy and Doug both graduating from Revelstoke High School.

When BC Hydro bought them out in 1965, they moved to Burns Lake, B.C. where Pennie finished high school. They resided there until 1986 when ill health became an issue and they returned to Revelstoke.

Cecil passed away in Queen Victoria Hospital in 1989 of emphysema. Lucy lived in Moberly Manor, and Queen Victoria Hospital where she passed away March 17, 2001.

Dorothy married Tom Young, an army veteran from Sidmouth, in 1960. They had three children:

Kandice married and has two sons, Nicholas and Christopher, all living in Revelstoke.

Keith died in 1982.

Kevin and wife, Sherilyne, have two children, Zachery and Bethany. They live in Tofino, B.C.

Dorothy remarried Don Pegues who works for initial attack in forestry. Dorothy began in 1981 working as a pharmacy tech, first at Donaldson's Drug that became Pharmasave in Revelstoke.

Following high school, Douglas served in the Air Force. He then became a bush pilot on Vancouver Island. While recovering from very serious burns

Pennie, Doug and Dorothy Banks. (Banks family photo)

suffered in a plane crash, he met and married Phylis. They moved to Tofino in 1969 where Doug and partner, Gary Richards, formed an air transport company consisting of float planes that they operated for over 20 years. Although Doug "retired," he still flies for the company's new owners. Doug and Phylis have two children: Kathy, married, and has two girls, Erin and Cassidy; Dan, married, and has a son, Riley.

Pennie moved to Burns Lake with her parents in 1965 where she completed high school. She and Albert Patterson married and have three children: Curtis has a son, Rylan, and lives in Burns Lake; Clifford has one son, Cole, and lives in Prince George; and Carren has three sons, Kyle, Lorne and Alan. She lives in Burns Lake.

Pennie remarried in 1983 to Ken Jones and has two stepsons, Dale and Brian. Over the years, Pennie worked at a variety of jobs, but the two she enjoyed the most were marriage commissioner and auctioneering. As her family puts it, Pennie has the "gift of gab" and was a very good auctioneer, working many including the annual Ducks Unlimited Auction. Sadly, she had to resign both positions because multiple sclerosis confines her to a wheelchair.

BITTNER

Heinrich (Henry) Bittner was born March 18, 1929 in Reichenau, Germany and emigrated to Canada in the 1950s. His family members were displaced and lost their farm in Poland when WWII broke out.

Heidi, Henry, Regina, Reinie and Edith Bittner. (Bittner family photo)

Henry was a trained butcher, and found work on Oscar Domke's farm and in logging in the Twelve Mile area. After a year and a half, Henry sent for his sweetheart, Adelheid (Heidi) from Mauschdorf, Germany and they were married a few days after she arrived. His German friends put together a lovely festive wedding party for the young couple.

At first they lived in Tony Ambil's log house below the ski hill. There they gave life to two daughters, Regina and Edith and a son, Reinhard (Reinie). Later they moved into their Revelstoke home on the corner of First Street and Pearson. Their three children are:

Regina and husband, Sigi Rothbart, live in Kamloops and have two children, Torsten and Emily.

Edith and husband, Mike Urso, live in Spokane, Washington and have two daughters, Lindsay and Brittany.

Reinie and wife, Rhonda, live in Revelstoke. They have two children, Jocelyn and Keyon.

Heidi passed away in 1986 of a brain tumor, and Henry passed away in 2005 of kidney cancer.

BOHM

Albert and Martha Bohm with daughters, Irma and Ellie, emigrated from Germany to Lethbridge, Alberta in 1954 where they worked on a sugar beet farm. That November they moved to Revelstoke, B.C. where they built their first home in the Big Eddy area. While there, their son, Waldemar (Wally) was born February 1955. Later that year, they moved to Twelve Mile and rented Oscar Domke's farm for about a year.

Irma and Ellie attended Twelve Mile School in grades five and seven. In 1956 the family moved to their home a few miles south of Revelstoke where they lived until moving to Bolton, Ontario in 1967.

Irma married Dieter Kaercher, a sheet metal worker and foreman. Irma was a stay-at-home mom raising their three daughters: Linda, Janet and Laura. They are retired and continue living in Bolton, Ontario. Janet has her own hairdressing business on Vancouver Island where she lives with her husband, Dan. Linda and Laura live near Irma and Dieter and each have two children.

Ellie, Wally and Irma Bohm. (O. Bernard photo)

Ellie lives in Orleans, Ontario near Ottawa.

Wally lived in Bolton and has two daughters and two grandchildren. He died in 2004 at age 49 years.

Martha died in 2001 and Albert died in 2003.

BRINKMAN

Bob Brinkman's house. (U. Podzun photo)

Robert (Bob) Brinkman moved to British Columbia from Manitoba before 1932 following a family dispute. He lived in Arrowhead for a short time before moving to the Twelve Mile area. He homesteaded three miles south of the ferry, his nearest neighbors being the Domkes. At first he built a log cabin above the creek, and then a two-story frame house with four rooms. Bob always lived alone. Although his brother came to visit a couple of times, the brotherly feud between them continued.

Bob was accomplished in many areas. In 1932 he was elected trustee of the Arrowhead School District. Not only did he have his own orchard of apples and other fruits, he had an apiary and liked to tell stories of how different hives had different characteristics. He traded honey to his neighbors (Millars and Domkes) for dairy products. Lois said "it was wonderful to have the honey during the sugar rationing in WWII." Ada Domke remembers the blue and white honey pails he filled with the honey he extracted himself, and shipped it to market.

His main source of income came from his trap line that ran across the west side of the Columbia River in the Cranberry area. He was gone for weeks at a time, tramping through the snow on snowshoes and staying in one of his two trapper's cabins. The neighbor kids were fascinated by the mink, marten, weasel and fox pelts drying on stretcher boards above his fireplace. As he sat in his rocking chair, smoking his ever-present cigarette hand rolled from Ogden's fine cut tobacco, he figured out how much money all those furs would bring him. After a good fur sale, he kept exclaiming, "Goodness gracious! What am I going to do with all this money." "Great Scott" was another of his favourite expletives. He was very informative, loved to visit and tell stories while he stirred—and stirred-- the six or seven spoonfuls of sugar he always put in his coffee. Bruce Kaduhr remembers the ballpoint pen Bob had, being so impressed that it didn't have to be dipped in ink repeatedly.

The Domkes were often recipients of fresh wild game from his hunting trips such as venison, goat and grouse. He shared bear grease with others to waterproof their logging boots.

One year he cut and peeled the cedar trees on his property into poles and had Oscar and Ben Domke skid them out with their horses. Ben still remembers how frustrated they all were in having to resize every pole because Bob had used a cotton tape to measure them, and unknown to him, the tape had shrunk. At times he sold firewood to the Twelve Mile School that he had Ben Domke haul with his truck.

One time a messenger pigeon perched on his shed next to the house. It had battled bad weather and was very tired. Bob let it rest there and after two to three days of recovery, it was on its way carrying a message clipped to one leg.

Being a bachelor, he learned to cook and bake. Every August his bread would mould over night. This puzzled him and as he ran down all the possibilities, he concluded it may have had something to do with his bees. Evelyn Domke remembers the time he invited her family for Christmas dinner. He began planning it in October. "We are going to have goose and fried potatoes with green onions. I will dig under the snow and get the green onions for the potatoes."

In 1949 Bob came down with throat cancer, followed by surgery in 1950 in Vancouver. He came back with a tracheostomy in his throat and ostomy in his stomach. The bandana he routinely wore around his neck now had the added purpose of covering the tracheostomy opening. Not owning a vehicle, Bob flagged down Ben Domke in his flatbed truck, and gave him money to buy a bottle of Australian "Emo" brandy. When Ben brought it back, Bob invited him in to eat. He took some home-canned strawberry juice, mixed it with "Emo," and poured it down a funnel in the hole in his stomach. He never tried to hide his problems from his friends. When he could no longer swallow food and his health began deteriorating, he sold his trap line to Ben, and his farm to the Ule Podzuns in 1954. He continued living in his original log cabin for a while and then asked Ben to put him on the train so he could die at his brother's home in Manitoba. Ben shipped his belongings to him. His brother told him that the train trip took its toll on Bob and he soon died.

BROWN

George Brown lived in the log cabin on the northwest bank above the ferry landing, later to be bought by Nippers. He lived there at least between 1937-44, as remembered by the Millars, his neighbors. He was an old bachelor gentleman and a great friend to the Millar children. Lois and Jim were fascinated by his method of dying Easter eggs with them, using onion skins and beets. When they moved, Ken was thrilled with Mr. Brown's gift to him of his fishing rod and rowboat, that Ken continued to enjoy for many years.

CROWLE

Sam Crowle and Emma Otte first met in Blue River, B.C., married in Revelstoke in 1946, and moved back to Blue River for a while. Sam's great-uncle, Sam D. Crowle, Sr. was one of the first pioneer ranchers in the Revelstoke area on the property where the current airport exists. He helped found the first school in Revelstoke.

In 1957 Sam and Emma traded their home in Revelstoke for Laboda's farm at Eight Mile and moved their family there. Sam worked in the logging industry and for Jim McKinnon's dairy farm.

When the school district began bus service to Twelve Mile in the fall of 1959, the Crowle children were among those who were bussed. They were transferred to Mountain View School in Revelstoke when they reached seventh grade.

In 1964, Emma and the children left Sam and moved to Fort St. John, B.C. There Emma worked as a camp cook, met Fred Wood and they married in 1970. She is currently retired in Canoe, B.C.

Their farm was bought out by BC Hydro in the 1960s. Sam moved to Revelstoke and passed away in 1990.

Sam and Emma have three children.

Nellie, David, Emma and John Crowle, 1990.
(Crowle family photo)

David was born in 1947. Most of his employment was in the trucking and oil patch work. Following surgery to remove a large brain tumor, he passed away in 1995 leaving two sons, Roger and Denny.

Nellie was born in 1948. She and her husband, Adam Auger, established a variety store in 1980 in Wabasca, Alberta, where they sell groceries, gas, furniture, hardware, appliances and more. They also own rental properties in various places. Nellie and Adam have five children, 20 grandchildren and three great-grandchildren.

Samuel John (John) has worked for years in the oil patch areas of Ft. St. John and Grand Pairie, and currently works in the trucking industry. His children are John Charles, Shane and Jody. They have given him eight grandchildren.

DEDOSENCO (DEDOOSENKO)

Meta and Rose Dedosenco,
Wedding 1934.
(Dedosenco family photo)

Demitry (Meta) Dedosenco and his father, John, operated the Dedosenco-McCormick sawmill at Eight Mile near Twelve Mile. They became friends of Mike and Mary Petrashuk and their daughter, Rosalie (Rose), of Twelve Mile while Mike worked for the mill. Meta and Rose married May 22, 1934 at the home of Mrs. Wickens who lived on CPR Hill in Revelstoke. They moved to Galena Bay where the Dedosencos had homesteaded and eventually obtained 500 acres.

Meta's parents, John and Christina, had an eventful life prior to moving to Canada. John was an official in the Imperial Guard of the summer palace at Livadia, Yalta, in Russia. He was the horticulturist for Czar Nicholas II and Czarina Alexandra at the palace. His wife Christina's family was also associated with the royal family. Due to problems between John and a Turkish admirer of John's sister, Czar Nicholas ordered the families to England where they were guests of the former Grand Duke Alexander and Elizabeth Romanov. Demitry (Meta) was born in 1898 in Crimea, Russia. Alistasia (Alice) was born in 1900. The rest of their children were born after they moved to Canada: Elizabeth, Annie, Violet and Helen. They first lived in Winnipeg, Manitoba before moving to Arrowhead in 1906, then Galena Bay, B.C. on the Arrow Lakes. John homesteaded and logged, eventually operating the Eight Mile sawmill with McCormick. John passed away on January 20, 1934 and Christina died in 1962 at age 84.

Alice had four children: Tiny, Evelynne (Rusenstrom), Lennard and Billy. Elizabeth moved to Yakima, Washington and had no children. Annie had a son. Violet, born in 1911, had no children. Helen, born in 1912, had two girls: Heather and Fern. She was an artist and contracted polio.

In addition to operating the sawmill with his father, John, Meta logged, trapped, raised bees, prospected, mined and worked on the Arrow Lakes.

Meta and Rose had three children while living in Galena Bay: Helen, born in 1936, in Galena Bay; Albert Dimitry, born in 1939, in Revelstoke; and Ronald Mathew (Ronnie), born in 1941, in Galena Bay. The children were able to attend the lower grades of school in Galena Bay, but for the higher grades Helen was sent to school in Arrowhead, and later to White Rock where she lived with her aunt,

Betty, while finishing high school. In July 1951 the Dedosencos moved to Twelve Mile where they lived with Rose's parents, the Petrashuks, so Albert and Ronnie could finish their elementary grades at Twelve Mile School.

While the family was living in Twelve Mile, Meta died of a heart attack on September 11, 1951. At the time, he was prospecting in the Pingston Creek mountainous area, above the west side of the Arrow Lakes. Just previous to this trip he had cut his foot while beach combing for logs and his foot became infected and was treated with antibiotics. The family has always wondered if this contributed to his heart attack. It was a sad day when Albert and Ronnie were called out of class to be given the tragic news about their dad.

Rose and the boys continued to live with the Petrashuks and Rose became the school's janitor. For their high school education in Revelstoke, the boys had to ride their bikes or catch rides to meet the bus at Greenslide. With the difficulty they had getting to school, Albert left after grade 10 and Ronnie left during grade 9. Through the years, however, Ronnie has been an eager, self-taught student of nature and history.

Several years after Meta died, Rose and Dick Camozzi married and lived in Revelstoke. Rose continues to live in Revelstoke after Dick's death.

Helen

After finishing high school in White Rock, B.C., Helen worked for the B.C. Telephone Company in Vancouver. She married Robert Smith, a Royal Canadian Mounted Police officer, in 1956. They continued to live in the White Rock-Vancouver area and raised five children.

Cheryl was born in 1958, has two children, Karla and Kim, and works in retail. Allyson was born in 1959. Wendy was born in 1961 and is a youth coordinator. Robert was born in 1963 and works in banquet and convention sales. Terrence was born in 1965, has two children, Tyler and Kylee, and is an RCMP. When Helen's husband died, she moved to Nanaimo, B.C. where she currently resides.

Helen Dedosenco Smith, 3rd from left. To Left: Bruce Kaduhr and friend, Patty. To right: Ronnie Dedosenco and Gloria Kaduhr Dedosenco. (Dedosenco family photo)

Albert

When Albert left high school, he worked with the surveying crew on the Rogers Pass. He caught the freight train in Revelstoke and stayed in the pass a week at a time. He began logging and working in his father-in-law's sawmill near Chilanko Forkes, B.C. (112 miles north of Williams Lake). His brother, Ronnie, joined him in logging there also. He moved to Williams Lake where he logged and worked for the Forestry for 14 years.

Albert Dedosenco, 2nd from right front at 2006 12 Mile Reunion. Back: Ronnie Dedosenco, Florence McLeod Johnson, Ada Domke Jarvis. Front: Gloria Kaduhr Dedosenco, Dorothy Banks Pegues, Della McLeod Johnson, Albert Dedosenco, Walter Kozek. (W. Jarvis photo)

He and his wife, Angela Pinette, have two daughters, Michelle and Leanne. In 2006 Albert moved back to Revelstoke.

Ronald

Ronnie and Gloria Dedosenco wedding, May 30, 1964. (Dedosenco photo)

Ronnie began an adventurous logging career during ninth grade when just 16 years old. He and Willy Bury formed Dedosenco & Bury Trucking, Ltd. While waiting for the Twelve Mile ferry in his Reo truck, the ferry missed the ramp and struck his truck, pushing it into the current. The ferry operator, in frustration, commented, "She wouldn't be twist." Another time in 1957, Ronnie barely escaped with his life when he was trapped in his logging truck that failed to make a turn on the Big Bend Highway.

Ronnie married Gloria Kaduhr, also of Twelve Mile, on May 30, 1964 after she finished high school.

Their son, Ronald Layton, was born in 1966, and in 1967 they moved to Puntzi Mountain near Chilanko Forks, B.C. to log. The tiny community had a closed radar air force base, weather station, small store and good fishing. That first winter, the temperature dropped to 65 degrees (F) below zero and formed frost on their living room walls. Gloria went back to Revelstoke and stayed with her aunt, Lil Gowanlock,

Layton Dedosenco, 1984. (Dedosenco family photo)

for about a month so their baby girl, Sherrie Lyn, could be born in a hospital in 1968.

The little family moved back to Revelstoke in 1969 and bought their first house. It was the 1,650-square-foot former Arrowhead teacherage that was moved from Arrowhead by Ivan Graham when BC Hydro took over the town. He deposited it on cement blocks over an unfinished basement hole near Joe Kozek's mill on Camozzi Road south of Revelstoke. They later moved to their present home on Nichol Road in the Arrow Heights area of Revelstoke.

In 1984, Ronnie began driving truck for the Highways Department on the Big Bend-Mica section, and continued there until his retirement in 2005.

Sherrie Dedosenco, 1981. (Dedosenco family photo)

Gloria completed the Micro-Computer Data Processing and Business Procedures course through Okanagan College in 1987 and used her skills at the BC Tel office in Revelstoke until 1991 when she was involved in a serious car accident. She spent the following years in and out of hospitals for facial reconstruction. She retired when BC Tel closed in 1993. In spite of her own medical needs, she has always been a tireless caregiver to her family.

Layton took a job for a company in Vancouver that moved buildings. As he was pushing the television and telephone lines out

Sherrie and Ronnie Dedosenco, 1979. Ron served 4-5 years in Revelstoke RCMP Auxiliary.

of the way for the building to pass under, he was seriously electrocuted in October 1988. After much medical treatment and rehabilitation, he now walks with the aid of forearm crutches, and is able to do amazing things with the hook prosthesis on his left arm. In 1996, he began competitive racing GoKarts up to 200 KPH for Westwood Karting Assn. He soon involved his two children, Jordan and Petra, in competitive racing. Petra won the B.C. championship for her age. Their home in Revelstoke is decorated with many first-place and other trophies.

Sherrie's life was tragically taken at age 15 years on May 15, 1983. She and her friend, Tina Boruck, were pushing their bicycles up "Red Devil Hill" after swimming at Williamson Lake south of Revelstoke when they were struck and killed by a drunk driver.

DEMERS

Percy Demers was born in 1909 before his family emigrated to Canada from France. There were two sons and three daughters in the family. Percy bought Joris Daem's property in Wigwam after Joris' house burned. He sold it to the Clarence McLeods in 1944 and purchased the James Millar farm on the west side of the Twelve Mile ferry.

Leona, Percy and Lois Demers, circa 1943. (D. Banks photo)

In 1943, Percy married Leona Herrmann of Sidmouth, B.C. They had three children while in Twelve Mile: Lois, Sharon and Richard (Ricky). When Lois was about five, the family had a wiener roast and invited the Nipper girls. Lois's dress caught fire and she suffered severe burns that required skin grafts. She was treated in the Queen Victoria Hospital for over a month. Mary Nipper remembers caring for Sharon and Ricky while the rest of the family were at the hospital.

When he could, Percy was involved in the community, helping with PTA projects at the school. Leona assisted with teas and canasta parties held at the school.

Besides farming and making silage for the animals, Percy worked at various other jobs including operating the ferry, logging and pole making for CRT and others. However, Leona had the wanderlust and several times Percy hired nannies from elsewhere to care for the children in their mother's absence. At times his sister, Sadie, lived with them to care for the children. The Asaph Domkes and the Kaduhrs in Twelve Mile, and the Stanley Nelsons of Sidmouth, also cared for the children at times. When money got tight, Percy finally ended up staying home to care for them.

Bruce Kaduhr remembers his parents lending Percy money so he could go to Vancouver to find Leona and try to bring her back to the children. When Kaduhrs invited him to meals, he ate small amounts and took the rest home to his children, being too proud to admit his extreme hardship. And when he died at age 43 on July 14, 1952, Bruce and others sadly remember the autopsy ruled death by starvation/malnutrition.

The year before he died, Percy found homes for his children. Lois lived in Vancouver with his sister, Elsie, until she moved into a foster home at age 15. Sharon and Ricky were adopted by John and Pearl Mamchuk of Six Mile (south of Revelstoke).

Sharon(5) and Ricky(4) Demers Mamchuk. (S. Folden photo)

Lois married Steve Baydak. They have two children and several grandchildren all living in the Vancouver area.

Sharon married Norman Folden. They live in Salmon Arm, have two children and five grandsons.

Ricky moved to Kelowna. He suffered severe head trauma in a fight, and spent the next seven and a half years in a wheelchair, before passing away at age 42.

DEVERALL

Audrey Munro was born in 1929 in Revelstoke, B.C. She enjoyed her early years and was honored by being chosen May Queen one year. After completing Normal School in Victoria in 1950, she taught a year in Revelstoke. In 1951 she and Edwin Deverall married and continued living in Revelstoke where he became a railway engineer for the CPR, and she continued teaching.

In 1958 Audrey taught the 11 children at Twelve Mile School.

Audrey and Edwin had four children: Robert, Judy, Edwin and Barbara. After raising their children they moved to Malakwa, B.C.

Ed passed away and Audrey lives in Oakside Manor in Salmon Arm, B.C. (2008).

DEVOLDER

Ted DeVolder emigrated with his parents to Canada from Holland. He trained in music and teaching. From September to November 1966 he taught grades one through six at Twelve Mile School. With the declining enrollment due to families moving away, he was transferred to Arrowhead to finish out the year.

He then taught Band at Revelstoke High School and is now retired in Revelstoke. He has two sons, Ted and Tim, both of Revelstoke.

DOMKE, ARTHUR

Emilie Domke, Olga Lange, Arthur Domke.
(O. Bernard photo)

Arthur Domke and Emilie Ittermann were married in the Ukraine and had two children, Emil and Martha. Martha married Leo Rohde and later moved to Twelve Mile. Arthur was a carpenter by trade. They emigrated from Germany to Twelve Mile in 1954 where they lived next to the Rohdes.

Arthur bought a horse and logged with Leo Rohde earning enough money the first three years in Canada to pay off his and Emilie's ship fare and buy property in the Big Eddy area of Revelstoke. Emilie helped the Rohdes with their children and farm.

Arthur and Emilie both died in Revelstoke, Arthur in 1978 and Emilie in 1997.

DOMKE, ASAPH

Asaph (Art) Domke homesteaded in 1934 near Blanket Creek 14 miles south of Revelstoke. In 1937 he and Kellina (Kay) Rabucha of Saskatchewan married.

Art was in 1901 in Mariendorf, Volhynia, Ukraine, in the Republic of Russia. His parents were descendants of the German farmers Catherine the Great brought to the Ukraine to farm. After his father was killed in World War I, his mother, sister and he, although being Russian citizens but of German descent, were treated as aliens by the Russians and were sent by rail boxcars into the Russian interior. They were first sent to Astrachan on the northern end of the Caspian Sea. It was a three-week trip in the middle of winter. To cross the Volga River, railroad tracks were laid on the ice and horses pulled across two boxcars at a time. They continued their trip by horses, camels and on foot and were moved continuously, seldom being welcome in the Russian villages. They rummaged around for their simple meals, at times even eating rotten potatoes left by the harvesters.

Needless to say, Art had no chance to attend a formal school, except for first grade, until he was 19 when his family finally moved to Germany. There he enrolled in a private boarding school of the Moravian Brethren. He found it a bit difficult entering ninth grade with only a first grade education but he began studies to be a teacher and planned to go to Brazil. After three years of studies, he couldn't resist an opportunity that arose to move to Canada. In 1924 with the combined efforts of the CPR, the Lutheran Church and a Canadian farmer, Mr. Steinke, of Pincher Creek, Alberta, his ship passage and first year's work were arranged. It was a common arrangement for immigrants to work off their fare in this manner.

Art then homesteaded in Edgewater, B.C. He suffered along with thousands of others during the Great Depression. He could not afford to purchase even the bare necessities to sustain himself on his little farm and resorted to setting snares to catch rabbits for food. So in 1934 when he heard of logging possibilities in the Revelstoke, B.C. area, he gave up his Edgewater farm. Hopping a CPR freight, he "rode the rails" through Rogers Pass to Revelstoke hanging on for his life at the end of a boxcar. He nearly got asphyxiated in the five-mile Connaught Tunnel in the midst of the coal-burning steam locomotive's fumes.

Oscar Domke, his cousin, had already obtained a homestead 14 miles south of Revelstoke in the Twelve Mile area, so Art took the 40 acres across the road on the mountainside and began the arduous task of grubbing out the huge charred cedar stumps left by the early loggers. He later purchased Huckle's 40 acres.

In the Cranberry Creek area south of his property in the Monashee Mountains, he began cutting and peeling cedar power poles, living in his logging cabin for weeks at a time, and leaving on foot only when supplies ran low. When Oscar's wife, Helen, introduced Art to her cousin, Kellina, they began corresponding. But Art was tired of trying to survive the Depression and upon hearing of the booming economy in Germany, he returned. There from 1935-36 he helped build the Autobahn, earned enough to buy some decent clothes, and bicycle.

Asaph and Kellina Domke wedding, September 22, 1937. (A. Domke photo)

Domke's log cabin, 1940. Note dry snags on mountain behind. (A. Domke photo)

He also was privileged to witness Jesse Owens become famous at the 1936 Olympics in Berlin. Always a keen observer and student of politics and history, he sensed that Adolph Hitler was developing into a problem for Germany, so he returned to his homestead south of Revelstoke and married Kellina.

Kellina was born in 1907 and grew up on a large wheat farm in Arelee, Saskatchewan. Her parents, Michael and Martha Rabucha, emigrated from Kharkov, Russia in 1901 to escape religious persecution by the state church. Kellina trained as a teacher at normal school but most teaching jobs were given to returning veterans in those post war recession years. She then studied nursing at Resthaven Sanitarium in Sidney, B.C. and fell in love with B.C. So Art didn't have to persuade her to move to the mountains. Their first home was Art's cabin in the Cranberry area where he cut and peeled poles. They always referred to it as their "honeymoon cabin." Being from the prairies, Kay had never hiked or climbed mountains, so this was her big chance. The bride was loaded up with the smaller household and personal items, while the groom packed a case of Pacific evaporated milk, flour and other groceries weighing about 110 pounds. (He had already packed up a small iron stove). Part way up the mountain, Art started relaying the supplies to relieve Kay of her burden. By the time they reached their little home, she collapsed weeping under the weight of the one remaining pot she was still carrying. In their "spare" time they built their log cabin on the homestead, completing it enough to move into that winter. Art cut and split the dried standing cedars left after the 1907 forest fire on the mountain behind their home site. He wrestled them down by hand. Their cabin had a porch, kitchen, living room, bedroom, closet, pantry and a side lean-to for the cream separator. They split roof shakes from the same cedars and that roof lasted for 60 years. They purchased salvaged doors and windows from Needham Brothers in Revelstoke. The total out-of-pocket cost of building the cabin was about $37.

The nearby mountain stream was diverted to run behind the house. This was used for household water and refrigeration. Across the creek they built an outhouse and a root cellar where they stored fruit, vegetables and canned goods for the winter. After months and years of grubbing, dynamiting the huge cedar stumps and trees, and taking advantage of the government land-clearing bulldozers, they had a beautiful farm where they raised hay for their cattle and horses, vegetables, fruit trees and commercial crops of strawberries and raspberries. They built log barns for their animals and hay. He loved woodworking and built their furniture, gates, fences and even a little furnished playhouse for their children. When Art was away logging for a week at a time, Kay and the children were busy from dawn to dusk keeping the farm running. Eugen and Ada learned to drive the pickup truck and tractor as children in order to do the farm work. Kellina never learned to drive.

Heavy snowfall in mid-1950s covering kitchen window of A. Domke's new house. (A. Domke photo)

During WWII, everyone of German birth was required to register with the authorities on a specific day each month. Even though Art was a naturalized Canadian citizen and was born in Russia, his rifle was taken from him and never returned, leaving his family without protection or the ability to hunt. He also had to register monthly at the courthouse in Revelstoke. Not yet having an automobile, he hiked five miles from his logging camp in the Cranberry and the 12 miles one way on the railroad tracks to Revelstoke.

One time he was able to catch a ride to town the day before his monthly registration date, and tried to check in at the office, but the bureaucrat in charge would not permit him to sign in a day early. Art walked home that night and walked back the next day!

Art continued working for various logging outfits with cedar power poles being his specialty. Since he was also a sawyer, he purchased a one-man portable mill from John Denter and sawed all the lumber for the new house they built in 1951 just north of their log cabin. This house was much larger, had a full basement, plumbing and a gasoline-powered generator for electricity. Their log cabin was then often rented to people who were working in the area temporarily.

Art taught himself the rock craft. He hand-dug a 20-foot-in-diameter swimming pool and cemented in its rock lining. It was fed by a small waterfall diverted from their little stream. Passersby frequently stopped to admire and at times purchase Kay's beautiful flowers, especially asters and gladiolas. By the time his projects were finished, that included a stone arch over the driveway, rock gardens and fence posts, they were forced to move because of the Hydro project.

Back: Amy, Janet and Emily. Front: Holly, Chip and Eugen Domke. (E. Domke photo)

They moved to Oliver, B.C. in 1966. Their homestead property was above the high water mark of the new reservoir and was developed into Blanket Creek Provincial Park. In 1984 Art and Kay moved back to Revelstoke. They and their children purchased property from Hydro on Montana Creek and built a vacation home. After suffering a massive stroke, Art died in 1993. Kay spent her final years in Extended Care at Queen Victoria Hospital in Revelstoke. She suffered from arthritis, and died in 1997.

Kellina and Asaph had two children. Eugen was born in 1939, and Ada was born in 1941. They both attended the Twelve Mile School through the eighth grade. Getting to school wasn't easy. They rode their bikes or walked depending on the road conditions and crossing the ferry every day always took extra time. Getting to high school was even harder.

Eugen (Gene) attended college in Tennessee where he met his bride, Janet Powell. Gene was a plant maintenance engineer in various hospitals. When his job took them to Saigon Adventist Hospital, he experienced the fall of Saigon first hand. Being a Canadian, he had no way out except for the compassion of an American friend who gave him his seat on the last

Ada, Will and Bill Jarvis, 2005. (W. Jarvis photo)

Matthew Jarvis, 2004. (W. Jarvis photo)

American plane leaving. Janet was employed in various aspects of the medical field. Her last position was in marketing. Gene and Janet are retired in Corbett, near Portland, Oregon and delight in traveling in their RV to warmer climes in the winter. Gene enjoys woodcarving among other hobbies. They have one son, Eugen (Chip), and two granddaughters, Holly and Emily. Chip and his wife, Amy, are employed in the skiing town of Vail, Colorado.

Ada graduated from business college and worked for various companies, and then graduated from Loma Linda University as an occupational therapist. She met her husband, William (Bill) Jarvis in Vancouver and moved to the United States when they married. They have two sons, William (Will), and Matthew. Bill is a university professor and they are both retired in Loma Linda, California. Ada enjoys her hobbies in arts and sports and Bill his model railroading and tennis.

CPR Ship Montcalm on which Asaph Domke returned to Canada in 1936.
(A. Jarvis photo)

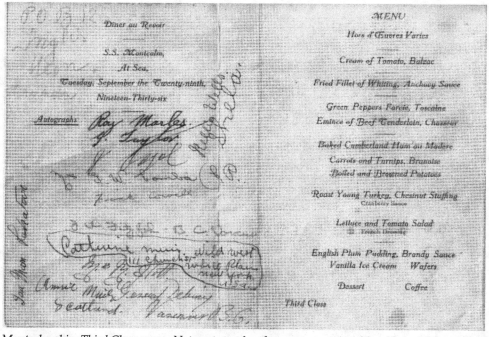

Montcalm ship, Third Class menu. Note autographs of passengers at Asaph's table and "General Delivery, Vancouver, B.C." address. (A. Jarvis photo)

DOMKE, OSCAR

Oscar Domke was born in 1903 in Emilufke, Russia to German parents. In 1928 he emigrated from Latvia to a farm in Saskatchewan and then moved on to Twelve Mile by 1930.

Owning one's own land was the goal of all immigrants, and Oscar was no exception. He obtained a 40-acre homestead two and a half miles southwest of the Twelve Mile Ferry, and later obtained the adjoining 40 acres. In 1933 Oscar met Helen Koronko through a friend and they were married later that year in Revelstoke. Helen was born in Arelee, Saskatchewan in 1910, and had worked as a nanny and domestic for various households. Helen and Oscar set up housekeeping in their initial one-room log cabin (that later became their chicken coop), built a small barn, and continued improving the buildings on their farm. Together they grubbed and cleared their land by hand, and later cleared more with a small CRT caterpillar and the government-sponsored land clearers.

Helen and Oscar Domke, wedding, 1933. (O. Domke family photo)

Oscar and Helen had three children: Benjamin (Ben) was born in 1934, followed by Evelyn in 1935 and Herbert (Herb) in 1942.

Their property along the road was fenced with split cedar rails and posts. In 1935 they built a two-story log house with two porches and a partial dark basement where they kept canning and some root vegetables; their large root cellar was dug into the mountain across the road. On the main floor was the kitchen, dining room with heater, living room and bedroom. Upstairs were two unheated bedrooms. The milk separator and gas-powered washing machine were housed in the back porch, and the front verandah came in handy for drying clothes on rainy or snowy days. Until the 1950s, their water supply was the nearby creek from which they carried buckets of water for household and laundry use. Laundry and bath water was heated in a large copper boiler on the kitchen stove.

Oscar and Helen Domke's log home. (O. Domke family photo)

In 1943 Ole and Pete Westerberg of Revelstoke framed up their large modern barn. In keeping with the neighborly spirit of the times, work bees from Sidmouth and Eight Mile shingled the roof. The volunteers were rewarded with huge chicken dinners prepared by Helen, cooking being her favourite hobby. Evelyn remembers finding Pete's wallet full of cash in the back of their truck after Oscar took Ole and Pete home one day, and was excited by the $5 reward he gave her.

Soon their small orchard of apples, pears, cherries, plums and green grapes was producing, complementing Helen's huge vegetable garden. They raised ducks, geese, chickens, milk cows and later Hereford beef cattle, and put up tons of hay to feed them. Oscar established an apiary and harvested the sweet clover honey each fall, extracting it with the honey extractor borrowed from Bob Brinkman.

In 1952 Ben and Henry Bittner dug a water line from their creek, under the highway to the house and barn. You could say it was another community effort, with Jack Nipper bringing his smelter tools to help install the plumbing in the kitchen. It was while operating his cat during this work that Ben came down with polio.

Oscar worked at various jobs. He joined the many relief workers in the early 1930s during the Great Depression. He first learned blacksmithing while working in his father's flour mill in Odessa, Russia, a skill he used while building the southern portion of the Big Bend Highway and working the gold mines in French Creek and area. He later opened his own small blacksmith shop across the road from their house where he made horseshoes for the loggers' and farmers' horses, logging tools and repairs, and sled runners for winter horse logging. He logged in the local areas, drove cat for Clarence Yount of CRT, built logging roads, and hunted.

Oscar worked away from home for days or weeks at a time, as did many of the men in the area, leaving Helen and children to take care of much of the farm work: gardening, canning, haying and animals. Her geese and ducks were her pride and joy. Not only was the meat delicious, the feathers made comfortable pillows and feather beds. Ben built the ducks a special little house and just before

Ole and Pete Westerberg building Domke's modern barn, 1943.
(O. Domke family photo)

butchering time, they disappeared overnight without a trace. Hawks and coyotes always left telltale feathers, but a human thief left nothing. Helen was heartsick. Another time, the geese were in the creek when lightning struck and killed most of them.

Helen's favourite excursions were into the adjoining Monashee Mountains with her neighbor cousin, Kellina Domke. She was known for climbing over windfalls and "shooing" off the bears in her quest for huckleberries. In the slough, Helen also picked high bush cranberries that were baked into delicious tarts. If she wanted some ready cash, she caught a ride to town and did spring cleaning for some of the businesses, especially Paula's Beauty Salon and George Williamson's Dry Cleaners. She also gathered up old woolens such as coats, pants and blankets from her home and friends, removed buttons, ripped them into pieces, weighed the wool, and sent it off to a factory. It came back in the form of gray, warm, itchy blankets. She never learned to drive an automobile, but her children taught her to ride a bike. However, she was too scared to ride it very far, especially after it got away, landing her in the little lake behind their house left over from spring flooding. Helen was a self-taught, accomplished musician on the guitar, organ, piano and harmonica. She donated her pump organ to Twelve Mile School to enrich its music class.

In 1946, Oscar bought Alf Olsson's blacksmith shop on the corner of Second Street and Campbell in Revelstoke, rebuilding a larger one on the same property in 1956. Together, he and his sons operated the

Oscar Domke poses in front of his first blacksmith shop in Twelve Mile.
(O. Domke family photo)

O. Domke & Sons Machine Shop, eventually opening branches in Kamloops, Cranbrook and Sparwood, B.C. The O. Domke & Sons Blacksmith Shop float won the "Most Original Float" prize at the Dominion Day parade in Revelstoke in 1949. It was a miniature blacksmith shop on wheels. Oscar was always one to seize on opportunities. He got the first distributorship in the area for McCulloch chain saws, much appreciated by loggers who had toiled in the woods with crosscut saws until then.

Oscar was Twelve Mile School's first representative to School District No.19 in Revelstoke in 1949 and continued serving on the Board of Trustees for 27 years. He continued his community service after moving to Revelstoke where Ken Millar remembers serving with Oscar on the water board for the

Big Eddy district when both families lived there. He also served on the Revelstoke City Council for seven years, on various city committees, and was one of the original members of the Okanagan College Council where he served for 10 years.

Their three children all rode bicycles two and a half miles each way to Twelve Mile School in the spring and fall, but in the winter, Ben and Evelyn rode in a cutter (sleigh) pulled by their horse and stabled it in Emil Rauchert's barn for a small fee while they attended school. They had many interesting experiences on the way to and from school. The dusty, gravel road took them in a hairpin turn to cross the Gold Creek (Sutherland) Falls bridge, past the beaver dam south of Ocepoff's, past

O. Domke & Sons Blacksmith Shop on wheels won the "Most Original Float" in Revelstoke's Dominion Day parade, 1949. (O. Domke family photo)

Thompson's German shepherd barking and nipping at their heels, and across the ferry to school. Sometimes kind-hearted folks with autos offered them rides, bikes and all. Herb and cousin, Ada, remember the time they were offered a ride by two happy men in a panel truck. They had no idea who they were but gave in to the tempting offer that saved them pushing their bikes up the long hill to Gold Creek bridge. The strangers loaded their bikes in the back and crowded the children into the cab, Herb in the middle and Ada on the passenger's lap. The bottle hanging out of the glove compartment gave away the reason for their excessive joviality! Herb and Ada were relieved to be dropped off at home without any mishaps.

Wanting to attend the circus they heard was coming to town, Ben and Evelyn thought nothing of hopping on their bikes and pedaling the 14 miles to Revelstoke in 1947. How surprised Oscar was to see them riding down Second Street when he stepped out of his blacksmith shop, so he gave them each 25 cents to enjoy the circus.

When World War II ended, Oscar, with the help of the Red Cross, began locating relatives who had been displaced in Europe during the war, and sponsored several family members who emigrated to Canada: Leo, Martha and Valentin Rohde; and Arthur and Emily Domke. Then in 1951 Oscar was overjoyed when the Red Cross located his brother, Adolph, who had survived the brutalities of prison camps, and was able to begin a new life in Revelstoke.

Magdalena and Ben Domke wedding, 1960. (O. Domke family photo)

When Helen and Oscar built a home and moved to the Big Eddy area of Revelstoke, they rented out their farm to various loggers and farmers. Later they built a duplex on Douglas Street in town where they were living when BC Hydro bought their farm in the 1960s. They retired in their new home in Langley, B.C. Oscar died in 1985 and Helen in 2003, and are both buried in Langley.

After finishing grade 10 at Revelstoke High School, Ben took general agricultural studies at University of British Columbia. Despite his weakened right leg from polio, he pursued his businesses of raising cattle and logging. Remains of one of his gypo sawmills can still be found on the far shore of

Echo Lake on Mt. Cartier. He built roads for B.C. Forestry and joined his father's welding and machine shop business. He also purchased Bob Brinkman's trapline and later sold it to BC Hydro which gave him permission to continue using as much of it as possible. Ben married Magdalena Vogel who had emigrated from Germany to Saskatoon, Saskatchewan. They lived in Revelstoke, Kamloops and presently Langley. They have two children, Benita and Berton, and four grandchildren.

When Evelyn graduated from Revelstoke High School, she received a $150 bursary from Queen Victoria Hospital to attend nursing school. She earned her undergraduate degree in nursing at Walla Walla College, and graduate degrees from Loma Linda University and San Jose State University. She enjoyed her nursing career that included positions of nursing administration, community college teaching, counseling, editing and reviewing nursing

Herb and Carol Domke, 2005. (W. Jarvis photo)

Evelyn Domke, junior nursing student, 1956. l(E. Domke photo)

textbooks. She married Bill Riegert of San Jose, California where they established their home and raised their two children, David and Karen. David is a Math and Music major and Karen an occupational therapist. Since retiring, Evelyn lives in Saratoga, California and now has time to pursue her many hobbies including gardening, travel and cooking.

Herb worked in the family's machine shop during his high school years and grew fond of the business world. He had to make the difficult decision as to whether he should continue his education in business or go into medicine. He chose the latter and finished medical school at Loma Linda University in California. He married Carol Rogers, a nurse, from Armstrong, B.C. and they set up a family practice in Victoria in 1969. A few years later, they each completed graduate degrees in public health to enhance patient care in their practice. Herb has also continued to be involved in residential and industrial development on Vancouver Island and in the Fraser Valley. Herb and Carol have two children, Heidi, a nurse in Oregon, and Mark who is involved in commercial transport in B.C. Mark and his wife, Karen, have two daughters.

DUNN

Margaret Dunn moved to Twelve Mile with her five children in 1950. While there, they lived in Thompson's house and the three older children attended Twelve Mile School. Charles Roger was in grade eight, Catherine Hellen in grade seven and Laverne in grade one. Colleen and Lauralee were under school age. In 1951 they moved from Twelve Mile.

Back: Margaret and Hellen; Front: Lauralee, Laverne and Colleen Dunn. (W. Kozek photo)

ENGLISH

Irene Campion was born in 1888 at Owen Sound, Ontario. She attended Owen Sound Collegiate and began her distinguished teaching career in Ontario at the age of 16. In 1910 she moved to Calgary, Alberta to attend Normal School then returned to Ontario and married Daniel MacRaney English in 1912. They began moving back west, arriving in Revelstoke in 1920. By then she had borne four sons: Dick, Jack and twin boys Jim and George. Two daughters were born in Revelstoke: Marion and Margery.

The family resided in the Lower Town section of Revelstoke for a number of years before moving to a house beside the old rink where Columbia River Manor now stands. When her children were older she resumed teaching. Endowed with a pioneer spirit, she didn't mind teaching in out-of-the-way schools such as Greenslide south of Revelstoke and then Twelve Mile from 1946-50.

While teaching at the Twelve Mile School, she lived in the two-room teacherage and rode her bicycle to her home in Revelstoke on some weekends. She became an integral part of the community, making lasting friendships with some of the parents. What many remember are the elaborate Christmas concerts she energetically prepared with her students each year. They also remember her for being a strict disciplinarian but also a tireless companion taking them on nature hikes to Echo Lake.

Irene English, right, in front of Twelve Mile School. (English family photo)

After Twelve Mile, she taught a short time at Beaton. Her grandson, Ken, remembers "a journey to Beaton by car and ferry to visit her at the school there." Her much-deserved retirement was filled with community activities in Revelstoke. She passed away in 1961 as a result of complications from stomach surgery. Her daughters, Marion and Marge, are still alive and live in the Salmon Arm area. Her grandson, Ken (Jim's son) lives in Revelstoke and is married to Cathy English, Curator of the Revelstoke Museum and Archives.

FISCHER

Vernon Fischer taught in the Twelve Mile School during 1961-62. There were 16 students in grades one through seven that year.

FLOYD

James Floyd is distinguished as the last teacher of the Twelve Mile School. He moved to the area from Alberta and taught in Arrowhead in the fall of 1966. When BC Hydro began displacing people, school enrollment dropped, and Jim was transferred to the Twelve Mile School November 1966 to June 1967. At that time, the school included grades one through six and the higher grades were bussed to Revelstoke.

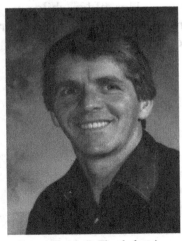

He has pleasant memories of the seven and a half months spent at Twelve Mile. "The children were great. The older ones were wonderful study buddies for the younger ones. The nature hikes we used to take along the CPR spur line were both fun and educational. On rainy days the old school was our gym."

James Floyd. (J. Floyd photo)

His bus trips to and from Revelstoke also left him with these favourite memories:

> I traveled between Revelstoke and Twelve Mile each day by school bus with Harold Rota as the driver and my tour guide. Harold, being an old Revelstokian, taught me so much about Revelstoke, its history and the people. As well, his stories covered Six Mile, Eight Mile, Twelve Mile, Sidmouth, Arrowhead and all points between and beyond!

When the school closed, Jim taught in Revelstoke schools where he continues to live.

FULTON

Mary Fulton and Ernestena Walters taught at the Twelve Mile School during 1941-42. Lorne Fulton attended school there from 1941-43. No further information is available.

FUNK

Ernie Funk of Arrowhead logged for Walter Shiell during the early 1950s. He helped grade the playground at the school when it was being upgraded. No further information is available.

GARDINER

Vivian Gardiner is renown for being Twelve Mile School's first teacher. School began in a couple of homesteaders' homes before the school building was completed that school year of 1930-31. It was her first teaching assignment, straight out of Normal School, and as Sharry Kelly put it, "It couldn't have been an easy assignment. She was young and very pretty."

She married Sylvester Camozzi, son of one of Revelstoke's early pioneers, Joseph Camozzi (Barry Camozzi's uncle). They retired in Powell River where he had worked in the pulp mill.

GOWAN

Mrs. P. B. Gowan taught at the Twelve Mile School from 1954-57. She used many motivational techniques in her teaching, giving prizes for good work, and instituting Open House for parents.

Her older children, Pat and Fred, came from Revelstoke to help her with the Christmas concerts.

Mrs. P. B. Gowan with students, 1954-55. Back: Sergei Astrahantseff, Ronnie Dedosenco, Susy Podzun, Emily Rauchert, Herb Domke. Middle: Genny, Larry, Kathy and Carolyn Rauchert. Front: Helen Nipper, Gloria Kaduhr, Ada Domke. (A. Domke family photo)

GOWANLOCK

Brooks Gowanlock and Lillian (Lily) Lutz married in 1940 in Vancouver, B.C. Brooks' parents, John and Mary, farmed in Saskatchewan. Lily's father was Reinhold Lutz who moved from Austria to homestead 200 acres in Duff, Saskatchewan (then the Northwest Territories). He moved his seven children to Vancouver in the 1930s. Lily's older sister, Lena, married Hickie Kaduhr in Vancouver also, so the families always were close.

Brooks was a barber by trade. He started in Chilliwack, then Vancouver and also had a shop at the CPR Hotel in Field, B.C. He was somewhat familiar with Revelstoke before the Kaduhrs moved with them to Twelve Mile on October 18, 1946. Together they located and purchased Cecil and Lucy Banks' farm on Drimmie Creek.

The two families resiliently withstood the week-long adventurous move from Vancouver to their new home. Brooks, Lily and five-year-old son, Russell, loaded up their Dodge car and trailer; their little boxer dog rode in a box fastened on the outside fender. Hickie, Lena, Bruce and Gloria caravanned with them in their 1929 "Green Hornet" Essex Super 6 car. On the Kamloops Hill, the brakes on the Essex burned out, requiring a couple of days in a motel awaiting repairs. Then between Three Valley Gap and Revelstoke, the trailer hitch on Gowanlock's car snapped, stranding the trailer on the railroad tracks. A train sped by just as they were pulling it off the tracks with a rope hitched to their car. But this was just the beginning of many adventures yet to come.

Brooks Gowanlock, 1935, Vancouver, B.C. (Gowanlock family photo)

Russell and Gordon Gowanlock on Katy, 1948. (Gowanlock family photo)

Gowanlock home. It was previously Ullman's and Banks'. (Gowanlock family photo)

The four adults and three children first moved into the one-room log cabin that had a table, four chairs and a sawdust-burning stove until Kaduhrs moved a little cabin of their own onto the property. It was quite a culture shock, especially to the sisters with no electricity, plumbing or telephone.

Gordon was born in 1947 after the family moved to Twelve Mile. At Queen Victoria Hospital, the nurses dubbed him the "fur coat baby" because of his unusual arrival. On the way to the hospital in a heavy snowstorm, Brooks and Lil skidded into a snow bank just as her water broke. They managed to dig out and get to hospital just in time to remove her fur coat before their baby was born.

They soon felt at home among their friendly neighbors and participated in the social events of the community, including the PTA, dances and sleigh rides. In the winter, Brooks hitched up their horse, Katy, to their large sled built on timbers, piled in some hay bales and went around the neighborhood picking up 10 to 15 passengers for fun winter rides. He also entertained everyone in his Santa suit at the school Christmas concerts. Russell played his "pioneer" part well. He remembers sneaking rides to Revelstoke on the steam train and then trying to figure out how to get back home! Swimming and playing in the slough, horseback riding, and playing with his cousins, Gloria and Bruce, are some of his fondest memories.

They tried various means of making a living, including the egg business, which failed when their chickens froze that first winter. Being from Vancouver, they had no idea of the severity of Revelstoke winters in those days. They raised their own vegetables, bought a sow, two horses and a cow so had plenty of food, regardless of the grim labor market. After trying his hand as ferry operator and barbering away from home, the family moved to Revelstoke in 1950 where Brooks opened up his own barber shop. Lil later got her hairdressing training in Vancouver and opened up Lily's Beauty Shop next door to her husband's shop. While in Revelstoke, Lily again became actively involved in community activities such as golfing, lawn bowling, alley bowling, and the Ladies Auxiliary.

Lil Gowanlock on Katy, 1948.
(Gowanlock family photo)

While Russell was enrolled in Revelstoke High School, he joined the Revelstoke Cadets and spent school holidays at the Vernon cadet school. He joined the reserves and as an army corporal, he trained and worked as a radio technician. From there he transferred to the Navy for four years, then to the Royal Canadian Air Force for five years. As a computer technician, he was the Western Canadian Service Manager for Honeywell and then for Compaq Computers until he retired in 2000. He and wife, Barbara (Bailey), live in Kelowna, B.C. They have a son, Stacy; a daughter, Lonnie; and eight grandchildren, Brendan, Brock, Brooke, Presley, Ashley, Jessica, Michael and Casey.

Gordon, Lily and Russell Gowanlock, circa 1990s.
(Gowanlock family photo)

Gordon logged on Vancouver Island, then trained as a heavy-duty mechanic and worked with the Highways Department in the Revelstoke-Mica district before retiring. He and Karen have two sons, Gordon and Derek, and she has one daughter, Tammy. They have three grandsons, Jonathan, Nickolas and Shawn; and two granddaughters, Angelina and Celina.

After Brooks died of a heart attack on September 21, 1961, Lil remarried Kurt Borstel in 1962. They lived at Mara Lake, B.C. for many years until moving to Sicamous (2008).

Russell and Gordon bought back part of their farm after BC Hydro bought them out in the 1960s. Gordon still plans to move back to this acreage, God willing.

HAMPTON

William Hampton spent a few years in Twelve Mile logging with Walter Shiell. During his short stay he was active in various community activities.

HANSEN

George Hansen operated a portable mill in the Cranberry area. Whether or not he lived in Twelve Mile cannot be confirmed.

HARRISON

Brothers Jack and Slim Harrison lived in the Twelve Mile vicinity while logging for CRT in the Cranberry area in the early 1950s. They moved to Revelstoke.

HASHIMOTO

Mary Hashimoto grew up and finished high school in Revelstoke. Interestingly, she and three Twelve Milers, Emily Rauchert, Herb and Ada Domke, were classmates. After graduating from Revelstoke Secondary School (RSS) in 1959 she completed teacher training at Victoria College in 1961.

Mary Hashimoto, circa 1967. (Hashimoto photo)

Mary taught at Selkirk School in Revelstoke and in Surrey, traveled overseas and returned home in the middle of the school year without employment. When Dave Mitchell, Director of Instruction, found out Mary was available to teach, he offered her a position at Twelve Mile School to finish out the school year, starting in January 1966. Nellie McKay was ill and took leave in December. Dave drove Mary to the school so she could visualize a one-room country school, and she agreed to try it.

Harold Rota, driver of the southbound school bus, picked her up in Revelstoke early in the morning. They picked up elementary students in Six and Eight Mile as they worked their way to Twelve Mile. After those students were dropped off, Harold met the older students from Arrowhead, Sidmouth and Twelve Mile and took them into Revelstoke. In the evening, the process was reversed. As can be imagined, those were long days for all. Later in the spring, Mary borrowed her brother's car so she could drive herself and save time.

Teaching 16 students in one room from grades one through seven was "like tutoring all the time: one, two or three students at a time. It was different from any other kind of teaching I've done before or since, but I know I quite enjoyed the unique experience," recalls Mary.

The most she had in any grade was three and there was only one in grades two and five. She had to be super organized, preparing lessons at least two days in advance so the worksheets could be copied and returned to her from the district office.

Mary Hashimoto Meehan (right) with husband, Pat, and daughters. (M. Meehan photo)

After Twelve Mile, Mary taught in Surrey, Toronto and Revelstoke. She was the first female principal in Revelstoke when Big Eddy became a stand-alone elementary school, independent of the Farwell School.

In 1979 she met Pat Meehan, vice-principal and then principal of RSS, and they soon married. After their two daughters were born, Mary retired from teaching to raise them. Pat's work took them to Kitimat and then Nanaimo in 1988 where they have made their permanent home and where they are now retired.

HEWKO

Mike Hewko was an early logger in the Twelve Mile area and established a sawmill at Ten Mile. Although it cannot be established that he ever lived in Twelve Mile, his name appears on the surveyors' map by P.B. Street and T.H. Plunkett on the property that the school was built on. The cabin that the Kaduhrs first moved onto their property had been Mike Hewko's.

HORSLEY

Mabel Horsley was another first-year teacher at the Twelve Mile School in 1940-41. She was a fun-loving young lady who made friends easily in the community.

She and Jack Petrashuk of Twelve Mile married and had a daughter, Ellen. They soon divorced and Mabel moved to Hope, B.C. with Ellen where they lived with Mabel's sister, Ellen Corbett. She taught in Hope and perhaps Coquitlam and later married George Ewert.

Mabel and her daughter, Ellen, are both deceased.

Center: Mabel Horsley with friends, Kellina and Helen Domke, Ben and Evelyn Domke, circa 1941. (A. Domke family photo)

HOWARD

Ross Howard moved to Twelve Mile in September 1947 from Malakwa, B.C. He lived in the ferry house when he worked for the Public Works Department operating the ferry. In 1948 he was severely injured when his fingers got caught in the cable on the ferry and pulled the tendons out in one arm.

Several people remember Ross in his other various jobs including the building of fire lookouts for the Forestry Department. He retired in the 1970s and is now deceased.

Huckle house on left. Eugen and Asaph Domke haying where Blanket Creek Provincial Park is now located. (A. Domke family photo)

HUCKLE

Nufree Huckle homesteaded the 40 acres located about one-half mile east of the present highway along Blanket Creek. The present Blanket Creek Provincial Park swimming lagoon was built on part of his original property.

He chose a beautiful knoll on which to build his rather large log cabin with one room and a loft. Not having a well, he hand-carried water quite a distance from the creek. When he died in the mid-1940s, Asaph Domke purchased the property to add to their 40-acre homestead. The Domkes always referred to that parcel as "Nufree's Place," and the children enjoyed playing in the vacant cabin because of its unique loft.

Not much has been found about Mr. Huckle. Ben Domke remembers him to be a small, hermit-type man who had worked at a mine near Keremeos before homesteading at Fourteen Mile. Ken Millar remembers Nufree coming to their place near the ferry to buy milk and eggs. Although he spoke little if any English, he would stay for coffee with Ken's mom, Dora, and they seemed to be able to communicate in some manner.

HULYD

The Damien Hulyds were among the first settlers in Twelve Mile arriving from the Ukraine sometime before 1920. Their son, Andrew, took out the homestead which was later purchased by Zibulaks and then transferred to Makarewiczes along the tracks and eastern side of the river.

The Hulyds sons were Jaron, Andrew and Roly (now Hold) plus two others. The family farmed, logged and made fence posts to sell.

They experienced several tragedies. On May 24, 1925 the brothers were working on a log boom in the river when Jaron disappeared without a trace. Then in August their loads of fence posts waiting to be shipped from the railroad siding were burned by an arsenist. The following month, Mr. Hulyd was injured in a car accident near Arrowhead. It was reported in the *Revelstoke Review* on September 16, 1925 as follows:

> A near fatality took place about a mile out of Arrowhead last night at about 6 o'clock when the car driven by Dr. Hamilton, of this city, went over an embankment below a narrow part of the road, and rolled down the hillside for about a hundred feet. The cause of the accident is given by Dr. Hamilton as being brought about by the steering gear breaking.

> In the car with Dr. Hamilton were Coroner W. I. Briggs, Provincial Constable O'Halloran and Mr. Hulyd, of Twelve-Mile South.

> Constable O'Halloran jumped from the car...and thus saved himself. Mr. Hulyd had a couple of ribs broken and was otherwise badly shaken up and scratched.

> Dr. Hamilton and Mr. Briggs were also very severely bruised and shaken up, but suffered no broken bones.

> Mr. Hulyd, who is an aged man and was suffering considerably, was conveyed to Arrowhead and given medical attention, Constable O'Halloran remaining with him and bringing him to the hospital here today.

The reason for the trip was to investigate and identify a man's body that D. J. Crawford found in one of the sloughs near Arrowhead while he was out hunting. Constable O'Halloran, supposing it might be the body of Jaron, picked up Mr. Hulyd on the way to Arrowhead. Although Mr. Hulyd couldn't positively identify his son, Jaron's wife later identified Jaron and he was buried in the Arrowhead cemetery.

After this tragedy, the family moved to Eight Mile, leaving their log cabin vacant. In the fall of 1930, the first school in Twelve Mile was held in Hulyd's unoccupied log cabin.

Jaron and his wife, Annie Bushko, had two children: Nettie and Marshall. Nettie trained as a nurse at St. Paul's School of Nursing in 1944, and Marshall served in WWII. Annie lived in Eight Mile until 1951 when she moved to Vancouver to live with her daughter, Nettie Grilish.

Roly and his wife, Tina, operated an experimental farm in Six Mile that was sponsored by The Farmers' Institute. They had one daughter, Lorraine, who married Bud Watson.

Andrew never married but later moved to Revelstoke and worked in Mulholland's pool hall.

Nothing could be found on the other two Hulyd brothers.

IWASIUK

Steve Iwasiuk was among the first homesteaders in Twelve Mile. His 40-acre homestead was across from the property that later became the school's. He built a one-room frame cabin atop the knoll with a view of Mt. Cartier.

His son, Arnold, attended the first Twelve Mile School in 1933-34.

In approximately 1935 he traded his property to Martin Schmidt of Alberta, and Martin later traded it to John Rauchert in the early 1940s.

JOHNSON

Mr. and Mrs. Vincent Johnson were newlyweds living in a house by the railroad crossing from 1949-50. He worked for Walter Shiell. When fire destroyed their tiny home that January, they moved to a house at Hewko's sawmill at Six Mile.

JOHNSTONE

Marjorie Johnstone taught the 10 students at the Twelve Mile School from 1937-40. Steve, Rose and Joe Kozek loved to play tricks on their teachers. They climbed on one of the stumps next to the school during school hours and looked at teacher Johnstone through the window with, "Ha, ha." Needless to say, Marjorie spoke to their dad. They put books inside their pants to protect themselves from the spanking they got from their father.

JONES

Fred and ? Bauer; Hickie and Lena Kaduhr; John Schmidt; Peter, Margaret, Paul, Ian and Rowena Jones, at Kaduhr's. (Kaduhr family photo)

Peter and Margaret Jones arrived in Twelve Mile from England in 1957 and lived there until 1961.

Peter was an ex-serviceman. After WWII with many houses bombed, minimal construction taking place, and refugees arriving, adequate housing for families was almost impossible to find. In 1956 England started finding homes for the Hungarian refugees during their revolution, leaving the British citizens with even less choices.

Since Peter had a trade as a motor mechanic, he qualified under the Canadian Immigration Act to emigrate to Canada. They crossed the Atlantic by ship, and across Canada by train, arriving in Revelstoke on a December evening. John Rauchert picked up Peter, Margaret and their three eldest children at the train station and drove them out to Twelve Mile. Margaret still remembers arriving at Rauchert's where the Astrahantseff and Dedosenco boys were waiting on the couch to welcome the new arrivals.

Immigration sent Peter to Burns Lake to work until spring. He was soon able to buy a car and they rented Gowanlock's house where they lived for two years while Peter worked in various garages in Revelstoke. He soon installed a water pump in the kitchen sink so Margaret wouldn't have to dip water out of Drimmie Creek. She especially remembers the mosquitoes, outhouses and Saturday evening dances at the Sidmouth Hall. The family soon became involved in the community with Peter even directing a successful play at the school Christmas concert.

In 1959 they moved to Eight Mile and then to Five Mile where they rented from Kabys and Saporitos respectively. Their three older children continued to attend Twelve Mile School, being bussed daily. They later moved to a large house on Douglas Street in Revelstoke. After Peter died in 1984, Margaret moved into Nimm's Manor in Revelstoke.

Peter and Margaret have five children and eight grandchildren:

David was born in 1948 in England where he began his primary education. He obtained his higher education at University of British Columbia and is a business consultant for UBC and the University in Kelowna. He is an avid mountain climber, having scaled many mountains throughout the world including part of Mt. Everest. David has also written several books including one on the Selkirk Mountains.

Paul Michael was also born in England in 1951, began school there and is a part owner in the Vic Van Isle Construction company in Revelstoke. He has one daughter.

Rowena was also born in England in 1954 and is in the printing business in Burnaby, B.C. She has two daughters.

Roy was born in 1959 in Revelstoke and works for Vic Van Isle Construction in Revelstoke.

Ian was born in 1961 in Revelstoke and does business in the Vernon office of Bell Pole Company. He has two sons.

Hickie and Lena Kaduhr pose by their beloved "Green Hornet" Essex. (Kaduhr family photo)

KADUHR

Hickie (Adolf) Kaduhr and Lena (Caroline Elizabeth) Lutz married in 1934 in Vancouver, B.C. They had two children, Bruce and Gloria. Lena's father was Reinhold Lutz who moved from Austria to homestead 200 acres in Duff, Saskatchewan (then the Northwest Territories). He moved his seven children to Vancouver in the 1930's. Hickie moved to Vancouver from Lemberg, Saskatchewan, where his parents, Gustave and Pauline Kaduhr farmed.

Lena's younger sister, Lil, married Brooks Gowanlock in Vancouver also, so the families always were close. Since Lena was plagued by asthma, Hickie and Brooks began looking for a climate that was more agreeable to her condition. From the days he had worked in nearby Field, B.C., Brooks knew of Revelstoke so they placed their focus there.

In 1945 the two families partnered up to purchase Cecil and Lucy Banks' 80 acres in Twelve Mile for $1,200 (40 acres were already cleared). The property was between the CPR tracks and Mt. Cartier east of the school.

Their move to Twelve Mile was filled with adventure that no doubt prepared them for the many yet to come. Hickie and Lena loaded up their large 1929 Essex Super 6 (lovingly named "The

Green Hornet") with their belongings and children, Bruce, age 11, and Gloria, age three. Brooks, Lil and son, Russell, age five, squeezed into their packed Dodge hitched to a loaded trailer, and the two families started out for Revelstoke.

Four days out of Vancouver, the brakes on The Green Hornet burned out on the Kamloops hill. They took a motel for two days during the repairs. The moment Gowanlock's car was crossing the tracks between Three Valley Gap and Revelstoke, the trailer hitch snapped, stranding the trailer on the tracks. No problem. They hooked a rope between it and their car and pulled it off the tracks just in time to avoid an oncoming train.

The two families arrived in Twelve Mile October 18, 1946, just a few weeks late for their three children to begin school.

At first they all moved into the one-room log cabin, but soon the Kaduhrs moved Mike Hewko's one-room logging cabin from the northeast corner of the school property, to the lower end of their land and added two rooms. The primitive conditions were quite a culture shock, especially to the ladies coming from the city. No electricity. No indoor plumbing—the only running water was in the nearby Drimmie Creek (then known as Twelve Mile Creek). No phone. No store. No church. Lena and Lil cried in disappointment but soon became part of the community with the warm welcomes received from neighbors. They quickly learned how to carry water from the creek, keep the kitchen stoves stoked, and fill the kerosene lamps.

The following spring, the freight truck delivered 200 four-month-old chicks to begin their egg business. They built a chicken house, bought a cow, two horses and a sow and were on their way to becoming great farmers. It was not to be. That winter all of their chickens froze to death! Hickie began horse logging for Walter Shiell in Wigwam and Trout Lake. In 1951 he became one of the Twelve Mile ferry operators, a position he held until it closed in 1969, when the valley was totally flooded.

They gradually upgraded their little home, installing a propane stove, lights, and refrigerator, as well as running water in the kitchen. They heated it in a large boiler for bathing and laundry. Unfortunately, one winter night in 1956 the propane refrigerator leaked poisonous fumes through their house, seriously affecting Lena who was rushed to the hospital for treatment.

The children thoroughly enjoyed country living with all of the outdoor games, pets, horseback riding, being pulled on a sloop by their horse through the deep snow, and water play. Hickie kept a close eye on Gloria and warned her constantly not to fall into the fast-flowing creek next to their house. Gloria enrolled in weekly piano lessons in Revelstoke and practiced on her grand piano in the heated bunkhouse next to their house. Neighbor children loved to try their skills on her piano.

Hickie Kaduhr shoveling himself out of his house. (Kaduhr family photo)

Bruce Kaduhr. (Kaduhr family photo)

Lena and Lil were soon actively involved in planning community social events such as sleigh rides, parties and dances at Twelve Mile School and Mt. Cartier community hall, Christmas concerts, and baby and bridal showers. Since Lena was one of a few ladies in the area who drove, she was always available to help neighbors in emergencies. She was an excellent seamstress, sewing beautiful clothes for herself and Gloria through her teen years, then for her grand and great grand children. She loved cooking and baking bread. When she and Hickie first married during the Depression they couldn't buy bread so he clipped out a bread recipe found in the Vancouver newspaper. It was such a good recipe, she used it until her last days.

The Green Hornet was good for entertainment in addition to transportation. Its wooden wheel spokes required periodic tightening when they dried out. Not a problem. Hickie just parked it in the shallow part of their creek and moved it in increments until all spokes got waterlogged. One morning he parked it against a snow bank at the top of the ferry approach when he went to work. The heat of the motor combined with the sun melted the snow just enough to release the car. It rolled right into the river when Hickie was on the other side with the ferry. Not realizing it was his car, he snickered thinking some fool had driven right into the river! When bachelor teacher Eric Norris boarded with Kaduhrs during his first teaching position at Twelve Mile School, he got to borrow the Essex because he was the "good boy," turning Bruce green with envy. Over the years, Hickie sold The Green Hornet several times, but always bought it back from its frustrated new owners because only he understood its idiosyncracies.

Bruce took the rest of grade six and finished grades seven and eight at Twelve Mile School with Irene English being his first teacher. After finishing high school in Revelstoke, his dad sent him to Vancouver to train as a Royal Canadian Mounted Police. But during his physical exam, his chest size at full exhalation lacked one-half inch of the required 70 inches. He was told to practice deep breathing for three weeks, then return. However, Bruce had other plans. That same day he joined the Royal Canadian Air Force and received six dollars in cash incentive pay for joining in 1953. On his way to St. John, Quebec for basic training, he took a train detour to Twelve Mile where Hickie gave him $60. Wow! That was the most cash he had ever owned. After basic training in 1954 he served for three years in Germany where he married and returned to Canada in 1958. He finished out his term in New Brunswick.

Bruce resides in Surrey, B.C. and is employed by Special Effects in the movie industry. Between contracts, he enjoys traveling the world and has played "tour guide" for his mom, and other family members. He has one son, Dearl, who is retired from social work and lives in Kelowna, B.C. He has four children: Sheldon, Crystal, Anastasia and Angelia. Each one has either completed or still attends college at this time.

When Gloria was in third grade, a spot was found on one lung. Fearing it was tuberculosis from which her Aunt Mary had died, she was taken out of school and made to take dreaded daily rests. At the end of that year the spot had disappeared!

Gloria boarded in Revelstoke with the Gowanlocks for her first year of high school before bus service was initiated in 1958 from Twelve Mile to Revelstoke. She and Ronald Dedosenco married in 1964. They had two children: Layton Ron and Sherrie Lyn.

Gloria Kaduhr, circa 1955. (Kaduhr family photo)

When BC Hydro bought out their family farm in 1969, Hickie and Lena moved to a government trailer in Revelstoke. Hickie transferred to the Needles ferry at Fauquier, B.C. He served as first mate on that ferry until his retirement in 1975. They then moved to Kelowna, B.C. He passed away December 21, 1995 following a stroke. Lena continued to keep her home in Kelowna and divided her time between Gloria and Bruce. She was able to enjoy trips throughout the world with her family, annual trips to Reno, Nevada and annual family reunions at Mara Lake, B.C. Over the years, she valiantly withstood treatment for persistent asthma, cancer and a serious car accident. She passed away January 10, 2007 at the age of 91 years.

KELLY

Marjorie Kelly, circa 1930. (Kelly family photo)

Allan Kelly was born on the Isle of Man, British Isles, in 1890, to John Kelly and Margaret Ann Kennish. In his youth, he apprenticed as a carpenter before moving to Canada. During WWI, he served in the Rocky Mountain Rangers guarding the CPR Columbia River bridge in Revelstoke from possible sabotage and then returned to England with his army unit. While in Revelstoke, Allan and Marjorie Smythe married in 1915. She was born in 1897 to Hugh Smythe and Amy Gibbon of Revelstoke (then Farwell).

Allan and Marjorie homesteaded about 90 acres three miles north of Revelstoke on the Big Bend highway that was just a narrow, gravel road at the time. Allan and his older sons spent grueling hours clearing their land but unfortunately it was too rocky to farm.

In 1929 Allan packed up his wife and eight children they had at that time and moved into the government house in Twelve Mile where he worked for the Highways Department as a ferry operator until 1935. Although his salary was only about $100 a month, it was a steady job. Unfortunately, after the national election during the 1934-35 winter, he lost his job because, as Sharry recalls, "he had voted for the losing party." This was a shocking blow to their family in the midst of the Depression. Forced to move back to their Revelstoke farm, they found a public work relief camp built on the northern part of their property for which they were not reimbursed.

Allan found work at a highway construction camp on the Big Bend Highway many miles north of their home. When WWII broke out, he worked at the shipyards and Boeing plant in Vancouver.

While in Twelve Mile, they became engrossed in community life. Marjorie was instrumental in having the first school built, and assisted her neighbors with business requiring proficiency in English. Her Kodak Brownie box camera was kept close at hand as she documented community and family events. She tended a large vegetable garden and kept milk goats. As an infant, daughter Joan could not tolerate cow's milk and so their goat-herding days began. Since the ferry house had no fence, the goats ran loose and Sharry, tongue-in-cheek, says they "probably caused some problems" for the neighbors.

During the winter of 1934-35, Sharry became severely ill with scarlet fever. Mrs. Rutherford, Robert Logan's housekeeper who had nursing experience in California, came to help Marjorie nurse Sharry, applying onion poultices to her chest to reduce her fever. When this didn't help, Marjorie took her to the Queen Victoria Hospital in Revelstoke. The road being impassable for their 1928 Chevrolet at that time of year, the northbound train was flagged down and Dr. Strong met them at the Revelstoke station with his car. Sharry recuperated at her grandparents' home (Hugh and Amy Smythe) and was able to complete grade two after Easter at Revelstoke Central School.

Kelly children on ferry dock, circa 1930. Back: Douglas, Jack, Kenneth; Front: Patrick, Sharry, Joan, Nordy, Christian. (Kelly family photo)

The Kellys have the distinction of having nine of their 10 children serve on behalf of the Canadian military.

John (Jack) was a Wireless Air Gunner in Europe serving on the bombing runs over Germany. When he was stationed in

Northern Ireland at Loch Erne, he flew in a Sunderland flying-boat aircraft off the lake, his unit following the Atlantic convoys to protect them from German submarines. Although they were shot down by a surfaced sub in the North Sea near Iceland, they managed to sink the sub. All of the German soldiers were rescued in a large life raft, but only half of the Canadian and English plane crew was saved when they were found by a ship from the convoy. Unfortunately, Jack was not among those rescued that fourth day of August, 1943. Kelly Peak south of Revelstoke was named in his memory.

Douglas trained in England as a transport driver and served with the First Division Seaforth Highlanders in Italy. He became friends with "Smokey" Smith who was in his unit in Italy and Holland. He contracted yellow fever, then returned to Canada in the fall of 1945. He died in 2006, leaving his wife and son, David.

Kenneth served in the Canadian Army, with Princess Patricia Infantry in England, and as a motorcycle dispatch rider on the continent. He met and married Nora Gardner of England. Upon his discharge, he taught school in Ontario for a number of years before moving back to Revelstoke. They had two daughters and one son. Kenneth died in 1997.

Phynoderee (Nordy) joined the women's division of the Royal Canadian Air Force Women's Division (RCAF-WD) during WWII and trained as a cook. She and her husband William Smith (RCNVR) had a son and daughter. She passed away in 1997.

Christian (Chris) trained in Calgary, Alberta and was a RCAF radio/wireless operator on Vancouver Island before serving in England during WWII. After discharge, he finished school in Ontario, married Helen Magill, and worked as an engineer for Aluminum Co. of Canada in Arvida, Quebec. They had two sons and a daughter and moved to California to work for Kaiser Aluminum until retirement.

Joan worked in Vancouver for Boeing Aircraft assembly before joining the RCAF during WWII. After training in Ontario as a radio operator, she served at remote stations on the west coast of B.C. She met and married William Cook of the Canadian Navy. Since being widowed, she continues to live in Port Moody near her two daughters and son.

Sharry enlisted in the Canadian Women's Army Corps (CWAC) the summer of 1943 after learning that her brother Jack was killed. She took basic training in Fort Vermilion, Alberta, and became an Instrument Mechanic for the Royal Canadian Electrical and Mechanical Engineers (RCEME). While in Vancouver, Sharry was able to renew her friendship with Rose Kozek of Twelve Mile who was married and had her first baby. She also met a Texas soldier, Charles Reynolds, who ended up in Vancouver from the Pacific Arena when the atomic bomb over Japan abruptly ended the conflict. They married in 1946 shortly after Sharry was released from service. They moved to Texas and owned their own plumbing and air conditioning business until retiring to the family ranch in Orange Grove, Texas. They have four daughters and two sons.

Hugh Patrick (Pat) joined the Royal Canadian Navy during WWII and served as a mechanic aboard ships. After discharge he returned to Revelstoke where he was involved in private delivery business and with the Fire Department-Ambulance Service. He and his wife, Dorrine Pleasant, have three sons and three daughters. He is retired and lives with his eldest daughter, Patti, in Kelowna, B.C.

Robyn made RCAF his career. He moved to Edmonton, Alberta when he retired. He and his wife, Grace Pearson, have one daughter and two sons.

Karran (Mona) and husband, Charles (Charley) Howe, have three sons and one daughter. They were happy to live in Lumby, B.C., away from the snow-shoveling days of Revelstoke. Charley passed away March 23, 2008.

Allan Kelly passed away in 1968 and Marjorie passed away in 1984.

KERNAGHAN

Eileen Kernaghan taught the 15 students at the Twelve Mile School from 1959-60. No further information is available.

Eileen Kernaghan at Christmas concert, 1959. Note the Canada P.O. mail bag that Santa is using. (A.Domke family photo)

KLAPSTEIN

Norman Klapstein and Nellie Dahl were married in 1941 in Ellerslie, Alberta. In 1956 they moved from Mission City to Twelve Mile where Norman worked in the logging business. They lived in Charlie Sartorous' sawmill camp at Blanket Creek.

At that time they had 10 children and the eight older ones attended Twelve Mile School, readily becoming friends of the local children. Even with a houseful of children, Nellie found time to bake her famous cinnamon buns, and visit with her neighbors.

Two years later they moved to Six Mile, then to Craigellachie where they lived for several years before moving to Quesnel and finally Prince George. Their last two children were born after leaving Twelve Mile.

Nellie passed away August 16, 1984, and Norman on January 29, 1994. Their children are as follows:

Elleanor and Abe Klassen of Sicamous have five children, 13 grandchildren and two great-grandchildren. Eleanor worked as a school custodian. Abe passed away in 2007.

Norma Klapstein, circa 1957. (A. Domke family photo)

Norma and Walter Chometsky have two children and three grandchildren. Norma is a retired bank clerk and lives in Vernon.

Ivan (divorced) had one daughter, and one grandchild who lives in Ontario. Ivan was a logging truck driver and passed away accidentally in 1995. His daughter died in 1999.

Ronald is retired in Nanaimo, and has three children and two grandchildren.

Kenneth and Marg (Gagnon) have three children and ten grandchildren. He owns a logging business and lives in Quesnel.

Dennis and Carol (Krueger) have one daughter and three grandchildren. He is a truck driver and lives in Quesnel.

Glenn and Cindy have one son, two grandchildren, and four stepgrandchildren. He is a truck driver in Nanaimo.

Robert and Peggy (Parr) have five children and six grandchildren. He is a truck driver in Slocan Park.

June and Merrill Giesbrecht have two children and two grandchildren. They live and work in Chilliwack.

Eugene (divorced) has three children. He lives and works in McKenzie.

Shirley and Chris Marr have three children and two grandchildren. They live and work in Chilliwack.

David (divorced) has three children and one grandchild. He lives and works in Nanaimo.

KOZEK

The Michael (Mike) Kozeks were among the very early settlers who came to Twelve Mile. Mike and his wife, Nastya (Nettie) lived in Poland (later Ukraine) and began worrying when WWI was imminent. They decided to move to Canada but Nettie was pregnant with Kashka (Kate). She decided to stay in the "Old Country" while Mike emigrated to Canada in 1910 seeking land and a peaceful life. (Years later, Nettie told her son, Walter, about the shells flying and having to hide in cellars while German and Russian soldiers went back and forth through their area.) Eleven years later in 1921 when Mike had saved enough money, he sent for Nettie and Kate. Nettie's brother came also and mined coal in Drumheller, Alberta. Nettie and Kate stayed with him over that first winter.

Mike initially lived in Winnipeg, Manitoba where the CPR offered to train him as a steam locomotive engineer, but he didn't like it. He was a farmer at heart and bought some land at Sunnyslope north of Drumheller. His attempt at growing oats proved unsuccessful because of the weather. When he heard through the grapevine that 40-acre homesteads were being offered for $10 at a place called Twelve Mile, he gave up his farm. They shipped their horse and belonging to Twelve Mile in a CPR boxcar, followed the "bush" logging road to the land they had purchased and settled in. That first year they lived in a logger's cabin where Walter was born June 25, 1922. That was the year of the large fire that engulfed the entire valley.

Homesteaders could keep their property if they cleared a certain number of acres and lived on the property. Mike cleared the land in order to survive, growing hay for the cow and oats for the horses. In those days, horses were used to pull out the roots of the huge cedar stumps after blowing them up with stumping powder. As other homesteaders also cleared land and burned the rubbish, the valley became full of smoke.

Initially there was no highway to Revelstoke, so Mike and other homesteaders caught the train to town on its way back from Arrowhead. He carried his purchases in a sack

Nettie and Mike Kozek. (W. Kozek photo)

thrown over his back as he walked home on the tracks. When the first road was built, Mike purchased a black Gray Dort car. Walter remembers that car in his pre-school years because it had a clock in it.

The rim had to be turned to wind the clock. His father had several other cars after that before he got his first logging truck.

In addition to their 40-acre homestead, the Kozeks obtained the adjacent Lawrence farm to the north and there in about 1925 built their two-story frame farm house (which still stands on skids after being moved onto Airport Way south of Revelstoke). The Lawrence barn was already there, built of 10 x 10 creosoted railroad bridge timbers, as well as an apple orchard and cellar. Mike cut the logs on his property, hauled them by wagon to a sawmill at Ten Mile (probably McCormick's) to be sawn into lumber for

Mike Kozek farm house, after it was moved eight miles south of Revelstoke. (A. Jarvis photo)

their new house. The mill was steam powered and included a planer. Their house had two bedrooms, living room and kitchen downstairs, and one big room upstairs. They lit the house with coal oil lamps and the barn with lanterns.

Walter and Kate Kozek in Vancouver. (W. Kozek photo)

When Gregory Astrahantseff bought the land between Kozek's and the river, an access road was needed. The lane was built between Kozek's two pieces of land, taking a piece off each side. This left the barn and well on the right and the house on the left side. When Walter came home from school one day, the house had been moved across the road! Pete Lonzo had skidded it with his small bulldozer once it was on greased log slabs.

Mike and Nettie had six children as follows:

Kashka (Kate) was born in 1911 in Poland; Walter was born June 25, 1922; Steve was born June 16, 1923; Rose was born July 1, 1924; Joseph (Joe) was born November 1, 1925; and Mildred (Minnie) was born April 23, 1933. All but Kate were born at home in Twelve Mile. Elizabeth Mazar was the midwife when Mildred was born.

Always trying to earn cash to support his family, Mike had many things going on. In the 1920s, he went back to Drumheller to work in the mine for a while. They sold cream, butter, eggs, produce and meat in town, and also shipped cream by five-gallon cans on the train to the NOCA Vernon Creamery. When his sons got older they went into logging and built a sawmill on their farm.

Nettie worked hard raising her family and doing farm work. One time she found a pea-sized gold nugget mixed with the gravel in a gizzard of a chicken she had butchered. They think the gravel was some they had brought for the chickens from a swampy, gravelly bank at Eight Mile.

All of the children also had to pull their fair share of the workload. When Mike went to Drumheller to work, the cow was "dry" and baby Walter needed milk. So 12-year-old Kate, who couldn't yet speak English, had to board the train to Arrowhead and purchase canned milk and other supplies. Mike had left a note at the store there allowing her to make the purchases.

Walter remembers many tales of his life on the farm. Some are recorded below:

After ninth grade I got my drivers license and on Wednesdays and Saturdays using the truck I'd haul cream, butter, and eggs to town. I picked up all the farmers along the way—Polly Astrahantseff, Shamons, Holds, Sytnyks—with their produce to sell in town. The way we hauled it and kept it cold—we put it in a box and cut with a scythe or sickle a bunch of green clover or grass and covered the milk in the box. It kept very cold all the way to town, even in the summer. Once I had a pint of cream left over that no one bought, so instead of hauling it back home, I bought a loaf of bread and Ukrainian garlic sausage (kobosaw). I ate and drank the whole thing. That was it!

We'd shoot gophers on the weekends with our .22 rifle. Once I shot a coyote right through the head with the .30 Remington. One misty summer morning, Dad came upstairs where Steve, Joe and I were sleeping. "Shhh, coyote." I jumped out of bed, got out the Remington and ran onto the upstairs verandah. I saw him sneaking up over the hill. I shot and missed, but woke up everyone else in the house. The black bears would eat apples off the trees, but we didn't have grizzlies on the farms. We didn't have deer in those days either.

Rose Kozek. (W. Kozek photo)

Mildred Kozek on right, Joanna Zibulak on left, 1947. (Makarewicz family photo)

The Kozek children all attended Twelve Mile School for their elementary through eighth or ninth grade education. It was difficult for any of the students to further their education without leaving home. Walter finished ninth grade in 1937 and then worked on the farm. Even though farmers wore coveralls or overalls on the farm, they always dressed up, usually in suit and tie, to go to town.

The Kozek's were bought out by BC Hydro in 1963. Mike and Nettie moved to Surrey, B.C. where they bought a house to be near Kate who lived in Vancouver. Walter and Steve had a mill on the farm. For compensation by BC Hydro, they received 24 acres on Airport Way, about eight miles south of Revelstoke.

Kay (Kate) married Charlie Robinson and lived in Vancouver until her death. Her daughter, Gloria, died of lung cancer, prior to her mother.

Rose married John Miazga in 1944 in Battleford, Saskatchewan. When they returned to Twelve Mile, the Kozeks put on a great feast complete with a five-tiered wedding cake. Rose and John moved to Vancouver where they both worked in the shipyards.

Mildred married Mr. Combatly. They have lived in Salem, Oregon for about 50 years where he was a mill superintendent and she operated her own real estate business until retirement.

Mike and Nettie both died in Surrey, B.C.

Walter

Walter was drafted into the army in 1942. In those days the young men received their notices by telegram. His was mailed from Revelstoke since they had no phone at that time. If the draftees didn't report to the army depot in Vancouver on the stated day, the RCMP came after them. Walter spent eight months in Holland but was not involved in combat. He completed his service in 1945.

Walter Kozek and Mary Ferby were married on November 9, 1946 after he was discharged from the army. When Walter, an army gunner, was on furlough from his station in Wainwright, Alberta in

1944, he visited his uncle, George Ewanchuk, in Drumheller. The Ferbys and his uncle's family were friends so Walter and Mary struck up a friendship and wrote letters while he was overseas.

Their wedding was a major social event in Twelve Mile. Although the ceremony took place at

Back: Mary Kozek, Lena Kaduhr, Mildred Kozek; Front: Gloria Kaduhr and Russell Gowanlock. (Kaduhr family photo)

the United Church in Revelstoke, the reception dinner was held the next day at the Kozek farm house. The entire community was invited and many still remember the event. Holopsi (cabbage rolls), old farm-style roast chicken and pork were served in abundance. The young guests were especially fascinated with the jello and whipped cream dessert served. Walter remembers their trip to their wedding dance at the Six Mile Hall:

It was the beginning of the baby boomers. My sister, Mildred, drove the car—1942 Ford V8. Mary and I were sitting in the back and Mildred and someone else (maybe Joanna Zibulak) were in the front. It had snowed four inches that evening. Going over the railroad crossing and turning left, the car slid into the ditch on its side. It was snowing like crazy, and we were all dressed up in our good clothes so we just stayed and waited. Joe and Steve were coming from the farm about a mile away driving my four-wheel-drive truck that I bought with the $700 I made in the army. They came around the corner and found us, hooked a chain to our car and pulled us out. Then we kept on going to the dance.

Walter and Mary lived with his parents over the winter. Jobs were hard to find, so they drove his old army truck to Vancouver, where they initially lived with his sister, Rose. Walter found work at a foundary making cast iron sewer pipes and all the fittings. He worked the big grinding wheel, grinding off the sharp edges of the seams. It was hot and sweaty work and the iron filings rusted on his coveralls. The job paid about $1.08 an hour. Walter also worked for Slade & Stewart Fruit & Vegetable Wholesale where he unloaded freight cars of fruits and vegetables. The job paid 75 cents an hour. Mary worked at Lions Gate Produce as a candle egg grader and packer. They were able to rent a house in Vancouver for $15 a month.

This was in 1948 when many were collecting unemployment insurance. The unemployed were told where all the jobs in the province were, but when they got there, the jobs had already been taken because about 40 fellows had already been there. Money for gas was scarce so it was a real hardship trying to drive around to jobs that were already taken. Walter and Mary spent two years in Vancouver before returning to Revelstoke.

From 1951-53 Walter worked in Revelstoke as a boilermaker's helper in the CPR shops. His job was to wash out the boilers of all the steam engines that came through Revelstoke. When diesels took over in 1953, he was out of a job again. The machinists were demoted to laborers (his job).

After that, he and his brother, Steve, started a sawmill on the family farm and continued logging. He is full of interesting stories of his logging days with his brothers from then on.

Sergei Astrahantseff hauled logs for them, but one day while logging on Hiren Creek up the Jordan, he couldn't start the loader. They discovered that the fuel lines had been chewed off by a porcupine. Another time, the critter had eaten the fan belts on the bulldozer, chewed the copper wiring, and ate the seats leaving behind the nails. To repair the equipment, they had to move the radiator, take off the hydraulic pump, disconnect all the oil lines and then replace the belts. However, it took several days for the belts to come after they were ordered. Walter explained how they solved that problem:

> We rigged up an electric fence to keep out the porcupines. We got an electric fencer, put chicken wire on the dry gravel road, put old rubber truck tires over the wire and drove the cat on the tires. Then we hooked a live wire from the cat batteries to the electric fencer sitting on the seat. This did discourage the porcupines from chewing up our equipment for a time until vandals came on a weekend and stole the electric fencer.

Walter and Mary had two children: Diane Carol, born August 7, 1949; and Alan Michael, born July 7, 1953.

Mary passed away in 1960 while living in Revelstoke. Since Walter had to work, he moved his family to live with his parents in Twelve Mile. Diane and Alan attended school there until Diane began high school in 1963 and Alan transferred to Revelstoke in 1966.

Mary Kozek with Diane and Alan, circa 1954. (A. Domke family photo)

Diane married Robert Lang in 1966. They have one son, Stacey, an engineer for CPR. He has three children: Matthew, Shannley and Amanda, all living in Revelstoke.

Alan lives in Vancouver. He is a tool and die maker for Richmond Ball that makes cans for the salmon industry.

Walter lives eight miles south of Revelstoke on Airport Way on the 24 acres received from Hydro as compensation for their mill. He continued to work at his nephew's sawmill, J. Kozek Sawmills Ltd., through 2007.

Steve

Steve was drafted into the army in 1942 but was released because two fingers on his left hand were missing and he couldn't hold the rifle properly. When he was a child, he blew off those two fingers while playing with blasting caps.

Steve and Walter started a small sawmill on their parents' farm in Twelve Mile using the small pension money Walter had received from his CPR job. Pine logs were $44 FBM. With Walter as sawyer, they sawed and sold lumber for $90 per M. When they halved the income they had some money left over but "never got rich on it."

When the Kozek farm and sawmill were purchased by Hydro, they logged in various areas.

Steve and his wife, Irene, had one son, Roger, and lived in Revelstoke, where Steve died.

Joe Kozek, circa 1940s. (W. Kozek photo)

Joe

Joe married Doreen Olsson-Fayette and had one son, Joey.

Before Joe bought property on Camozzi Road in Revelstoke on which to build his mill, he moved his portable sawmill to many areas including the Big Bend, Jordan, Akolkolex by Echo Lake and Sidmouth. The logs were skidded right to the mill so they didn't have to haul them. When he logged around Cranberry (now Corsier) Lake with Sartorous, Walter hauled the logs to the Sartorous mill by Blanket Creek below the falls. They used a six-wheel-drive International stake truck (6x6) and carried up to 20-foot-long logs. As Walter puts it,

> The road wasn't too good. There was a hole filled with a bunch of rubbish and when I went over, the truck was leaning, then pretty soon it turned over on its side. So I went back up the hill and told Joe, "The truck tipped over on its side, we have to get a cat and pull it out." We left the logs there and took the truck back up for another load.

They hauled in the summer and winter. One day in March it snowed 16 inches. That's the time Walter climbed on top of the logs and took a picture that showed the valley all the way to Revelstoke from Blanket Creek.

Joe built up J. Kozek Sawmills, Ltd. and Walter scaled logs for it. After Joe passed away, his son, Joey, continues operating the mill.

In 2007, Joey's son played hockey on the University of North Dakota's U.S. college championship team.

KRAMER

Olga Lange emigrated to Canada in 1952, sponsored by her mother's cousin, Asaph Domke. She lived with the Domkes and worked hard on their little farm that year to pay off her ship fare. One time when they were burning the trees and stumps that the bulldozers had piled up from land clearing, she stepped into what looked like cold ashes and sunk down to the burning coals below. The pain from the burns was excruciating and her cousin, Ada, remembers her agony to this day.

During that year she met Eric Kramer. The following year they married and continued to live in Twelve Mile.

Olga's family was of German descent, living in the Ukraine. After her father was taken away by the Russians in 1937 and World War II broke out, the family became refugees. When Germany tried to transport them and others to Germany by rail cars after the war ended, their rail yard in Cotpus, Poland was bombed. She never saw her mother or sisters again, but her grandmother was uninjured. Olga suffered severe injuries to her head and spine resulting in paralysis. She recovered in Bavaria and was hired by the Hiltels to care for their children. Since her grandmother had also died by now, they became her new family. After her uncle and aunt, Arthur and Emilie Domke, located her, she moved to the Hamburg area and then sailed for Canada at age 18 on the *Bevabra*.

Back: Olga, Ed, Eric Kramer; Front: Judy, Brian, Lillian Kramer. (Kramer family photo)

Eric was born in Edenwold, Saskatchewan. Since he farmed with his parents, four brothers and two sisters, he was exempt from the Canadian military draft. One summer in the early 1940s he and

Siegfried Sauer took a motorcycle trip to Kelowna, B.C., with Siegfried riding in the sidecar. That summer they worked in a packinghouse, but returned to the farm in the fall because of their "army relief" status. When the war ended, Eric moved to B.C. and worked at the Copper Mountain mine for a couple of years. There he met Hans and Lotty Podzun and moved with them to Twelve Mile.

Eric farmed with the Podzuns and logged in the area until hiring on as an operator of the Twelve Mile ferry where he continued working until it closed.

After Eric and Olga married, they purchased some property from Ferdinand and Emil Rauchert, and moved a shack from the Big Eddy west of Revelstoke onto the corner by Zibulak's road. Moving it was quite an operation because the roof had to be removed so it would fit the various bridges on the way to Twelve Mile. As their family grew, they added more rooms.

When BC Hydro bought them out, they moved to Colbeck Road in Revelstoke. Olga worked in various restaurants to support her family.

Eric and Olga had four children: Edward (Ed) Eric, Lillian Bernice, Judy Elaine and Brian.

Ed has three children: Kenny, Tyson and Cindie, and lives near Vancouver, B.C.

Lillian and Colby Robison have two sons: Ryan and Clayton, and live in Golden, B.C.

Judy has two daughters: Jamie-Lee Stacy and Jeni-Rae Stacy, and lives in Chilliwack, B.C.

Brian has two children: Tyler and Tara, and lives in the Okanagan area.

After her second husband, Peter Bernard, died, Olga moved to Kelowna, B.C. Eric moved to Vernon, then Chilliwick, B.C.

KUPCHENKO (KUPCHANKO)

Nick Kupchenko, a bachelor, homesteaded on the west side of the river between McMahons and the Domkes. He built a one-room log cabin along the small creek that ran through his property. In the 1940s he began working on the CPR section from Wigwam to Arrowhead and later became a steward for the CPR dining cars out of Revelstoke. In 1945 the Ocepoffs purchased his farm.

LAMONTAGNE

Guy Lamontagne moved from Saskatchewan to Kaslo, B.C. when only 17 years old and began his logging career.

In the 1950s, he lived with and worked for John Rauchert in Twelve Mile for seven years, using his own logging truck during part of that time.

When Guy and Donna Berarducci of Six Mile married, they moved to Sidmouth; then built their own house a few miles south of Revelstoke. When BC Hydro bought their home, they purchased and moved some of the houses from Six Mile flats to property on Gawiuk Road east of the airport, and rented them.

Guy is remembered by his friends and family as an ambitious, fine gentleman who was always willing to help where needed. In November 1969 he lost his life tragically in a hunting accident.

Donna and Guy had four children: Aaron, now in New Westminster; Dianna, deceased; June, now in Sicamous; and Dean, deceased. Donna currently lives in Malakwa.

LAWRENCE

When the Mike Kozeks arrived in Twelve Mile in 1921, they purchased the Lawrence property and took a 40-acre homestead next to it. The Lawrence property had a barn that was well-built out of railway bridge timbers, a well and a root cellar. It is uncertain if the Lawrences were early loggers, or homesteaders.

LINDSAY

Ruth Lindsay was born in Nelson B.C. in 1913 to Percy and Alice Lindsay. She had one sister, Dorothy. They moved to Revelstoke where Ruth graduated from high school and went on to finish teacher training at Victoria Normal School. Her sister also became a school teacher.

Ruth taught at the Twelve Mile School from 1936-37.

Her teaching eventually took her to Prince George where she met and married Gordon Stock. They had three children and continued living in Prince George. Ruth stayed at home to raise their family while Gordon worked as an airlines mechanic.

In their later years, they moved to Surrey, B.C. where Ruth still lives.

LOGAN

Robert Logan, a bachelor, homesteaded the property on the west side of the river that was later purchased by the Millars, then Demerses, then Podzuns. He farmed there from the 1920s until the mid-1930s.

Bob was known for the apples and grain that he raised on his farm. On November 8, 1935 the *Revelstoke Review* described the samples of Golden Pippin apples that Bob sent to them. The paper wrote a glowing report about their size, shape, color and flavor! He also boasted that his wheat reached a height of six feet, oats five and a half feet, and Timothy hay five and a half feet. His farm animals included Charlie, his sway-backed horse which the older Kelly children enjoyed riding.

He depended on his neighbors to help work his fields, however. Walter Kozek once ploughed Bob's field and his plough kept getting caught in underground roots. Likewise, when the Millars purchased the farm, they discovered that Bob had taken a shortcut in order to clear enough land to obtain title to the homestead. They found that he had chopped off the roots of the stumps and trees and covered the rest with soil. When Jim tried ploughing the fields his plough also kept getting caught in all the buried roots.

In addition to farming, Bob did some prospecting and in March 1934 the *Revelstoke Review* reported that he staked a rich gold lead. Its whereabouts was not given.

Mrs. Rutherford, his housekeeper who received nursing experience in California, assisted Mrs. Kelly in nursing Sharry through her bout with scarlet fever during the winter of 1934-35.

LOZIER

Diane Lozier attended Twelve Mile School during the 1966-67 school year. No further information is available.

LUSCHNAT

Roderick (Rod) Luschnat emigrated to Canada from Berlin, Germany in 1924. He and Asaph Domke met on the Canadian Pacific Steamship *Montclaire* sailing for 10 days from Liverpool to Quebec City. After a year working off their fares with individual Alberta farmers, they homesteaded side-by-side in Edgewater, B.C. for several years. With money and jobs scarce during the "Hungry 30s", they abandoned their homesteads and struck out in separate directions. Rod rode a freight train to Vancouver in 1931. The two men and their families remained lifelong friends.

Even though Rod became a naturalized Canadian citizen in 1935, he experienced much unjust discrimination due to his telltale German accent. One that hurt him the most was losing his shingle mill in Port Coquitlam when B.C. Electric boycotted it. Ironically, after Canada entered WWII, Rod was conscripted into its army in 1943.

After the war, he started a sawmill in Port Coquitlam and purchased a bulldozer with which he contracted for land clearing and logging. He shipped it by CPR flatcar, and drove his truck to Twelve Mile in the spring of 1948. There he lived with the Domkes and in logging camps while building roads and logging for Columbia River Timbers (CRT) in the "Cranberry" area and Columbia valley south of Revelstoke.

Back: Kellina, Asaph and Ada Domke, Rod Luschnat; Front: Phyllis Luschnat, Eugen Domke, Sylvia Luschnat. (A. Domke family photo)

Rod's family did not move to Twelve Mile, but visited him there. When he completed his logging contracts, he returned to his home in Port Coquitlam and worked as a steam engineer for various companies including Alcan in Kitimat, B.C. He eventually established a demolition business in Port Coquitlam that was successful until his retirement. His wife, Filomena (Phyllis) Chine, and he had four children: Sylvia, Diana, Roderick II and Anita.

Rod passed away in January 1, 1998. Phyllis, their three children, five grandchildren and five great-grandchildren all continue to live in the Vancouver vicinity.

MACRAE

Mrs. Margaret MacRae taught at the Twelve Mile School from 1943-45. She and her son, Ronnie, who was a student there, lived in the teacherage. She is remembered by her students as being strict and "prim and proper."

MCINTOSH

D. McIntosh taught the 14 students at the Twelve Mile School during the 1960-61 school year. No further information is available.

MCKAY, JACK

Mr. and Mrs. Jack McKay and sons Harvey and Bernie moved to Twelve Mile for a short while in 1946 while they logged their timber limit. The Kozeks had built roads for their logging operation.

MCKAY, NELLIE

Nellie McKay finished out her teaching career at the Twelve Mile School from the fall of 1962 through the fall of 1965. She was forced to leave that winter because of illness. She lived in the teacherage of the third school and her students remember her to be a competent and caring teacher. When she moved from Revelstoke to care homes in Sicamous and Kamloops, some of the students' families kept in touch with her. She passed away about 2007.

Nellie McKay, circa 1962-65. (B. Weston photo)

MCKINLEY

Mr. and Mrs. Jerry McKinley rented Oscar Domke's log house from 1957-59 while he logged in the Cranberry area with his caterpillar.

Eugen Domke drove to work with him. He remembers "hanging on for dear life because Jerry drove like crazy over those rutted logging roads." He also recalls the day Jerry found a cute bunny in the bush, and took it home to his children in his lunch box, but unfortunately the rabbit didn't make it.

The McKinleys had three children. Their oldest daughter, Doreen, finished grades three and four at Twelve Mile School.

They moved to Revelstoke where they bought a service station.

MCLEOD, CLARENCE

Clarence McLeod was born in Ingedine, Michigan and moved to Empress, Alberta where he and his first wife homesteaded. They had two sons, Kenneth and Douglas, and moved to Barrier, B.C. to log.

After Clarence and his wife separated, he met Annie Smith in Revelstoke. She was born at Hall's Landing, just south of Sidmouth, B.C. They moved to Wigwam to log with Dan McLeod, Clarence's cousin. There they first bought Ollie Passmore's property that had a frame house, and eventually the adjoining farms which belonged to Robinsons and Percy Demers. The Akolkolex River ran through their property and formed a large grassy delta in the river. They raised up to 300 head of Hereford cattle, butchered and sent the beef by train to the Revelstoke butcher shops, and sold it to their neighbors. They also raised chickens. Their team of horses was an important part of Clarence's logging operation. He established a pole yard between the train tracks and Columbia River next to the CPR bridge crossing the Akolkolex River.

The only way out of Wigwam was by boat or by train that ran two to three times a week from Revelstoke, through Twelve Mile, Wigwam and Arrowhead. They used the CPR section foreman's phone to connect with Arrowhead. Two rings got the station in Arrowhead that transferred their call to Crawford's General Store. They read off their list of groceries that were boxed up and shipped to them on the next train. Their mail was delivered by train twice a week.

Della was born October 1, 1937 in Revelstoke's Queen Victoria Hospital. Annie went to town by train and stayed with friends until her baby was to be born.

Florence surprised everyone by arriving during the December 17, 1938 Twelve Mile Christmas concert. The school's teacherage was the delivery room!

The girls had no neighbor children to play with so entertained themselves. They fished for dollys and trout below the falls in the Akolkolex River, picked wild huckleberries on Smith Creek, played in the snow and with their farm animals.

Trying to get an education was a real challenge. For the first three grades, the girls and Annie lived with friends in Arrowhead so they could go to school. Then Annie home schooled them for grades four through six. For grades seven and eight, Della and Florence attended Twelve Mile School, first rooming and boarding with Gowanlocks. When Brooks and Lil moved to town, Annie stayed in Twelve Mile through the week with the girls in the Mulvehill house along the tracks near Drimmie Creek. For the first two years of high school, Annie and the girls moved to Kamloops. Della withdrew from school after finishing tenth grade, and Florence finished eleventh in Revelstoke.

Annie McLeod and Joanna Zibulak with Della and Florence McLeod on CPR tracks between Twelve Mile and Wigwam, circa 1943. (Makarewicz family photo)

One winter while living with Gowanlocks, Della and Florence wanted to go home for the weekend, but it was snowing. After supper they walked five miles on the train tracks, arriving home at 9:00 that dark night. Boy, were they in trouble. They were not to go anywhere after dark because of cougars along the tracks. Della shrugs her shoulders saying, "But what were we supposed to do? It's dark most of the winter and we weren't scared." They usually caught a ride back to Twelve Mile on Monday mornings with the CPR section man, Nick Moreno, who patrolled the tracks with a little handcar known as a "jigger."

Even though they were isolated, the McLeods modernized their home with indoor plumbing. The water gravity-fed from a water tank on the mountain above. Clarence kept a 1949 Ford car in a garage near the Twelve Mile School and accessed it by a small boat that he docked along the river. At times the slush and wind prevented the boat from landing, so he'd have to return to Twelve Mile and wait with his supplies for the next train.

In 1957 their house, barn and shop burned down. Annie got up at five in the morning to light the fire and warm up the house before Clarence came home. The girls had already left home so she was alone. The chimney had never been cleaned. Residue built up until a chimney fire blew the stove pipes right out. Since the wind was blowing south towards the hay barn, it immediately caught fire also. They lost everything.

After BC Hydro bought them out in the 1960s, Clarence and Annie moved to Greenwood, B.C. Their property was above the high water line of the reservoir and is currently being farmed. They found out later that they could have bought their farm back from Hydro, but they weren't aware of the details in time to do so.

Annie died in 1975 in Greenwood, B.C., and Clarence died in 1981 in Revelstoke.

Della married Carl Johnson in 1955. They had seven children and 12 grandchildren. John lived in Mara, B.C.; Owen in Ft. McMurray; and Harvey in Cochran, Alberta. Sheila, David, Irene and Susan all live in Calgary. Carl died in 2002 and John died in 2006. Della continues to live in Revelstoke.

Florence married Ike Johnson, Carl's brother, in 1956. They live in Sicamous, B.C., have five children and 11 grandchildren. Dorothy, Anita, Brenda and Jeff all live in Revelstoke; and Les lives in Malakwa.

Clarence, Annie, Florence and Della McLeod, 1945. (McLeod family photo)

MCLEOD, WILLIAM

William (Bill) McLeod of Campbell River, B.C. completed his teacher training at Victoria Normal School in 1950. That year he began his distinguished teaching career at Twelve Mile School (1950-51).

William and Judy McLeod in front of W. L. McLeod Elementary School, named in his honor, Vanderhoof, B.C., 2007. (W. McLeod photo)

Setting up housekeeping as a young bachelor in the school's teacherage was delayed because his trunk of personal belongings did not arrive until October 2 due to the Greyhound bus strike. Bill soon experienced the warm hospitality typical of Twelve Milers, however. Olympe Astrahantseff brought him a ling fish for lunch that first day, and left him some fishing tackle.

A room full of 17 students, grades one through eight, is a challenge for anyone, not to mention a rookie teacher in a country school. He was grateful for help from Helen Hammond, an experienced primary teacher in Revelstoke, who ably mentored him through lesson planning. Bill said, "I scratched my head many times as I tried to juggle instruction among all the grades, and especially wondering what to do with the little girls in the lower grades." In the following years, he wondered how the little girls fared in later life and was thrilled to learn that Emily Rauchert had been the principal of a school in Revelstoke from which one of his pupils transferred.

Bill still recalls with a chuckle the morning after the school's Halloween party. Part of his daily routine was to arise early and get the fires going to warm up his teacherage and the classroom. But on November 1, 1950, rather than throwing off heat, his stove sent out billows of smoke. He immediately pulled out the wood and discarded it outside. That's when he discovered a cardboard box over the chimney. And that's when he also discovered the roof's ladder was mysteriously missing. *Ah, ha!* An idea struck him. He blew the box off with his shotgun and hid the evidence. As school progressed through the day, only innocent looks were exchanged between teacher and students, with no one owning up to the prank to this day.

For the next four years, Bill taught at South Slocan and then moved to Doe River near Dawson Creek as principal of Grades one through 10. This proved to be a fortuitous move, for it was there he met and married Judy Bell of Fruitvale, B.C. in 1956. She and her sister, Dawn Bell, taught the lower grades. Bill then served as principal of Bridge River Superior School (1956-60) and at Vanderhoof Elementary School until 1983. He was honored to have the Vanderhoof school named "W. L. McLeod Elementary School." He held a district position until retirement in 1986.

Bill and Judy have three sons, a daughter, three grandsons and one granddaughter. In 1999 John Ryan, their son-in-law with paraplegia, rode his handcycle across Canada raising about one million dollars to benefit spinal cord research. Bill and Judy were privileged to follow along and cook for him and his crew of nine during his 133-day trek from May 1 to September 15.

MCMAHON

Hugh John McMahon owned the property between Nick Kupchenko's (later Ocepoff's) and Thompson's properties. He was a bachelor when living there in the 1930s. Hugh worked at various jobs for the forestry and cooked in logging camps.

Hugh's parents were Thomas McMahon and Eliza Jane (Brill) who lived in the Big Eddy area of Revelstoke. He was one of their six children: Thomas (Tom), married Margaret Sinfield who wrote *Pioneers of Revelstoke* (1986) and also the words and music to the Revelstoke song; Roy; George (married Mildred Jones); Lloyd (married Violet McNair); and Minnie (Beckwith). George served in Italy with the Seaforth Highlanders in WWII. Roy and wife, Rosie Saporito, farmed at Seven Mile against the mountain where lime deposits were found, a commodity valuable to farms with soil having high acid content.

Hugh's father, Thomas, died in 1910. Eliza married James Irvine, and then William Henry Thompson of Twelve Mile in 1933. When the marriage didn't work out, she moved in with Hugh at Twelve Mile for a few years before moving to Tom and Margaret's in Revelstoke. Eliza died in 1944.

Hugh married Patricia Addison in 1947 in Revelstoke and they later moved to Vancouver. When he died in 1958, she went back to Twelve Mile to try and claim his property without realizing it had been sold.

MCQUEEN

Jim and Carrie McQueen homesteaded at Crawford Creek south of Wigwam in 1913. They moved to Twelve Mile for about a year in 1917 and then returned to their farm. Their children were Jessie, Bertha, Dorothy and Thomas.

MAKAREWICZ

Nick was born in Laznisko, Poland, June 22, 1921. At age two, his father was killed in the war and Nick went to live with relatives. At 14, he was rounded up with other young village boys by the Russians while invading Poland. The Russians sent the young men to Siberian slave labour camps. Somehow Nick and his brother, Alexander, managed to survive the camps. When Churchill and Stalin made their pact, Stalin granted amnesty to the Polish prisoners, and 25,000 were sent for special training with the British. Nick and his brother became separated as they boarded separate trains commanded by either the British or Russians. Nick last

Nick Makarewicz with Victoria Cross and other WWII medals. (Makarewicz photo)

heard from his brother via a letter from Turkey. Nick fought with the Polish 2nd Corp under the British 8th army, which took him to North Africa, Turkey, Italy, France, Iraq, Iran, Palestine and Egypt. The soldiers experienced very dangerous conditions while trying to sleep in the cold deserts in Iran and Iraq. They bundled up, slept under their tanks with sentries posted to protect them from the Arab nomads who tried to slit their throats and steal their goods. As a Corporal, Nick was a tank commander when his regiment captured Monte Casino in Italy. The battle broke Hitler's Gustav line. An Italian officer witnessed Nick's heroic actions during the battle, leading to his award of the Victoria Cross, Britain's highest military honor. Interestingly, the Polish 2nd Corp were not allowed to march with the victors due to a British commander's ruling.

When the Polish soldiers were released by the British in 1945, they were given the opportunity to emigrate to Canada. Nick's mother told him not to return to Poland as there was nothing left of their country. The soldiers also heard that men returning to Poland were being treated as traitors and shot. Nick and some buddies ended up on a sugar beet farm in Lethbridge, Alberta, and later Nick moved to the coal mines in the Sparwood, B.C. area. He then moved to the Shelter Bay-Beaton area to work as a faller for Celgar through Walter Shiell. Nick was a real extrovert and easily made friends including Ken and Marge Miller during his Beaton days.

Nick and Joanna Zibulak married May 16, 1953. Joanna's family had an established farm in Twelve Mile, and is included elsewhere in this book. While Nick was logging in the Beaton area, he attended a dance in Revelstoke and met Joanna there. They re-met at another time when Nick was cutting wood for the Kaduhrs in Twelve Mile, which led to their marriage.

When Nick and Joanna married, they lived on and farmed Zibulak's farm (Joanna's parents' farm) in Twelve Mile and Nick began working on the Twelve Mile Ferry where he continued until it closed in 1969. He then continued his employment with the Highways Department until retirement.

Joanna and Nick had seven children: Gail, born 1954; Janice, born 1956; Linda, born 1958; Bob, born 1959; Sharon, born 1961; Bonny, born 1962; and Sheila, born 1965.

Nick and Joanna Makarewicz wedding, May 16, 1953. (Makarewicz family photo)

Gloria Kaduhr recalls that Joanna always took time to rock each of her babies to sleep. When she was due with her next child, she walked the railroad tracks to the Kaduhrs to be driven to the hospital while Nick was working.

Gail suffered a hip dislocation when delivered by forceps. It wasn't diagnosed until she was 14 months old. The Shriners, through their friend, Wallace Huffman, arranged an assessment in Vancouver. At 18 months she experienced her first surgery and full body cast. Several surgeries followed until she was six years old and starting school. The Shriners paid for all the surgeries that were performed in Portland, Oregon. Her parents took her there by train by way of Vancouver, while friends and neighbors pitched in on babysitting the rest of the children. Kellina Domke always enjoyed looking after the little ones when it was her turn.

The children have fond memories of their years growing up on their farm in Twelve Mile. Joanna inherited her parents' (Zibulak's) farm when they passed away and she and Nick continued to build it up into a productive farm of 160 acres. They raised pigs and chickens and up to 100 head of beef cattle to sell in stores in Revelstoke and to logging camps. They built a modern home complete with indoor plumbing, a new barn, hay sheds and implement sheds.

Gail Makarewicz on Shriners' Float, Revelstoke parade, 1950s. Makarewicz family photo)

The children learned to work at early ages and Gail calls herself "Dad's first boy." One time when she was 12, she drove the tractor pulling a trailer load of hay from Mike Nedelco's farm near Revelstoke. Another time when Mike and Nick were getting ready to fill the truck with hay but were shorthanded, they wanted Gail to drive the truck, a standard shift that she had never driven before. Mike, a large, heavy-set man, climbed onto the box and Nick gave her some brief instructions. As the young Gail tried to get the truck going, Mike flew out of the back of the truck with the first jerk, and the truck took off. There was a lot of yelling and screaming. When Nick baled hay, the children ran behind the baler to pull out the bales and load them into the wagon.

Joanna did the chicken butchering. She grabbed a chicken in one hand, axe in the other, and used the huge tree stump by the chicken coop to finish it off. The girls remember trying to do homework at the kitchen table at the same time their mother was cleaning the chicken. "The smell!! Oooh, we're not going to eat that! But when it was cooked, it tasted so good."

When the larger animals were butchered and hung up, many people were informed ahead of time. The German people came with buckets to catch fresh blood for making blood sausage. The liver was the best on butchering day. "Mom breaded it and fried it for supper. It was so tender and puffy you could cut it with a fork," recalls Gail.

Life on the farm was good. It is no wonder the Makarewiczes, like many others, did not wish to give up their beautiful farm to BC Hydro's unfair offer. They paid for an independent appraisal, hired an independent lawyer and went to court, all to no avail. Hydro would not budge on its low appraisal. Nick and Joanna were paid about 80 percent of the appraised value.

While the Makarewiczes were fighting for their farm and hadn't moved out yet, others were leaving just ahead of the hired *torchers*. One day when Nick was still working on the ferry, the workers came and started burning the tool garage. Joanna hurriedly got Nick from the ferry in time to pull his tools out of the burning building. It was a horrifying experience.

They built a new house by the Illecillewaet River bridge in Revelstoke. Their farm house was moved to Catherwood Road south of Revelstoke, where it partially burned and was rebuilt.

Nick passed away August 11, 1996 in Revelstoke. Joanna continued living in their home until she passed away August 29, 2005.

Hildegard Mantei marriage to Robert Krause. (A. Domke family photo)

The children all live in British Columbia. Gail has two children: Lee and Jill; Janice has two: Ty and Annie; Linda has one son, Seth; Bob's sons are Jordon and Connor, and his daughter is Paige; Sharon's sons are Alex and Nicholas. Bonny and Sheila do not have children.

MANTEI

Olga Domke Mantei emigrated to Canada from Dusseldorf, Germany in 1955 following WWII which devastated her family. Her husband, Theodore Mantei, a soldier in the German army, was one of the war's casualties leaving his wife and three daughters to fend for themselves.

When Olga's brother, Asaph Domke, of Twelve Mile arranged to sponsor her to Canada, she adopted her granddaughter, Helga, and brought her along, in search of a better life. They lived with the Domkes for a year. Helga attended grade two at Twelve Mile School and quickly mastered English.

That first year Olga enjoyed knitting *Siwash* or *Indian* sweaters, socks and mittens for everyone in the family using the wool from Domke's sheep. From her wartime experiences, she could not tolerate anything going to waste so she plucked the sheep's wool off the barbed wire fences around the farm and stuffed it into quilts. Through that first winter she persevered with her English lessons from her family.

Farm life suited Helga just fine. She mothered and played with all the animals, naming the calves, kittens and lambs, and dreamed of having her own horse someday.

Olga and Helga moved to Kelowna where Olga worked in the fruit industry. She met and married Henry Sauer and after several years they built their dream home in Barrier, B.C. They have both passed away.

Olga's second daughter, Hildegard, emigrated to Canada in 1958, living with the Domkes for a short while before also moving to Kelowna and Barrier. She married Robert Krause and they had four children. They are both deceased.

Helga married Jack Pennell, manager of Willow Ranch near Kamloops. She finally realized her dream of having her own horse, Cheekie, and participated in roundups, branding and all the challenges of ranch living. Though retired, they still participate in ranch life on a limited scale on their own small ranch south of Kamloops.

Olga Mantei-Sauer, Helga Mantei, Henry Sauer. (A. Domke family photo)

MARAUN

Otto Maraun was born in Buschow, Germany in 1931. He was orphaned during the war and lived in an orphanage with his only younger brother. Tragically, his brother was killed when a hand grenade that he found on the playground blew up while he was playing with it.

When Otto was 19 years old, he emigrated to Canada and worked at the Copper Mountain mine in British Columbia. There he developed a friendship with Hans and Lotty Podzun. After they moved to Twelve Mile, Otto partnered with them in farming and logging. Otto was an honest, humble young man, who stayed partners and friends with the Podzuns over the years through thick and thin in the various business ventures that they shared.

Otto began corresponding with Thea Hoheisel of Stuttgart, Germany with encouragement from matchmaker, Lotty. After about a year of letter writing, Thea and her four-year-old son, Robert, arrived in Revelstoke in 1965 and they were married soon after. Robert says it was quite a culture shock for his mother and him coming from a large city.

Robert remembers helping to pack up Otto's and Podzun's belongings when BC Hydro bought them out in 1965, and moving with them to Canim Lake near 100 Mile House. Here they established "Canim Lake Farms." They grew turnips, potatoes and cabbage, and raised cattle until 1969.

While trying to unjam the potato digger, it malfunctioned and pulled Otto's jacket and right arm into the machinery. The muscles in that arm were permanently injured. However, he maintained use of his right hand, and continued to do heavy work.

Brian, Thea, Otto, Yvonne and Robert Maraun. (S. Podzun photo)

They sold the farm in 1969 and Otto and his family returned to Revelstoke. When he became hospitalized with arthritis in the winter of 1972-73, the doctors suggested a warmer climate. Otto and Thea decided to buy property and move to Belize where Otto worked with the Podzuns in their cinder block factory.

Otto and Thea returned to Revelstoke in 1983, hoping to enjoy their retirement years, but it was not to be. He passed away in 1998 of a diabetes-induced stroke. Thea passed away in 2002 of a brain blood clot.

Robert finished high school in Belize and returned to Revelstoke in 1979. He married Jutta Bartsch and now operates the Begbie Machine Shop. They have two sons and a daughter.

Otto and Thea had two children. Yvonne was born in 1967 in 100 Mile House. She lives in Prince George, and has one son. Brian Andrew was born in 1972 in Revelstoke where he continues to reside.

MAZAR

Thomas (Tom) Mazar and Elizabeth (Civetta) Kupchanko married in 1918. They moved from the mining area of Drumheller, Alberta to Twelve Mile in 1922 where they homesteaded the property on the east side of the river and south of the highway. When fire destroyed their house in September 1922, they moved to Canmore, Alberta where Tom obtained work in the mine. They returned to Revelstoke in the spring of 1923. On their farm in Twelve Mile they built a two-story frame house and frame barn, and farmed the land. In addition to farming, Tom worked on various projects including the building of the Big Bend Highway.

The Mazars were an integral part of the community. Elizabeth used her midwifery skills to deliver several of the babies including Mildred Kozek and Jim Millar. Danny Gawiuk remembers riding his bike from Six Mile to visit them and go fishing. He still remembers the time they gave him a dog, Prince, to take home in the front basket on his bike.

Their three older children, Mack, Dorothy and Thomas (Tommy), developed lasting friendships with the neighbour children and helped on the farm. Dorothy was born in Canmore, Alberta. Mack, Tommy, Jim and Judy were born in Revelstoke. Their youngest son, Fred, was born in Rimbey, Alberta in 1944 and now lives in Okotoks, Alberta.

Elizabeth and Tom Mazar on their new farm in Winfield, Alberta. (W. Kozek photo)

As was the case with all the early settlers, educating the children without a school was a problem. The family returned to Drumheller in 1928 for a short time, but returned to their homestead in Twelve Mile in 1930 when the first Twelve Mile School was completed.

While WWII was on, Tommy, being a patriot, wrote a letter to the Provincial War Savings Committee in Vancouver. It was published in the *Revelstoke Review* on February 7, 1941 under the heading, "12 Mile Boy Is Enthusiastic War Saver," and exemplified the feelings at the time to "smash Hitler by buying war savings stamps and certificates."

A young man, Leo Rebelato, worked for the transport company that picked up their milk and cream cans for shipping to the creamery and became close friends of the family. Dorothy and Leo married in 1940 and moved to Revelstoke where Leo owned his own butcher shop on the corner of Fourth and Victoria. They later moved to Vancouver. He worked as a butcher for Swifts Meat Packers. They continued to live in Vancouver until their passing, Dorothy in 1995 and Leo in 1997. They had one child, Sheila, who lives in Vancouver.

Mack Mazar, RCAF, 1946. (W. Kozek photo)

In 1942, the Mazars traded their Twelve Mile farm to Ferdinand Rauchert of Winfield, Alberta and started mixed farming. Tom and Elizabeth lived there until 1962, retiring to Wetaskiwin, Alberta. Tom passed away in 1971 and Elizabeth in 1996.

Mack served in the RCAF during WWII. He worked as a CPR engineer for 38 years until his retirement in 1984. In 2006 he passed away, at age 82, in Kelowna, B.C. where his wife, Nola, continues to reside.

Tom, Jim, Dorothy holding Judy, and Tommy Mazar, 1943. (Makarewicz family photo)

Tommy joined the Canadian Navy in 1949 and moved to Victoria where he married and raised four children. He and his wife, Olive, are retired and still live in Victoria.

Jim became a Civil Engineer. He and his wife, Bev, raised two children and live in Calgary, Alberta.

Judy lives in Canmore, Alberta with her husband, Wally Walenstein.

MICHELS, ALEC

Alec Michels was second of eight children born to Peter and Effie Michels. In 1914 they moved from Salt Lake City, Utah to Sidmouth to farm. Alec and his siblings attended school at Hall's Landing.

Alec began working on the Twelve Mile ferry about 1943, first as a spare, then full time. He also worked on the Sidmouth ferry from time to time. He was a bachelor and lived for a time in the government ferry house, then in one of Petrashuk's cabins while boarding with them.

While living in Twelve Mile, Alec was occasionally called upon to help with community situations. During the 1945-46 school year when the school closed because of low enrollment and the planned consolidation of country schools, he drove the few students to the Greenslide School.

In September 1949, when a geologist was missing in the mountains around Cranberry Creek, Alec joined the search party because he knew the territory well. Planes and men searched for the geologist for several days. "He finally returned to camp with a broken ankle after being five or six days overdue in the mountains alone with no axe, and no gasoline to light a fire to signal the plane which he saw but could not contact," read the report in *Revelstoke Review*, September 29, 1949.

Alec and Robert Brinkman became good friends. They drove to Revelstoke in Alec's car for supplies. One time when they were returning, quite "jolly," they picked up Ben and Evelyn Domke who were walking home from school. Because it was so crowded in the tiny car, Ben sat on Bob's lap, petrified they wouldn't make it home. (It was common in those days for drivers to give pedestrians a lift.)

Although Alec never married or had children, he made friends with some of the young people. Ron Dedosenco owes his cribbage skills to Alec's tutoring. Alec often visited his great niece, Diane

Visser, and her family wherever they lived, even driving boxes of fresh fruit from the Okanagan to their Burns Lake home for them.

When Alec retired from the ferry in about 1951, he moved to Wigwam and worked for Clarence McLeod for a while before moving to Savona, B.C. to be near Diane and Hank Visser. There he lived in his mobile home for many years until becoming ill with lung cancer. When Diane and her family moved to Smithers in 1978, he moved and lived with them until his death in 1978.

MICHELS, HARRY

Harry Michels was born in 1901 in Utah, USA, the son of Peter and Effie Michels of Sidmouth, B.C. and brother of Alec Michels. In 1926, he and Annie Shaw of Galena Bay married and had three children: Merle Peter, Jack Raymond and Peggy Ann.

Although their primary residence was Sidmouth, where they lived on the Michels family farm for a while, they logged in various areas in the Columbia valley. Annie is renowned as the best pole maker in the region, as well as being an excellent seamstress—a talented lady!

When they made poles for the CRT on the mountain south of Mulvehill Creek in Twelve Mile, they lived in the log cabin on the west bank north of the ferry landing. There the children played with their neighbor children, the Millars. Even after they moved to Revelstoke, Harry and Annie returned to Twelve Mile to make poles.

Harry Michel's sons: Merle and Jack Michels. (Merle Michels photo)

Harry passed away in 1953.

Merle continued in his parents' tradition of logging and also worked with BC Hydro. He and his wife, Marjorie Benyard, have three sons, and are retired in Kamloops, B.C.

Jack and his wife, Barbra Gaualin, have two sons and two daughters. Jack died in 1999.

Peggy and husband, Barry Brown, have two daughters and a son.

MILLAR

James (Jim) Millar was born in 1898 in Scotland. He and Dora Monteith (born 1903) married in Arrowhead, B.C. Dora taught school in Beaton and Arrowhead before her children were born. Jim was an engineer on the CPR boats on the Arrow Lakes. They moved with their first two children, Ken and Lois, to Twelve Mile in 1930 when Jim began operating the ferry.

In 1932 Dora and children went to Salmon Arm to care for her father. While his family was away, Jim lived in the government ferry house on the east side of the river with Ed Mulvehill and spare ferry operator, Alec Michels. Jim visited his family as often as possible, but that wasn't easy because he had no holidays or days off from his ferry-operator job. He held that job from 1930-44.

Jim and Dora Millar. (Millar family photo)

When they purchased the Bob Logan property on the west side of the ferry landing in 1937, Dora, Ken, Lois and Audrey moved back to Twelve Mile. Jim, Jr. was born in Twelve Mile during the heavy snow season of 1939 and was delivered by Jim and neighbor Elizabeth Mazar. They also purchased Hugh McMahon's property when it was sold for unpaid taxes after Hugh left it in the late 1930s. They sold it to BC Hydro in the 1960s.

Ken remembers the huge forest fire of 1937 that burned until fall. It seemed to start around Mt. McKenzie and consume the valley and Mt. Cartier to about Eleven Mile. Ashes fell like snow and they watched the flames through the night.

Dora is remembered by her neighbors as a gracious hostess. She always took time to visit with young people and any lonely neighbors who came by for "a coffee." They cut huge blocks of ice in the river, pulled it out with ice tongs, sledded it to their ice shed. There they buried it in sawdust and then let snow cover it. When spring and summer came, they still had ice for their household use, including the making of homemade ice cream. Dora preserved fruit and vegetables for winter use from her huge vegetable garden. In the summer they sold raspberries and strawberries to stores in Revelstoke. They also sold their excess dairy produce to Lena's Restaurant in Revelstoke. Since sugar and butter was rationed during WWII, the Millars and Bob Brinkman worked out a mutually sweet trade—his honey for their dairy. He didn't mind walking the two plus miles from his house to the south because it gave him a chance to visit.

Wild huckleberries were a special treat to the early settlers, with good crops usually bearing near Blanket Creek. The Millars picked enough to eat and preserve for the winter.

George Brown, a bachelor, lived in the log cabin on the riverbank to the northwest of Millars. At the same location, Lois remembers playing with Jackie Michels, who was Harry Michels' son and Alec's nephew.

Ken, Lois and Audrey attended the Twelve Mile School, but Jim didn't start school until they moved to Beaton. Audrey started school at age five in order to meet the minimum number of students required to keep the school open. This was a common practice of the small rural schools to assure continued operation.

The Millar children easily became friends with neighboring children. Evelyn Domke still remembers the fun Audrey and she had at school making playhouses among the hazelnut bushes behind the school. The Millar and Domke children walked the two miles back and forth to play together. In the summertime, there was always swimming in the back eddy between Kozek's and the river on the east side of the river. Millie Kozek Combatly remembers her first kiss being from Ken!

Ken and Tommy Mazar were good friends, but now Ken wonders why Tommy's mom ever let them play together. It seems like Tom was always getting hurt in some way. When the two boys were digging out some of the roots that former owner, Logan, buried, Ken's shovel flew up, giving Tommy a bloody mouth. Another time Ken was trying to imitate a circus act he had seen. He had Tommy bend over and reach with his hands back between his legs. Then Ken gave a mighty pull on one hand. But

Lois, Ken and Audrey Millar, circa 1939. (Millar family photo)

instead of flipping Tommy over to land on his feet like a polished circus act, he landed face down in the gravel like a circus clown!

It was always a treat when the Crawfords and other Arrowhead friends stopped by to visit and picnic at nearby Mulvehill Falls.

Ken had "a lot to do with the Domke family as a young boy." He was sent over to help Helen with the haying when Oscar was away.

I don't remember how much haying we got done. It seems we spent most of the time cranking some old truck. Another of my jobs was helping Helen take her cows to visit Mike Kozek's bull. That was always a chore and it seems to me now there wasn't a lot of time between trips-- either for one of our own or one of Helen's. Just the thing a young boy wants to do! Part of our life growing up though. My very first job for pay (I was 11 or 12 I think) was helping Pete and Ole Westerberg build Oscar's new barn. They needed some kid to climb up to the top of the rafters and tie a rope on one of them so they could move them along. Needless to say, I was scared as could be because the rafters were just sitting there and were really waving around. I remember they paid me $8 for three days' work. I thought I was rich. Actually, the pay rate was far better than my first full-time job on the lake boats at age 16. That paid $50 a month.

Unfortunately, Millars' bordering neighbor, William Thompson, was not as friendly as the others. He was easily annoyed and thought nothing of injuring their small dog with a thrown chisel. Another time James found their other dog near death from a gunshot wound at the hands of Mr. Thompson.

Jim operated the Twelve Mile ferry for 14 years. In June 1944, the Millars sold their farm to Percy Demers and moved to Beaton where they bought the *SS Beaton* (*Beaton Boat*) on the Arrow Lakes. Jim and Frank Sutherland were partners. The boat was initially steam driven but was later converted to diesel. In 1951 Ken took special training in Vancouver and received his official captain's papers.

In 1957 when the *Beaton Boat* was having some generator trouble, Jim stayed behind to work on it after the rest of the crew went home. Some time later in the night he was turning his truck around on the dock and slipped over the side into Arrow Lake. Dora had an uneasy night not knowing why he was gone so long. The accident wasn't discovered until morning when the crew went to work, so it was not known when he drowned.

Dora remarried after Jim's death and lived in Beaton until BC Hydro bought her out in 1966. They moved to Princeton, B.C. to be near Audrey, but Dora's second husband died soon after their move. Audrey passed away in 1971 of diabetes and Dora continued living alone. When she was about 85 years of age, she suffered a tragic fall down some stairs and fractured her skull. Sadly, she never completely recovered from this serious injury and spent most of her last years in hospital until her death in 1996 when she was 93, not really knowing her children or her surroundings.

Ken, born in 1928, married Marjorie Smith, a school teacher, who coincidentally had done her practice teaching at the Twelve Mile School in 1949 and later taught in Beaton. Ken worked the boats on the Arrow Lakes and Columbia River for 30 years and for 20 years on Francois Lake northwest of Prince George. They lived in the Big Eddy area of

Back: Naida, Lorilynne, Jamie, Glenda, Marilynne Millar. Front: Ken and Marge Millar, 50th wedding anniversary, with children. (K. Millar photo)

Revelstoke for a while and there resumed friendship with the Domkes, Ken serving with Oscar on the Big Eddy Water Board. Ken and Marjorie have five children, 10 grandchildren and two great grand children to date and are retired in Comox, B.C.

Lois, born in 1931, completed Normal School in Victoria with her sister Audrey in 1951. She began her teaching career at Albert Canyon. When she married Clayton Masur, she taught in the various areas where her husband was transferred to by his employer, the CPR. They retired in Revelstoke. Lois passed away April 3, 2008.

Audrey, born in 1933, completed Normal School in Victoria with her sister Lois in 1951. Her teaching career was spent in Princeton, B.C. where she and husband Clayton Hamilton lived until her death from diabetes in 1971.

Jim, born in 1939, also pursued a career in education, teaching in various places including Beaton, Prince George and Nanaimo. He taught math at Vancouver Tech and coached athletics in the Vancouver area. Jim is retired in Vancouver and Palm Springs, California.

MILLER

Walter E. Miller homesteaded the property along the tracks south of the train station before 1921 until about 1940.

He was known for his wonderful vegetable crops. On October 24,1940 *The Revelstoke Review* reported that his "gargantuan sugar beets" were on display at Clarence Sheedy's barber shop window in Revelstoke. He lived alone, did his own cooking and was known for baking apple pies. The housekeepers who answered his ads "usually left on the next train out." Apparently the accommodations didn't meet their expectations!

Neighbors were fascinated by his creative methods of ridding his property of the black cedar stumps that plagued all homesteaders in the valley. He designed his own stump puller by attaching a cable to it. Then his horses wound and tightened the cable around a drum until the stump gave way.

His black hands from wrestling the charred stumps and his "fierce" boar that was allowed to run free scared the neighboring children.

It is not known where Walter moved to, but some remember his having a daughter living in the Mt. MacPherson area out of Revelstoke. Fred and Katherine Zibulak purchased his farm and their grandchildren, the Makarewiczes, remember walking past "the old Miller barn" which stood into the 1960s.

MINION

Newton Minion completed normal school in Ontario and married Etta McCann of Saskatchewan. Teaching jobs were scarce and so was money. As a result, his teaching career took some detours. They tried farming in Saskatchewan, but with dust storms and other hardships of those 20 years, they gave it up. They shipped their household belongings in two railroad boxcars and moved to Salmon Arm, B.C. with their four children, Wilbur, Harold, Evelyn and Lorna. There they rented land and farmed in the Mt. Ida district. After 10 years, Newton worked at Farmers' Exchange.

When Newton retired from Farmers Exchange, he returned to his first love—teaching. He taught at Clearwater in northern B.C. and then at Twelve Mile School during the 1957-58 school year. He and Etta lived in the teacherage of the new (third) school. When Etta became ill, they moved back to Salmon Arm near their children, but Newton continued with substitute teaching.

Newton died at age 89 years, and Etta at age 94 years.

MITCHELL

David Mitchell taught at the Twelve Mile School in 1935-36. No further information is available.

MOBLEY

William Charles (Bill) Mobley and Elsie Emmeline Jones-Mobley moved from Revelstoke to Twelve Mile in 1944 with their children, Ronald, Lorraine, Helen and Alyce. Bill grew up in the Tappen, B.C. area where his father, C. W. Mobley, had a big game and angling guide business for many years. He was one of the earliest settlers in the Sunnybrae area.

Bill operated the Twelve Mile ferry until 1947. Even though the four Mobley children were a great boost to the school's enrollment when they arrived, the school closed the first part of the 1945-46 year. Bill and Alec Michels, the two ferry operators, were commissioned to use their own cars to take turns driving the students to the Greenslide School until the Twelve Mile School reopened in November 1945.

The Mobley family lived in the ferry house on the east bank of the river part of the time. Like other women in the area, Elsie had her hands full with the children, taking care of a huge garden, canning, as well as doing other household chores, all without modern conveniences. The children also did their share of the chores including laundry by hand. They were especially fond of their black cocker spaniel, Gip, so named because his tail had been cropped. During the heavy snowfall of the winter of 1947, the Mobleys had their supplies shipped from Revelstoke to Twelve Mile by train where it was Ronnie's job to haul them home from the station in the deep snow.

Back: Bill Mobley. Middle: Helen, Elsie, Lorraine, Ron. Front: Alyce. On Twelve Mile Ferry. (Mobley family photo)

The children enjoyed the various school activities, including participating in the Christmas concerts, and some classmates became their lifelong friends. Alyce remembers participating in her first Christmas concert at school, singing a duet with Russell Gowanlock, "Good Morning Merry Sunshine." They repeated it after receiving a standing ovation.

In 1947, the Mobleys left Twelve Mile for the Sunnybrae area 15 miles from Salmon Arm. Bill worked at various jobs including selling for the Fuller Brush Company, driving taxi and working in mills.

Ronald William (Ronnie) was born in 1930. He joined the army and served in Korea in the early 1950s. Later, he worked in the Kamloops, B.C. liquor store. He and his wife, Joan, had a son and two daughters. Ron passed away in 1993.

Lorraine Elsie, born in 1932, and her husband, Earl, had four children. After Earl passed away, she married Leon Richardson and they live in Vernon, B.C.

Helen Marie, born 1934, married Larry Toebosch after completing high school. She worked in a bakery and telephone office. She and Larry worked together in his trucking business for several years. Helen later trained and worked as a long-term-care aide in Salmon Arm at Bastion Place and felt her calling was working with the senior citizens. In 1992 they moved to a 160-acre cattle farm in the Notch Hill area of Sorrento. Tragically, Larry was accidentally killed on their farm in 2002, so Helen sold their cows and leased out part of their farm. Her loneliness has been assuaged by her youngest daughter, Tara, her husband and young son moving into a nearby house on the farm. Helen and Larry had four children and now have three grandchildren. Her oldest son, David, lives in Canoe, B.C. Gary lives in Surrey, B.C., and daughter, Tia, lives in Seattle, Washington.

Alyce Wilma, born in 1940, and husband, Chuck, had three sons and one daughter. She lives in Quesnel with her second husband, Leon Renaud.

Bill and Elsie lived in Sunnybrae until they died, she in 1967 and he in 1982.

MORGAN

The Mina Morgans moved from Kamloops to Twelve Mile in the fall of 1950. He was a miner and they had two children of preschool age. No further information is available.

MULVEHILL

Ed Mulvehill was born in London, England in 1872 and emigrated to the United States. He moved from Indiana to B.C. about 1903, spending time in the Nelson district before moving to the Revelstoke area about 1914.

He logged, farmed and trapped. He sold his mink, bear, marten, beaver, weasel, rat, lynx and coyote pelts to F. B. Wells Furrier in Revelstoke from 1914-1917.

In Twelve Mile, Ed had a small house on his homestead by the railway tracks north of the property that the school was built on. He later sold it to Nettie Kozek and it was rented out to various folks including the McLeods and Walter Kozeks.

In addition to being remembered as a kind and friendly bachelor, he is known for being Twelve Mile's first ferryman on the small wooden ferry moved from Sidmouth in 1923. When the ferry

Mulvehill Falls. (E. Domke photo)

operated two shifts per day, he shared the job with Allan Kelly and James Millar for a few years before retiring. Ed is further immortalized by having Mulvehill Creek and Falls named for him. That area has now been developed into the Mulvehill Creek Wilderness Retreat.

When Ed died in his home of apoplexy July 20, 1938, he had one brother left in Hammond, Indiana whose son, a police officer, had been killed earlier by the notorious Dillinger gang.

MYERS

Samuel Albert and Pearl Myers moved from Nelson, B.C. to Eight Mile when they bought Paul Kozak's farm in 1957.

David Myers on his way to catch the school bus to Twelve Mile School. (P. Myers photo)

Their son, Samuel David (David), attended school at Twelve Mile from 1962-67 when the school district began bussing elementary children from Six and Eight Mile to Twelve Mile. As families' lives were disrupted in the 1960s when their homes were expropriated by BC Hydro, Pearl took in children from various places so they could attend school. These included children from Trout Lake and the Westons of Twelve Mile.

David continued his education at Revelstoke High School, then Simon Frazer University and University of Victoria. He has a daughter, Megan, and currently operates his own logging business.

With the termination of Sam's and Pearl's marriage, he moved to Duval, Saskatchewan where he later died.

Always ambitious, Pearl continues to work her farm and owned Creative Flowers at People's Drug in Revelstoke from 1979-94. She has also authored two books of historical fiction: *The Long Whistle* and *Lean Into the Wind*, both by Trafford Publishing.

NASH

Ronald Nash attended Twelve Mile School during the 1957-58 school year. No further information is available.

NELSON

Ernest, Ruby and Wilbert Nelson attended Twelve Mile School during the 1954-55 school year. No further information is available.

NIPPER

Jack Nipper was born in Poland/Austria in 1890. The family name, Nippeir, was later changed to Nipper. During WWI he was taken prisoner and cooked in a German concentration camp. On his left hand, he lost fingers two, three and four that his daughter, Mary, thinks were removed one at a time for punishment while a prisoner.

After he emigrated to Canada, he married Nettie Ostrikoff July 30, 1930 who was born in Verigan, Saskatchewan January 1, 1910. They lived in Trail, B.C. where Jack worked in plumbing/maintenance at the Cominco lead and zinc refinery. They had four daughters: Sophie Margarite, born in 1931; Annie, born in 1932; Mary, born in 1937; and Helen Pauline, born in 1938.

In 1947 they moved to Twelve Mile to be near Nettie's mother, Pearl Ocepoff. They purchased the farm on the west side of the river next to the ferry dock. The Michels name appears on the 1918 Department of Interior property map. They shipped their belongings from Trail by Glover's Moving, and the family travelled by train and boat.

Their main house was a one-room log cabin with a front porch overlooking the river. Next to it was a one-room cabin with a heater where the girls slept. Since the girls were all school aged, their attendance was a nice boost to the waning school enrollment.

1948, just a year after moving to Twelve Mile, was a disastrous year for the Nippers. That June the river overflowed its banks big time with the water coming up to the door of their cabin and flooding their garden area. The following month, Jack badly cut his left thumb while chopping wood,

John (Jack) and Nettie Nipper wedding, July 30, 1930. (Weston family photo)

resulting in nine stitches. It's no wonder the girls longed for their nice big house with modern conveniences they left behind in Trail. They remembered the fun they had playing in their basement. Sophie and Annie drew pictures on a huge roll of paper, then unrolled it while the audience, Mary and Helen, watched the "movies" with their flashlight.

They raised chickens for eggs and poultry, and pigs for meat. One year they bought five turkeys from Kaduhrs. Mary remembers trading Helen Domke a turkey for a duck one Christmas so the families could each taste a different meat. Since Nippers didn't have cows, they purchased milk, cream and butter from Helen Domke. Jack was a great gardener and raised huge beets, cabbage and other vegetables in raised plots with paths between. Next to their house he raised huge tiger lilies that bus passengers waiting for the ferry enjoyed. Root cellars used to store canning and root vegetables were a must in Twelve Mile and Nippers' was under the little shack the girls shared.

The girls all helped with outdoor work. Jack borrowed Percy Demers' horse from next door to pull in logs. Then he and the girls sawed the logs into firewood, split and piled it for the cook stove and heater. Sophie and Ann even helped their dad dig a well but Ann remembers the river water tasting better than the well water!

The Nipper kitchen was the closest thing to a coffee shop that Twelve Mile had. Being next to the ferry, it was a regular break stop for the ferrymen and others who had to wait to cross the river. Jack, ever the gracious host, served tea and freshly baked pie and bread. He loved to cook, never used a written recipe, and neighbors were always welcome and served foods he had freshly prepared. Nettie also was known for her tasty bread. Jack liked certain handcrafts and entered a very fine horsehair brush into the hobby show in Revelstoke.

Mary Nipper Leitz with husband, Vern, and daughter, Arlene. (Weston family photo)

Ada Domke used her bicycle to teach Mary how to ride, holding the bike while Mary peddled on the rutted, rocky road between the Nippers and Ocepoffs. One trip, and she had it mastered. Were they ever excited when Uncle George Ocepoff gave Mary and Helen each boys' bikes of their own.

Neighbors remember Nippers' large, floor model radio they brought from Trail. At night after homework, the family all sat around it listening to their favourites: Arthur Godfrey, Ozzie and Harriett and Red Skeleton. In the morning, it was The Breakfast Club with Don McNeil. Jack especially loved listening to music.

The family had no car so took rides to and from town with neighbors. In 1951 Mary had a frightening experience. She was riding home from Revelstoke with Jules Fiset in his small pickup when he suffered a heart attack and drove off the road between Twelve Mile hill (rock bluffs) and the railroad crossing. Being just 14 years old, Mary did not know how to drive or she would have tried taking over when she noted the problem. To this day she remembers the frightening experience, his bleeding from ears and nose, slogging through quicksand-like material, climbing out of the ditch and walking to her aunt Tiny Rauchert's for help. Her uncle Emil got out of bed, called the ambulance and police and went back with Mary. She stayed to answer their questions.

The girls berry picked for various farmers and then Sophie and Ann worked at the King Edward Hotel in Revelstoke. Being an excellent seamstress, Sophie was hired as an instructor by the Singer Sewing Company in Vancouver. Ann was also an excellent seamstress and sews for other

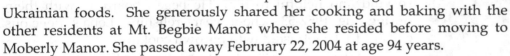

people to this day. She also learned knitting and eventually knit garments on a special machine.

Jack was always on some type of medication (Helen used to give the little aluminum containers to her friends to play with). He may have had chronic pain and although it hasn't been confirmed, this may have contributed to his ending his life April 7, 1956, at age 67.

When her girls left home, Nettie moved in with her widowed mother, Pearl Ocepoff, who lived on a farm about a mile to their south. Sophie and husband, Gordon Weston, took over the Nipper farm.

When BC Hydro relocated Pearl to Salmo, B.C., Nettie moved with her. After her mother died there, Nettie returned to Twelve Mile to live with Sophie and Gordon and then moved to Revelstoke. She loved to bake bread and cook perogies, cabbage rolls and other

Ann NipperForlin. (A. Jarvis photo)

Helen Pauline Nipper. (A. Domke family photo)

Ukrainian foods. She generously shared her cooking and baking with the other residents at Mt. Begbie Manor where she resided before moving to Moberly Manor. She passed away February 22, 2004 at age 94 years.

Ann married John Forlin and lived in Fruitvale, B.C. where they raised their family of four. Her husband passed away 1988 and she continues to live in their home.

When Mary left Twelve Mile, she worked for Cominco and other jobs in the Trail area. She and Vern Lietz married, had six daughters and one son, and now live in Kelowna, B.C.

Helen (Pauline) married Lawrence Bolen and had five children. She died of a brain tumor at the early age of 39.

Eric Norris in school's front door, 1953. (E. Norris photo)

NORRIS

Wilson Eric Norris (Eric) obtained his Temporary Teaching Certificate from Victoria Normal School. While looking for a teaching position, he worked on the CPR in Revelstoke. When Dave Story left his teaching position at the Twelve Mile School December 1951, Eric seized the opportunity to finish out that school year.

In January of 1952 he moved from Armstrong to Revelstoke and hired a taxi to take him to his new job. He traveled light, thinking he would purchase his groceries and supplies when he got to the "town" of Twelve Mile. Luckily, the taxi driver discovered Eric's plans and took him shopping first.

He settled into his new quarters in the two-room teacherage and began the never-ending job of planning lessons for the 16 students in grades one through eight. He worked late into the night writing lessons on the two large chalkboards. As he reminisces:

> The chalkboards were actually painted canvas which wobbled as you wrote. The grades one and two were the most difficult to keep busy as they finished their assignments before I was through with the rest of the grades. To keep them occupied, I had them put together jigsaw puzzles, one of the map of Canada and the other of the United States. They could soon solve these puzzles blindfolded.

> Periodically the School Inspector would give us a surprise visit. He would find diligent pupils, neat notebooks, and ready answers to his questions. We always tried to impress him with a tidy, organized classroom. Our efforts always gave us very favourable reports.

Eric was rehired for the following school year, 1952-53, and felt fortunate to be teaching in a neighborhood where everyone helped one another. Since he did not have a car of his own to drive to town for supplies, he depended on the goodwill of others. Movie night was always a treat. Movies were shown once a month at the school with the traveling movie projector run by the gas generator.

They usually included one comedy, one newsreel and one play. They were always well attended, and when they were over, Eric had electric lights the rest of the evening powered by the generator.

Eric became lifelong friends of the Kaduhrs who were so kind and helpful to him. He began boarding with them during the 1952-53 school year, relishing Lena's delicious cuisine, that contrasted with his own cooking.

After leaving Twelve Mile, he taught mainly in the Surrey-Vancouver area. He and his first wife, Jean, married in 1956 and had three children, Barbara, Clayton and Kenneth. In 1968, he married Norma who was a teacher, librarian, School District helper and homemaker. Together they raised the three Norris children on a small farm in Surrey.

Norma and Eric Norris, 1973. (E. Norris photo)

Following 37 years in education, most of it in administration, and with 24 of those years at Old Yale Road Elementary, he retired. Norma soon followed suit. Together they moved to Armstrong in 2003 where they enjoy farming their 60 acres.

OCEPOFF

Paraskovia (Pearl) Kerynsky was born in 1884 in Russia. When she married John Luktin, of the Doukhobor sect, they were exiled to Siberia for his refusing to participate in the military. From there, they emigrated to Saskatchewan, Canada with a group of Doukhobors including the Lordly Peter Verigan. Pearl and her daughters, Polly and Nettie (Ostrikoff), both born in Canada, moved to Trail, B.C. where Pearl met and married Paul Ocepoff. Paul had served in the Russian army before emigrating to Canada. They later moved to Shoreacres, B.C. Paul and Pearl had three children: Peter, born July 7, 1920; George, born December 3, 1921; and Fannie (Tiny), born August 13, 1924.

In 1945, a few months after Tiny and Emil Rauchert established their home in Twelve Mile, George located Nick Kupchenko's homestead also in Twelve Mile for his parents to purchase. Paul, Pearl and Peter moved into the one-room log cabin next to the creek. They later added on another room and cold storage room.

Nettie Nipper, Pearl and Paul Ocepoff, Helen Nipper with Dick, their dog. Taken in front of the Ocepoff home. (Weston family photo)

They raised their own chickens and had a horse, but purchased their milk and butter from neighbors, Asaph and Kellina Domke. On their way to school the Domke children placed the dairy products in a little box on the gatepost and picked up the empty milk bottles with payment inside on their way home. Paul and Pearl didn't have a car, as was the case with many of the farmers then, but there were always neighbors and relatives to drive them to Revelstoke for food and supplies.

Paul was a hard worker and carried heavy loads that were fastened to the two ends of a long pole cradled across his shoulders. His friends remember how he loved to discuss history and politics. They raised hay, but because they had no cows and just one horse, they asked their grandson, Larry Rauchert, to help cut the hay and sell it. Pearl was always a gracious hostess and when company dropped in, she served tea with fresh homemade bread and jam. She always entertained her relatives at Christmas and Easter. Her tradition was to keep some of her Christmas fruitcake until Easter. She dyed Easter eggs with onion skins to give to her grandchildren and neighbors. Ada Domke remembers them well:

"At Easter she gave each of us children several special onion-dyed eggs. Over the years, I've come to appreciate them even more. They were in fact stained in a mosaic pattern which were works of old world art: the orange shades reminding us of the everlasting sun, the browns representing mother earth and her bounties, and the yellows symbolic of Christian love and kindness. What beautiful memories!"

Paul is known to his family as the "Grandpa that got lost." In the early 1950s he went out for a walk and did not return. For about a month afterwards, Pearl kept a glass of fresh water and a piece of bread on her table by the window, hoping for his return. Although the RCMP brought out their tracking dog, his

Pete Ocepoff. (Weston family photo)

George Ocepoff. (Weston family photo)

body was never found. After that, their son, Peter, moved in with her so she wouldn't be alone.

Peter worked in the logging industry and also served in the Canadian army. He never married or had children. He passed away in 1975 near Nelson, B.C.

George worked on the CPR section gang for a time, and left the family over a dispute. He has passed away.

In the 1960s BC Hydro relocated Pearl to Salmo, B.C. and Nettie moved there with her. Pearl passed away in 1982.

OZERO

Louis Ozero initially owned the property in Twelve Mile near the railway crossing that Rohdes later lived on. It is not known whether he lived on it, or merely had it for logging purposes. He eventually moved to Six Mile and bought Camozzi's place near Montana Lake.

PATRIQUIN

Virginia Patriquin attended Twelve Mile School during the 1958-59 school year. No further information is available.

PETRASHUK (PYTRASHUK)

Safron (Mike) Petrashuk (aka Pytrashuk), born in 1882 in Romania, married Odokia (Mary) Mylnyk of the Ukraine. They emigrated to Canada, first working in the Drumheller, Alberta coal mines. However, Mike's first love was farming, so upon hearing of the opportunities south of Revelstoke, they moved to Mt. Cartier (Six Mile) and then to Twelve Mile about 1921. They homesteaded 40 acres on the Revelstoke-Arrowhead highway, just east of the Lawrence (later Kozek) farm.

Mike, Mary and Rose Petrashuk. (Dedosenco family photo)

Mike and Tom McCormick from Six Mile built Petrashuk's first house on their farm. They produced enough vegetables, eggs, chickens and cream to sell in Revelstoke. A friend and neighbor, Jaron Hulyd, always helped Mary with the chicken butchering.

In addition to farming, Mike logged, and made fence posts for Hulyds to be shipped by train.

Mike and Mary also acquired a second 40-acre plot on the east side of the train station against the mountain. They later sold it to John Ullman (Almen?) who built a log house along Drimmie Creek.

On August 9, 1925 tragedy struck. Mary was home with nine-year-old Rose and 18-month-old Betty asleep in her buggy. It was late at night when they heard the dog frantically barking. They escaped in time to witness their home go up in flames. The police noted that an arsonist had set fire in the small woodshed back of the kitchen area where Mary had hung beans to dry. Footprints were noted around the house leading to the road. They moved into a little cabin on their property. Rose never forgot how unbearable the mosquitoes were while living in that tiny cabin while her dad and McCormicks rebuilt their home.

Mike and Mary had three children: Rosalie (Rose), John Safrone (aka Phonic and Jack), and Elizabeth (Betty). Mike and Mary both valued education and read newspapers and books that they used in educating their children before the first school opened in Twelve Mile.

Rose was born October 5, 1916 in Erickson, B.C. Until she was 12 years old, she was mostly self-taught at home, reading her father's books. Then she attended the first Twelve Mile School that began in the fall of 1930 in a small log cabin. She recalls that there were only about four or five students and they could not have a school built until there were at least nine school-age children. Rose married Meta Dedosenco. They lived in Galena Bay and Twelve Mile.

Jack was born in 1918. He was also self-taught initially using his dad's books, until he attended Twelve Mile School for a short time. He first met Mable Horsley when she was a young teacher at the school in 1940-41. They married and had one daughter, Ellen. He later married Mariette (Molly) Lillian Dufour on July 18, 1964. His hobbies were fishing and building cars from parts of other old cars. He joined the army in Vancouver and because of a heart condition was trained and worked as a mechanic. He also worked in public works in Hope, B.C., as a

Betty Petrashuk. (Dedosenco family photo)

mechanic in Smithers, B.C., and manager of a Sandman Motel.

Betty was born in 1924 at Mt. Cartier (Six Mile) and attended Twelve Mile School through 1939. She left Twelve Mile with her friend, Rose Kozek, to pick fruit in the Okanagan. She then joined the army, was trained as a welder and worked in the Vancouver shipyards. She and Oscar Cyr married and had four children: Sharon, Richard, Michel and Dennis. Oscar passed away in 1961.

Jack Petrashuk, 1931. (Kelly family photo)

Rose and Betty Petrashuk, Joanna Zibulak, on Joanna's new bicycle. Note huge, charred cedar stumps in background. (Makarewicz family photo)

Mike Petrashuk died November 26, 1958 in Vancouver of cancer. Mary continued living in their Twelve Mile home until 1966 when BC Hydro bought her property. Before she had a chance to move, Nettie Kozek found her lying by her woodpile where she had suffered a stroke. Harry Joseph drove Mary to Hope. She lived briefly in Hope and Chilliwack before passing away in Hope, B.C. where she is buried.

PODZUN, HANS

Hans Podzun and Lotty were married in 1942 in Schleswig Holstein, Germany. Hans had been drafted into the German army during WWII and spent some time in Russia and North Africa where he was taken prisoner by the United States. As a prisoner, he was sent to Arkansas to pick cotton under the grueling sun. Fortunately he later got a job in the mess hall where he actually gained 70 pounds! After some years, he was sent for a short stint to Canada and England and then to Germany in 1946.

He found Germany shattered with low morale, no food or employment and most business being done through the black market. Hans and Lotty, of adventurous spirit, decided to go to Africa to start a coffee

Podzun families: Back: Hans and Ulli; Middle: Fred and Hans; Front: Susy, Grandma, Lotty, Inge. (S. Podzun photo)

plantation. They were in the process of trading their house for a boat when the opportunity came to emigrate to Canada immediately. Hans signed the agreement with the Canadian government to work in a copper mine on Copper Mountain in B.C. Lotty and Susy joined him about six months later. After Hans had bought a tiny house, a car, paid off their travel fares from Germany and saved some money,

Hans, Lotty and Susy Podzun moving to Demers farm from Thompson farm, circa 1955. (S. Podzun photo)

he started to dream about owning land. With Lotty and their 10-year-old daughter, Susy, they spent countless happy days looking at abandoned farms throughout B.C. They all finally fell in love with and purchased Thompson's farm in Twelve Mile in 1953. It was complete with many types of apple trees and bushes loaded down with huge blackberries and raspberries. They later bought Demers' farm. Susy was enthralled with a wealth of books left behind in the Demers house and enjoyed contented years of reading. Lotty was a great housekeeper and soon had the little house tastefully decorated. She planted weeping willow trees and made beautiful rock gardens filled with many flowers.

It was difficult for Hans to find work to supplement farming. He peeled poles part time for John Rauchert and later was fortunate to find a good-paying job in a sawmill nearby. When he was laid off from the sawmill, he became fearful, not knowing how he was going to support his family. But he regrouped his thoughts and ideas and found a way to start his own business. For the rest of his life he boasted to friends and acquaintances, "Getting laid off was the best thing that happened to me. After that I never worked for anyone again. I always had my own business and gave jobs to others." It was a win-win situation for him.

Lotty worked closely with Hans on their farm. Neighbors remember her driving the tractor in the fields in makeup and dresses. Otto Maraun, a young German immigrant, joined them as a friend and business partner. They bought Asaph Domke's sheep one winter. It was a totally new experience for them. While shearing the first one, it died. Hans had put it on its back to make it comfortable, not knowing that sheep suffocate in that position because they cannot right themselves. Frantically, Hans drove around trying to find someone who could teach him to do it correctly. Lotty loved spinning the sheep's wool on her spinning wheel and knitting for her family. When they got tired of the pesky sheep, they butchered them and sold the mutton house-to-house in the Italian community in Revelstoke. Hans became upset when a customer complained that the "meat tastes like wool." The Podzuns with Otto raised milk cows, pigs and beef cattle. One time they had hundreds of chickens, but when the price of eggs dropped too low to pay for the feed, Hans fed the eggs to the pigs. Then he put up a big roadside sign for quick disposition, "Chickens for Sale, $1.00 a Piece." While the chickens were selling, Lotty and Susy plucked, cleaned and canned chickens in glass jars for their family for what seemed like weeks on end.

The ironic part of Hans' love for farming was that he was unable to kill an animal. At butchering time, he had his friend, Heinrich Bittner, a professional butcher, do the job. Later Otto took over. Hans would go into the bedroom until the butchering was over so as not to hear the animal cries. Afterwards he had no problem cutting up the meat and making sausages. On one occasion Lotty had to oblige when a chicken dinner was planned and there was no one around to help. She didn't like it but her hunger for meat gave her the courage.

Hans Podzun with Lilly. (S. Podzun photo)

In addition to farming, Hans and Otto bought a bulldozer and started their own successful logging business. Unfortunately the day came in 1965 when BC Hydro bought them out as well as the other farmers in Twelve Mile. It was a bittersweet experience for the Podzuns to leave their beloved farm. Hans was thinking of semi-retiring, but when the doctor gave him a clean bill of health, he chose to partner with Bill, a retired horticulturist from Kamloops, to start a vegetable farm and cattle ranch at 100 Mile House, B.C. Growing about 365 acres of cabbage and turnips was a huge success in the northern climate. People came from far and wide to see the operation. They had never seen such a large root cellar for storing vegetables and so much planting and harvesting machinery. The Podzuns were even chosen to be on television. However, their plans were struck down when Bill suffered a severe heart attack.

Hans and Otto knew nothing about vegetables, so everything around them fell to pieces and they were forced to sell and move again. This time they chose a small town where they found "eternal sunshine," in the small country of Belize. The English language and English laws of Belize were appealing to them and it was easy and inexpensive to live there. Hans started a factory under thatch roofs where cement and decorative blocks were made as well as fancy Mexican cement tiles, cement pillars and cement stair railings. From Revelstoke, Otto and his family joined the Podzuns in 1973.

After 20 years living a life of peace and fullness in Belize, Hans became ill. He moved back to Revelstoke with Lotty and spent about a year in Queen Victoria Hospital and extended care. He died in 1996 at age 75. Lotty died five weeks later at age 74.

Susy attended the Twelve Mile School from 1953-58, high school in Revelstoke and Salmon Arm, and University

Susy, Lotty, Hans and Douglas Podzun in Belize. (S. Podzun photo)

Susy Podzun by her hand-carved doors with Mayan motif. (S. Podzun photo)

in Vancouver and Germany. After finishing school, she joined her parents in 100 Mile House to help in the business that overwhelmed them. She also took part in their move to Belize. It was there that she got to know the Catholic Nuns in their flowing white habits, doing merciful work among the natives and living a life of poverty and prayer. They had been started by a German Order and still had German Sisters among them. Susy felt called to join them and has labored with them for 30 years. She currently lives in Maryland, USA where she teaches Fine Art in a Catholic High School and has her own art studio and small gallery. Some of her art can be found on her website: *divineinfants.com.*

In 1962 Douglas Podzun was born in Revelstoke. He was barely three years old when the Podzuns left Twelve Mile. He lives in Belize with his Mexican wife, Maria, and their two sons, Wolff and Hans. He built up Corozal Bay Resort in 2000 on the shores of the Caribbean that has become one of the best vacationing spots in Belize. Information about their resort can be found on the web at *corozalbayresort.com.*

PODZUN, ULLI

Ulrich (Ulli) Podzun and Inge Neumann met in Rendsburg, Germany and were married there on September 18, 1948. On November 24, 1949 their son, Friedrich (Fred) was born in the same city.

Ulli and his older brother, Hans, were truly blessed to have come through the terrible WWII unscathed. The two brothers were always close and when Hans and Lotty decided to emigrate to Canada with daughter, Susy, Ulli and Inge elected to go as well with the men going first. Initially Ulli and Hans worked at Copper Mountain mine near Princeton, B.C. About six months later in November 1951, after Ulli had built his family's first home in Canada, Inge and young Fred followed, along with Lotty and Susy.

In the summer of 1954, shortly after the birth of their youngest son, Hans, Ulli and Inge moved to Twelve Mile following Hans and Lotty who had moved there in 1953. Ulli and Inge purchased Robert Brinkman's homestead about three miles south of the ferry. Bob then moved into his original log cabin and continued living there until he moved to Manitoba.

As a young boy, Fred was fascinated by Bob's stories, by his bandana covering his tracheotomy, and by the bees kept at the back of their property. But what amazed him the most was how Bob had painted the horizontal kitchen wallboards all different colors. That was Fred's favorite feature of the house. As with most, if not all, of those country homes, there was no electricity or indoor plumbing, except for the kitchen water pump. And there was always an outhouse.

After Bob left, his log cabin became Podzun's pig barn. Always ready for excitement, Fred delighted in watching his dad and Uncle Hans catch the squealing pigs on butchering day. The family used Bob's hand-built beehive boxes for various other purposes and one became a cargo box in the back of their beloved 1952 Fargo. Over its many years of use, it continued to emit the pleasing scent of honey and wood.

One evening the Podzuns returned home to find their house on fire. Fortunately they were able to save a few precious items. They immediately moved into Asaph Domke's log cabin until they could decide what to do. The community banded together and gave them clothing, dishes and cooking utensils. Some of the golden coloured coffee cups are still in Fred's possession.

Living three or four miles south of the rest of Twelve Mile's settlement, not yet in school and with only his Collie, Rolph, for company, it was difficult for Fred to find playmates. He found that hanging around neighbours, Asaph and Kellina Domke, he could hone his conversation skills. At other times he and their eight-year-old niece, Helga Mantei, played together with the farm animals. He was excited to finally begin school at Twelve Mile in 1955. As a curious six-year-old, Fred was fascinated by the activities related to the ferry. One winter when the Columbia

Fred, Inge, Hans and Ulli Podzun. (S. Podzun photo)

River froze over and he was riding it on his way home from school, workers deployed sticks of dynamite at the end of very long poles. The exploding dynamite broke up the massive ice flows allowing the ferry to cross.

In 1956 Ulli and Inge purchased a home in Revelstoke on Tenth Street next to a forest where Fred and Hans built tree houses and played as they grew up. Over the years the family often visited Hans, Lotty and Susy, maintaining the relationship with Twelve Mile. To Fred, his uncle and aunt's farm seemed to continually change as they acquired additional acreage and cleared more land.

In 1965 Ulli and Inge's farm was expropriated by BC Hydro along with the others in the valley. During the following summer, Fred and other high school students found work as "root pickers" in the larger Twelve Mile area picking up the debris that had been left after all the houses, barns and outbuildings were demolished and the land was cleared down to the topsoil. Fred remembers, "at times the mosquitoes were overwhelming and we had to wear head nets, gloves and long-sleeved shirts during most of those hot and dusty days." Then in the summer of 1970, Ulli and Inge's son, Hans, worked for the Parks Board surveying the Twelve Mile area for a boat launch and picnic area, often encountering bears, deer and other wildlife. Ironically, it turned out that the Podzun farm was one of the few that had been spared being cleared, possibly because of its elevation. For years the site of Brinkman's house could be found, but slowly the fields grew over and the apple trees succumbed as nature reclaimed the homestead.

Over the ensuing years, Ulli worked as a surveyor throughout B.C. for the Department of Highways and often found himself away from home for a month or more at a time. This was hard on the family. Ulli continued to educate himself until he obtained his Engineering Technician degree and was eventually offered a stationary position as a Superintendent on the west coast. In the fall of 1971 Ulli and Inge moved to North Vancouver with their son, Hans. He unexpectedly found himself far from Revelstoke to finish twelfth grade. At that time Fred was in Kelowna enrolled in the founding class of Okanagan College along with several other Revelstoke Secondary School students.

In 1974 after years of hoping to eventually live in the Okanagan, Ulli was offered a new position as a Dam Inspector for the Ministry of Environment, and he and Inge moved to Kelowna. This was to be the happiest period of his working career as ironically he traveled the back roads from Princeton, near the area where he had previously worked many years before, and all the way to Revelstoke. He inspected the vast network of country dams that exist unbeknownst to most of the population. In the course of this work, Ulli met a variety of interesting people from all walks of life and spent many years in the countryside that he loved so much.

Eventually Ulli retired and thoroughly enjoyed his remaining years in Kelowna, until he passed away after a short illness in 1994. Inge continued living in their last family home, surrounded and comforted by her two sons, until her passing in 1998.

Fred began demonstrating his artistic talent in grade school. He refined it in high school in the form of cartooning on classmates' notebooks, and finally made it one of his vocations. He illustrated children's *Big Books* that could be coloured and read by several children at the same time. They were used in British Columbia schools in the 1980s. He has also produced many pen and ink drawings that have been sold in limited editions over the last three decades. Mostly, however, he still enjoys drawing cartoons. The pleasure of this has resurfaced in his talented niece, Bailey, who draws insightful and humorous cartoons amongst other pictures while attending the University of Victoria. Fred is currently a Project Manager and has lived in White Rock for many years.

Hans has a Notary Public practice in Richmond and lives near his brother. Hans remarried and lives happily with his wife, Colleen, and younger stepchildren, Conor and Brogan. Hans' son, Brody Podzun, was born in New Westminster, B.C. in 1986. His daughter, Bailey Podzun, was born in Richmond, B.C. in 1989. They both attend university (2008).

As Fred puts it, "The years spent in Twelve Mile South proved to be a stepping stone to enriched and fulfilled lives in B.C. for the Podzun family, and the memories found in old photographs from those days will likely be passed down through the generations."

POFFENBARGER

The Poffenbargers lived in Wigwam. Since the closest school was at Twelve Mile, their son Wayne Rodney attended grades 1-3 there during 1953-56. He boarded at the Astrahantseffs during the week while in school.

POITRAS

Ron Poitras attended Twelve Mile School during the 1966-67 school year. No further information is available.

RAUCHERT, FERDINAND AND EMIL

Ferdinand Rauchert was born October 19, 1873 in Rusterchietz, Poland. He and Maria Schlese married November 1898 in Ukraine. They emigrated from Volhynia, Russia with their three children, Olga, Caroline and John, to Minot, North Dakota in 1905. On February 15, 1906 their youngest son, Emil, was born in Hamburg, North Dakota. The family moved to the Winfield District near Wetaskiwin, Alberta in 1914.

Ferdinand traded his Winfield property for Mazar's farm of approximately 22 acres in Twelve Mile around 1942 and moved there with his son, Emil. Emil later purchased another 10 acres.

Ferdinand Rauchert. (J. Rauchert family photo)

Emil met Fanny (Tiny) Ocepoff in Shoreacres, B.C. After their engagement party there, they were married in Revelstoke on April 14, 1945, with Joe Kozek attending as best man.

Emil logged in the area with his brother, John. He mowed hay for neighbors Petrashuks, Astrahantseffs and Ocepoffs, and sold cedar stumps to the brewery in Revelstoke for five dollars a cord. After starting part time as a ferry operator, he was employed full time. He loved his job and always sang, "Cruising down the river on a Sunday afternoon," and always wore his captain's hat with pride. Because he lived so close to the ferry, he was aroused from his sleep to take people across the river after ferry hours, the fee being one dollar.

Emil loved taking pictures and he even had a movie camera. He was proud to show his slides. He also enjoyed music and played his mandolin, banjo, violin and sometimes his guitar, at times playing for the local dances. He made his own violins in Twelve Mile and later in Canyon when he moved. Each of his

Back: Fanny (Tiny) Ocepoff Rauchert with her parents. Front: Paul and Pearl Ocepoff. (Weston family photo)

children and grandchildren received one of his hand-made violins.

In the late 1950s during the Cold War years, Emil and Tiny were contacted by the RCAF Ground Observer Corps to report by phone to the Department of National Defense of the RCAF the

Emil Rauchert (right), Air Defence volunteer, with three National Defence officials, upon close of program. (E. Rauchert photo, RMA)

movements of aircraft over the area. The size of the airplane, elevation and direction were recorded. Their son, Larry, and Ruth Rauchert also were involved in this operation.

Tiny enjoyed her vegetable and berry garden. They also bought fruit in Kelowna, canning and jamming up to 200 jars of berries and fruit each year. They also harvested the morel mushrooms that were plentiful in the spring. In the fall, bears eagerly came close to the house to clean up the fruit that dropped off their trees.

On their farm, they also had horses, cows, chickens, ducks, pigs and goats. After purchasing a small tractor and baler, they sold their horses that had been used for plowing and haying.

Although their home was well built, it initially did not have plumbing or electricity. They later had propane lights, refrigerator and stove but continued to use a wood heater in the winter. In the 1960s Emil built a 12-volt power system for electric lights, that their children especially enjoyed when their Christmas tree was lighted up.

Tiny was one of the few ladies in the community who drove a car, so she took other ladies on shopping trips in Revelstoke.

Ferdinand lived in his own little house between the main house and the ferry.

Larry, Rosalie (Rose) and Lorna attended the Twelve Mile School. During part of that time the classes included Kindergarten up to the seventh grade and the eighth-graders were bussed to Revelstoke.

In the summer, Rose and Lorna earned one dollar a crate picking raspberries for the Astrahantseffs.

In 1965 when BC Hydro bought their property, Hydro contracted with them to burn their own house and barn before moving. Emil and Larry documented the buildings burning with their movie camera.

The family, including Ferdinand, moved to Canyon, B.C. in 1965. They soon became active in the community. Tiny and Emil joined a carpet bowling league, and joined the Branch 28 Seniors in Creston where they played in "Tiny's Band." She played the drums and Emil the violin. The band also included piano, accordian, guitar and banjo.

Emil and Tiny had seven children:

Larry Henry, born in 1946, has three children: Lori, Larry John (stepchildren) and Natasha. He lives in Langley, B.C. and is a building inspector. Lori had four sons and two grandsons.

Rosalie (Rose) Linda, born in 1949, has one son, Jason, three grandsons and one granddaughter. Rose and her husband, Burt Olson, live and work in Peace River, Alberta.

Lorna Mary, born in 1950, has one son, Wesley. She and her husband, Lorne Selden, live in Lister, B.C. Their infant son, Billy Allen, passed away in 1972 in Creston.

Sandra Pearl, born in 1960, moved to Canyon with her parents. She was involved with the Endicott Center for challenged children until its closure and is now working at Cresteramics in Creston, B.C.

Infant twin boys, Eric Emil and Frederick Paul, died of pneumonia in Revelstoke when they were about six months old.

Infant son, Richard Ferdinand, passed away at a very young age also in Revelstoke.

Emil passed away April 19, 1990, and Tiny continues to live in Creston (2008).

RAUCHERT, JOHN

John Rauchert was born in Wolwachowka, Volhynia, Russia on April 7, 1904, to Ferdinand and Maria (Schlese) Rauchert. He had two sisters, Olga and Caroline, and a brother, Emil, who was born after they arrived in the United States. The family emigrated in 1905 first to the United States and then to Usona District near Wetaskiwin, Alberta in 1914.

During those first 10 years in Alberta, John survived the Great Depression by herding sheep, drilling water wells, threshing grain, cutting railroad ties, logging and being foreman of the Knobhill Sawmill near Winfield, Alberta.

He homesteaded west of Hoadley, Alberta and a happy misadventure led him to the nearby Glanfield homestead where he met Ruth Glanfield. They married June 7, 1942 at Warburg, Alberta.

Ruth was born in Winmarleigh, Lancashire, England in 1923, to Frederick and Isabel Glanfield. She had a brother, Fred, and two sisters, Lucy and Peggy. The family emigrated to Canada in 1929 and homesteaded near Winfield, Alberta. Two younger brothers, Oliver and Brian, were born in Alberta.

After they married, John trucked on the Alaska Highway, hauling material for the Liard River Bridge and the White Pass and Yukon narrow gauge railroad that connected Skagway to Whitehorse.

John's father, Ferdinand, and brother, Emil, moved to Twelve Mile first. Then John, Ruth and baby daughter, Emily, joined them in 1944. They shipped their belongings by CPR boxcar that was delivered to the siding in Twelve Mile. John hoped to find a good job with his 1938 Maple Leaf truck. They obtained 40 acres (across from the school) from Martin Schmidt by trading their Ford truck for the land. This property had originally been homesteaded by Steve Iwasiuk. One wonders what went through Ruth's mind when she first set eyes on her new home, a little gray, one-room shack sitting crookedly on top of a hill. As their family grew, they built a new frame, two-story house in 1953 by the road right across from the school.

John always found logging jobs and obtained his own timber rights on Mt. Cartier, taking out cedar poles and logs. His first timber rights were turned over to him by Dick Sawyer. Dick also encouraged John to buy a trailer for his logging truck. He started out with a little gas tractor but when it gave out Mr. Ogawa helped him obtain a new Caterpillar tractor with payments of $900.00 a month. He also had a skidder with rubber airplane tires and a gin pole for loading logs onto the truck. When logging was closed in the winter, he worked on the ferry. He expanded his operations with more equipment and logged with the Kozek brothers west of Revelstoke. He logged until 1966 when he sold his quota to Saskatchewan Co-Op in Sicamous, B.C.

Ruth and John Rauchert with: Kathy, Genny, Donna, Emily and Carolyn, circa 1951. (J. Rauchert family photo)

Ruth was kept busy with her children, planting, harvesting and preserving food from her large vegetable garden as well as household chores typical of a pioneer woman. There was endless laundry and cooking to be done, all without the conveniences of running water and electricity. When the children were young, she used her treadle sewing machine to sew pretty dresses for the girls. What was fascinating to others was her ability to read a book while knitting sweaters at the same time. When they had a telephone installed, Ruth was one of the Ground Observers for the Department of National Defence during the Cold War years. Whenever a plane flew over, she dropped whatever she was doing, ran to the phone and called in the information. Her identification was "Bravo Foxtrott 5-5 Black. The Corps operated from 1951 to 1960.

As the children got older they pitched in with the chores, which were many. In the summertime Gregory and Polly Astrahantseff hired them to pick strawberries and raspberries, which were sold in town or shipped elsewhere by rail. Even though it was hard, hot work, they were glad for the extra spending money, which could be as much as $10 by the end of the season. Carolyn remembers a summer when some pretty girls from town came to pick berries. They were "all dolled up" in good blouses and pedal pushers in contrast to the local pickers in work shirts, old jeans and hats with mosquito netting hanging down. The "pretty girls" flirted with the boys all day, running up and down the rows of raspberry bushes, throwing fruit at each other and screaming. They never came back and it was rumored that they had filled their little baskets with grass topped off by a layer of berries.

It was special to the girls when Ruth came along to pick berries with them. She knew how to fill those little baskets in no time. On the days Ruth picked, Polly made a special lunch for them. The girls still remember her delicious, pink borscht served with sour cream, fresh, crusty bread, long slices of crispy, cool cucumbers with lots of salt, and raspberry turnovers with thick cream for dessert.

John loved sports. If he was off work during school hours, he crossed the road from his house to the school to play softball with the students. Evelyn Domke still remembers the time she was on second base and John was up to bat. "He hit the ball and it hit me on the forehead. I just stood there. Everyone was yelling, 'Are you okay?' Luckily, the ball was rather spongy and I was fine but just a little stunned."

John was also a hockey enthusiast. Every winter he and the children cleared and packed down an area of snow. Then they took turns pumping and carrying water to flood it. A magic rink appeared after a good freeze. Probably no other kids could skate right out of their house onto a rink. It was open for the entire neighborhood to use, and one year John formed the local boys into a hockey team. After days of coaching and practicing, they took on a team in Revelstoke, but it apparently didn't go well and he came home disgusted and gave up the idea in the future. It didn't stop him, however, from at times driving all the way to a Penticton game and returning home at about 3:00 in the morning. In 1955 the Penticton V's won the World Cup against a Russian team. They also won the Allen Cup, so John took his family to the Okanagan to view the cup displayed in the window of the restaurant owned by the Warwick brothers, Grant, Dick and Bill, who were the hockey heroes.

John adored his children and loved to surprise them. One day after work he knelt on the ground with his black lunch bucket and gathered his little girls around him. As Ruth stood there, hands on hips, wondering what he was up to, he slowly opened the lid and out fluttered a scared, little brown bat. As the girls screamed, it circled their heads and flew straight through the open window of their upstairs bedroom.

Genny, Kathy, Larry, Carolyn and Emily Rauchert on ferry, circa 1951. (J. Rauchert family photo)

Another time, John brought home the leftover food the Forestry Service gave him after helping with a forest fire on Mt. Cartier. The girls especially loved the cans and cans of sardines that they ate all summer on their picnics.

Before Christmas John took his children into the bush to cut their Christmas tree. As is often the case with a free-growing tree, the side growing next to a larger tree has fewer branches. This didn't stop him from balancing it out by drilling holes to add in branches where necessary. He and Ruth took their family to Revelstoke to enjoy the Christmas lights since Twelve Mile did not have electricity. There was always a huge, lighted fir tree in the center of the intersection of McKenzie Avenue and Second Street as well as many other decorated homes and businesses. To top off their evening out, they brought home hot dogs and ice cream for supper.

John and Ruth had five daughters and two sons. They all finished high school in Revelstoke despite the difficulty they had catching rides to and from school before a bus was scheduled to Twelve Mile. Ruth always encouraged her children and grandchildren to pursue a higher education. Their children are:

Emily Recknell, born in 1943, is a retired school teacher living in Manitoba. Her daughter, Glenda Garrison, is an executive assistant to a Member of Parliament in Ottawa.

Genevieve (Genny), born in 1944, is a retired school teacher. Her husband, Terry Wilson, is a retired businessman. They live in Golden, B.C. and have two sons. Robert and his wife, Runa, are both teachers. Doug is the branch manager for Century Valen, and his wife, Karen, is a social worker with the School Division.

Kathleen (Kathy), born in 1945, and husband, Alan Reimer, have one son. Their young daughter passed away in 1982 of cystic fibrosis. Kathy is working in the field of environmental management. They live on Salt Spring Island, B.C. Their son, James, is a student at the University of Victoria (2008).

Carolyn, born in 1947, and husband, Ronald Nutton, have one daughter and one son. They are retired and live in Delta, B.C. Sandra is married to Ron Teljeur and they have three young children. Byron is a biologist working with the Department of Fisheries in Prince George, B.C.

Donna Tagseth, born in 1950, has three children. Patricia is married to Rob Ciarniello and they have two children. Shannon is married to Lee Odgers and they have two children. Shawn is married to Lopa. Donna is a real estate agent and lives in Kelowna, B.C.

John Rauchert family, 2004. (W. Kozek photo)

Roderick, born in 1953, died accidentally in 1960.

John, Jr., born in 1961, is married to Beverley Turner. He works in the Distant Education Department of Southern Alberta Institute of Technology (SAIT). They live in Calgary, Alberta.

John, Ruth and John, Jr. left Twelve Mile in 1968 when BC Hydro expropriated their home. "History repeats itself" was a truism for John and Ruth. They loaded their belongings, including their caterpillar, into a CPR boxcar on the Twelve Mile siding and shipped them back to Alberta. Ruth finally got her modern home which they built on their cattle ranch near Hoadley and the West Blindman River near relatives. When they no longer could manage the ranch they moved back to Rimbey, Alberta. Ruth suffered from rheumatoid arthritis and passed away in November 1993. John moved to Golden, B.C. in 1999 to spend his last years near Genny. He passed away December 22, 2004, just three months short of his 101st birthday.

REVELLE

Helen Revelle attended Twelve Mile School during the 1955-56 school year. No further information is available.

RIBALKIN

Winnie and Nick Ribalkin attended Twelve Mile School for part of the 1953-54 school year. No further information is available.

ROBSON

William (Bill, Sandy) Robson logged with Walter Shiell first in Nakusp then in Twelve Mile between 1947-51.

In 1948-50 Mrs. Robson and daughters Roberta (Bobbie) and Evamae (Eva) joined Bill in Twelve Mile, and the girls attended school there. They lived in the log cabin by the railroad crossing (which later burned down when the Vincent Johnsons lived in it). Their other five children lived in Nakusp.

Bobbie and Eva easily made friends with the other school children and thought nothing of walking after school, through the snow, to Domkes to slide down the mountain on pieces of cardboard boxes, then home again in the dark.

Bobbie married Mr. Chabot and they live in Vernon.

Eva passed away.

ROHDE

Leo, Martha and son Valentin (Val) Rohde arrived in Twelve Mile March 1, 1950. Leo was born in Russia of German descent and served as an officer in the German army during WWII. After being released by Britain from a POW camp, he met Martha Domke near Tolstaglope, Germany. She and her family had also moved there earlier. They married in 1947. After Val was born they emigrated to Canada, being sponsored by cousin Oscar Domke. When their payback year was finished, they bought the 40 acres by the railroad crossing in Twelve Mile from John Rauchert and lived and farmed there until 1958. They sold their home to Hickey Kaduhr, who later sold it to the Schmidts, and moved to the Big Eddy area of Revelstoke.

Leo began his logging career in Canada by making poles, first learning the trade from Martha's cousin, Asaph Domke, who was considered to be the area's expert pole maker. Leo logged for various companies including Mike Kozek, John Rauchert, Walter Shiell, Celgar, and various sawmills including Downie Street Mill.

At the time Leo began pole making in the 1950s, pole makers were paid by the foot for each pole, and the contractor kept back 10 percent until the poles were trimmed in the pole yard. The reason was that some poles were too skinny or the tops weren't big enough so they had to be trimmed, thus decreasing the footage. He remembers the trust Mike Kozek showed him when he paid Leo for the 500-pole contract in cash and in full without withholding the ten percent. When Leo asked Mike why he wasn't holding back 10 percent, Leo will never forget his reply, "Do you think I don't trust you?"

He remembers also the kindnesses to him by John Rauchert. John offered him a pole- making job, then sold him his first land on monthly payments, moved the Rohde shack from Asaph's property, and arranged for him to purchase a logging horse from Walter Shiell for $200. He earned enough that first summer with his horse, Billy, to buy his first pickup, a 1943 half-ton Dodge. When the snow was too deep to log in the woods, Leo cut poles on his own property and used Billy to skid them to the road.

When Martha's parents, Arthur and Emilie Domke, emigrated to Canada from Germany in 1954, they lived next to each other both in Twelve Mile and then in the Big Eddy area of Revelstoke.

While in Twelve Mile, Rosalinde and Nellie were born. Roland and Gary were born after they moved to Big Eddy. Valentin and Rosalinde began their education at the Twelve Mile School. The family grew their own vegetables and meat from their cows, pigs and chickens. After living meagerly and at times almost starving in the old country, they were thankful for a bountiful country and the opportunity to own their own home.

From the Big Eddy, Martha and Leo moved to the Arrow Heights area of Revelstoke where they continue to live. Martha suffered a massive stroke a few years ago and is cared for in Extended Care at

Rohde family. Back: Nelli, Valentin, Rosalinde. Front: Roland, Leo, Martha and Gary.
(L. Rohde photo)

the hospital. Valentin and Kim have a daughter, Erica. He has a business near Mara Lake. Rosa and Henry Grusen recently moved to Nakusp, B.C. and have two daughters, Elaine and Christina. Nelli and Glen Richardson have two sons, Jason and Kyle. Nelli has been active in Revelstoke City Council, School Board and various other civic activities. Gary and Niki live in Revelstoke and have two sons, Tyler and Travis. Roland and Lori live in Revelstoke and have a daughter, Ashley, and son, Logan. Gary and Roland are both with the CPR.

ROMANSKY

Mike Romansky's name pops up here and there as stories are told, but no one seems to know much about him. Mrs. Kaduhr thinks he came to Twelve Mile from Nanaimo. Everyone agrees he was a drifter-nomad type and lived in Twelve Mile from about 1948 into the early 1960s.

Mike worked for various people, sometimes just for room and board. For about one and a half years he lived and logged for Ben Domke. He'd work for one or two days, then "I don't need to work anymore," he would tell Ben. The Astrahantseffs looked after him for a while where he did chores for his keep. He also worked for Kozek's mill for a while, living in one of their camp shacks. Sometimes he worked as a ferry deck hand. Bruce Kaduhr remembers that at one time Mike lived in their root house. He remembers that Mike stored cabbage under the snow where it didn't freeze. Then he fried it into a tasty dish.

Both Ben and Bruce agree that Mike fantasized a lot. He felt women were after him, and also claimed to have had a Strativarious violin at one time but a girl friend burned it. He may have gone back to his brother's in Saskatchewan, although it hasn't been confirmed.

SCHMIDT

John George and Edna (Plester) Schmidt arrived in Twelve Mile in 1955 with their family from Hoadley, Alberta. They were friends of the John Raucherts and came to log for John.

John's father, Martin Schmidt, had emigrated to the USA from Germany during the Boer War (1899-1902) and married Alvina Moss. After John was born they moved to Alberta. According to the Raucherts' records, Martin owned 40 acres in Twelve Mile across from the school. Around 1944 he traded it to John Rauchert for a Ford truck

At first John and Edna rented Brooks and Lily Gowanlock's log house in Twelve Mile. In 1956 they moved to Vancouver Island for a brief period of time, but came back. They lived in the "ferry house," for a while until they bought Hickey Kaduhr's property (formerly Rohde's) north of Petrashuks by the railway crossing. There Reginald Seed of Sicamous assembled their new prefab home.

John worked for Celgar as a faller while Edna tended her large garden and children. They easily made lifelong friends with the community people. Karen remembers the time she shoveled snow off their roof, then jumped into the hard-packed snow below. Needless to say, she spent the rest of the winter with a broken foot in a cast. When the cast came off that spring, she was so excited, she immediately went for a bicycle ride, crashing through the railway guard and ending up seeing Dr.

Karen, Alvina and Larry Schmidt. (Kaduhr family photo)

Armstrong again—with a broken arm. "You mean you call her a girl?" he commented in disbelief to Edna.

In 1967 BC Hydro bought Schmidt's property, transported their house on a flatbed truck to Sunnyside Road across from the Revelstoke Airport where it was unloaded onto a new basement. Their son, Jack, bought the house in 1981 and continued living there for about 10 years. John and Edna had five children.

Alvina Jean was born in 1944. She attended Twelve Mile School for grade seven and part of eight until the eighth graders began being bussed to Revelstoke. She trained as a special front line worker, lives in Revelstoke, and has two daughters and a son.

Karen Ann was born in 1945 and attended grades 5-7 at Twelve Mile School. She's been a homemaker but currently resides in Moberly Manor in Revelstoke. She has two daughters, a son and three grandchildren.

Larry Roger was born in 1950 and attended grades 2-7 at Twelve Mile School. He is a truck driver and lives in the Kamloops/Burns Lake area. He has two daughters and three grandchildren.

John Edward (Jackie) was born in 1955 and attended grades 1-6 at Twelve Mile School. He is a logger and lives in Revelstoke and the Philippines. He has three sons and three grandchildren.

Randy passed away at three months of age.
John and Edna both passed away in Revelstoke.

SHAMON

Olga Perich was raised in Alberta and Manitoba, being one of 11 children. Her father was a minister, so the family moved quite often as he ministered to various congregations. Olga received her teaching credentials at Camrose Normal School in Alberta and began teaching in Vegreville, Alberta. There she met Walter Shamon and they married in July 1934. Their first child, Barbara, was born in 1935.

When Walter heard of work opportunities on the Big Bend Highway in B.C., they left their Alberta farm and moved to Revelstoke in 1936. His mother and brothers, Mike and Steve, lived south of Revelstoke at Mt. Cartier. Their son, Walter, Jr. was born in 1937.

When money became tight, Olga began teaching again at Albert Canyon, 1941-42. She took Barbara and little Walter with her by train on Mondays and returned

Walter and Olga Shamon, 1942. (Issy Shamon photo)

Olga Shamon, back left, with friends. Front: Walter, Jr., -?-, Barbara Shamon. In front of Twelve Mile School, 1942. (Issy Shamon photo)

to Revelstoke for the weekends. They lived with the Rake family while in Albert Canyon.

In the fall of 1942, Olga began teaching at Twelve Mile School. Again, she took her two little ones with her and lived in the teacherage during the week and went home for the weekends. Even though Walter was not yet of school age, he sat in the classroom with the 11 students. In addition to teaching all eight grades in one room and caring for her children, she had to get up through the night to add wood to the stoves so her home and school stayed warm through the winter.

Before her third child, Isabel (Issy), was born in April, Olga turned her teaching job over to her sister, Rose Slym, from Calgary to finish out the year from March until June. Barbara remembers that spring as if it were yesterday:

So mom and her two children were living in the back of the school, without a phone and she's pregnant. I remember how frightened I was of the ferry and the rushing water. Mom obviously was concerned that if she went into labor early she would need help, so we rehearsed over and over again what I was to do if she needed me to go for help. Assuming it was night, I was to take a lantern and walk to the ferry and wake up Mr. Millar who ran the ferry. Mom told me to walk on the side of the road and swing the lantern as I walked. I was to knock and wake up Mr. Millar. Thank God, I never had to do it. It seemed like a heck of a long way from the school to the ferry, especially if it had to be walked by a seven-year-old—in the dark—by herself!

After raising her children, Olga returned to teaching from 1957-70 in the Revelstoke School District. She retired in 1970. On August 3, 2003 she passed away at age 93 years in Vernon, B.C.

Barbara (Flock) lives in the Palm Springs, California area and Issy (Leveille) lives in Vernon, B.C.

SHEPPARD

Judith and Wayne Sheppard attended Twelve Mile School during the 1955-56 school year. No further information is available.

SHIELL

Walter Shiell was born and raised in Needles, B.C. After he and Celia Waterstreet were married they spent many years logging in various areas of B.C. including Salmo, Nelson, Nakusp, Beaton, Twelve Mile and Revelstoke.

Walter and his partner, Sandy Robson, set up their logging operation in Twelve Mile from 1947 to approximately 1951. They logged cottonwood and birch from the islands in the Columbia River. The wood was sold for plywood. Cottonwood trees were cut into eight-foot lengths and shipped by railcar to Vernon. Only the butts were usable because it was clear wood.

Walter used horses in his logging operations, working them all summer and stabling them in the old Louis Ozero barn by the railway crossing. At the end of the season, he loaded them in boxcars and shipped them to the prairies where they were turned loose for the winter. One spring Leo Rohde purchased a Clyde/Belgian horse, Billy, from Walter for $200. He said the horses that came back in the spring were skinny with long hair and needed to be "beefed up" for their summer work.

Celia Shiell's 100ᵗʰ birthday, January 2008, celebrated with: Back: Pat and Seamus Monaghan; Middle: their children. (D.Tucker photo)

While in Twelve Mile, the Shiells lived in the two-room cabin on Ferdinand Rauchert's farm. They raised their niece, Pat Waterstreet, who like all the older Twelve Mile students, had to board away from home for her higher education, first in Revelstoke and then St. Mary's in Calgary, Alberta. She trained as a nurse, married Seamus Monaghan and continues to live in Alberta. They have three children.

When their work was completed in Twelve Mile, Walter and Celia moved to Revelstoke and continued in the logging and pole business for several years. He then worked at the Bell Pole yard and trapped in the Goldstream area. They retired in Lethbridge, Alberta near Pat. The Shiell family farm in

Needles was bought by BC Hydro in the 1960s and Walter's brother, Fred, later purchased back part of it and continues to live there.

Walter died in Lethbridge March 17, 1996. Celia continues to live in Lethbridge and recently celebrated her 100th birthday in January 2008.

SLYM

Rose Perich was born in 1902 in Laniuk, Alberta (later changed to Two Hills). Her family moved to Winnipeg from 1917-20 where Rose got her teaching certificate. A young person in those days could get a teaching certificate after grade 10. She and John Slym married and moved to Calgary, Alberta.

In the spring of 1943, Rose finished out the school year from March to June at Twelve Mile School for her sister, Olga Shamon, who was on maternity leave. Rose returned to Calgary where she lived until her death in the early 1980s.

SMITH

Marjorie Smith did her practice teaching at Twelve Mile School during 1949. She then taught at Beaton and married Ken Millar, formerly of Twelve Mile.

STOLLER

John and Pat Stoller moved with their family from Golden to Twelve Mile in 1966. John was originally from Switzerland and Pat was from Winnipeg, Manitoba.

As most logging families were inclined to do, they followed the jobs. John and his two brothers, Robert and Herman, contracted with BC Hydro to burn slash as the valley was cleared for the reservoir. John, Pat and six of their younger children rented and lived in the frame house that Hydro bought from Asaph and Kellina Domke.

Charleen, Elizabeth, Rudy and Shelly attended Twelve Mile School during 1966-67. Danny and Latricia were still preschoolers, and Max and John (Bonzo) were already working away from home.

The following year the Stollers moved to Revelstoke where Charleen (Zacker), Rudy and Max still live. John passed away in 1973 in Revelstoke and Pat followed in 1995 in Creston, B.C.

John's brother, Robert and his wife, Pat, lived in a mobile home across the small creek next to Domke's house while he burned slash for Hydro. Robert drove his daughter to the ferry every day to catch the bus to Revelstoke High School.

John's second brother, Herman, and wife, Bonnie, also lived in a mobile home on Domke's homestead while also burning slash for Hydro.

STORY

David Story was born in Penticton, B.C., and spent his early childhood in Nelson. When he was 12 years old he and his family moved to Revelstoke. It didn't take Dave (or "Duve" to his friends) long to become active in high school sports, especially baseball and basketball; and he was known for livening up a gathering with his piano playing.

Upon completing teacher training at Victoria Normal School, he accepted a teaching position in 1951 at the Twelve Mile country school. First-year teachers are challenged under the best of circumstances, let alone trying to teach 16 students in grades one through eight in one room! His students were pleased when he participated in their ball games and enjoyed "music class" with him accompanying their singing on the old pump organ.

Not only did he set speed records driving back and forth from Revelstoke on the rough gravel road, his teacher friends also have stories to tell. That fall he gave them the ride they'll never forget as they drove together in his car to the teachers' convention in Oliver, B.C. They were Audrey Millar (Arrowhead teacher), Lois Millar (Albert Canyon), Bill Husband (Arrowhead) and Bud Stovel (Glacier). They were billeted in various homes in Oliver and those who stayed in orchard homes loaded the car with boxes of apples to bring back.

By December, David decided teaching wasn't for him. From 1957-1993 he worked for the CPR and continued making Revelstoke his home. As an adult he was always a key player in the sports programs, playing in men's fastball, coaching Little League, and serving as President of Revelstoke Little League during the 1960s. He was also a strong supporter of Revelstoke Minor Hockey and later became active in Revelstoke's Senior's Bowling League. Dave was a communications technology pioneer and became known as "Satellite Dave" when he installed one of Revelstoke's first satellite dishes in his yard enabling him to share up-to-the-minute National Hockey League scores with his buddies long before sports channels existed.

He married Loretta Jones in 1955 and they had four children. Jerry (Butch) and wife, Maureen, live in Surrey, B.C. and have two children. Mike and his wife, Jane, reside in Port Moody, B.C. and have two children. Jean and husband, Jeff Weston of Twelve Mile, are in Revelstoke and have three children. Bev and husband, Kevin Fleming, live in Sicamous with their two children. Dave and Loretta have nine grandchildren. Their family was blessed with musical talent. Jerry (Butch) continues to play with his sons, Colin and Sean, in their group, "3 Storys High." Their latest CD is "Stokin." Mike restores pianos under his company's name, "Story and Co. Pianos."

Loretta passed away in 1982 and David died in Revelstoke in 1995.

SUTHERLAND

Ron Sutherland attended Twelve Mile School during the 1943-44 school year. No further information is available.

THOMPSON

William Henry Thompson (Scotty) moved to Twelve Mile from the Vancouver area before 1922. He had a daughter in Vancouver who he visited occasionally, and there are reports that he may have had a son who lived in Twelve Mile for a while before he returned to Vancouver. On his homestead, William built a four-room log cabin on the southwest side of the river near the ferry. Over the years lilac bushes that he planted along the road in front of his house, bloomed beautifully.

During part of the winter of Twelve Mile's first school year, 1930-31, the students were taught in Thompson's living room while the first school was being built.

Neighbors remember William to be a small man with a big mustache. His fingers on one hand had been shot off at the knuckles, and the rumor was that he had been badly injured while serving in the Boer war (1899-1902). He never had an automobile, but took rides to town with neighbors for supplies and grain.

William was known for baking delicious Scottish shortbread, and for playing his harmonica and singing at socials at the school. He grew a large field of mangels, a root vegetable of the sugar beet family used to feed farm animals. He left them in the

Maggie McPhee Thompson, 1948. (Weston family photo)

ground until spring, shoveled the snow off, all by hand, then sacked and shipped them in boxcars. In 1940 he received recognition from the Agricultural Department in Victoria for a new variety of Netted Gem potato. It was expected to have a higher yield and be much larger than the ordinary varieties per the March 14, 1940 article in the *Revelstoke Review*. He also raised and shipped crates of strawberries.

On November 15, 1933, William married Eliza Jane Brill-McMahon-Irvine in a quiet ceremony in Twelve Mile. "Reverend B. H. Balderston performed the ceremony in the presence of friends and relatives of the bride and groom." (*Revelstoke Review*, November 17, 1933). Apparently, the marriage didn't work out and Eliza Jane soon moved in with her son, Hugh McMahon, who owned the adjoining property.

Maggie McPhee and son, Jimmy, came from Vancouver to live with William in approximately 1946 when Jimmy was nine years old. Their relationship has never been clear. In the late 1940s, Maggie bore baby daughter, Chrissie. Maggie was active in the community's social activities such as teas and canasta parties, and enjoyed the community dances held at the school.

Young people in the area generally feared Mr. Thompson because of his unpredictable nature. His German Shepherd dog chased and nipped at the heels of the Domke children every morning that they rode their bikes past his property to school. Ada built up speed, then raised her legs to the handle bars to pass his farm safely. Various neighbors

Jimmy Thompson, 1948.
(A. Domke family photo)

remember seeing "Old Man Thompson", as he was often referred to, chasing Jimmy around the farm fields wielding a piece of blackened stump, and at other times a scissors. On other occasions they saw Jimmy locked up in a picket fence pen next to the house. Jimmy went to school with bruises and black eyes. Unfortunately, in those days such abuses weren't usually reported. One day when Lena Kaduhr and Maggie were picking strawberries in the Thompson patch, Lena found a pistol in the ground. Maggie admitted to burying it as she was afraid Old Man Thompson would kill Jimmy with it. She gave it to Lena and it was identified to be a WWI .44 revolver.

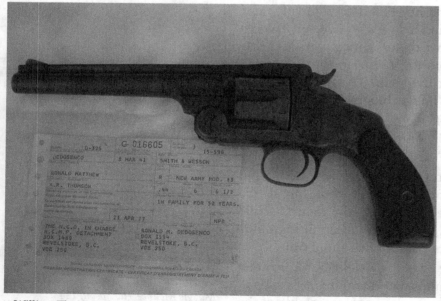

William Thompson's WWI .44 revolver. (W. Jarvis photo)

William feuded with his neighbor, Hugh McMahon, to his south, and with the Millars to his northwest. He shot and badly wounded one of Millar's dogs and badly injured their other dog. In 1948 when Ben Domke was crossing the ferry on his way home, he heard gunshots just south of the ferry. As he passed Thompson's, he found Asaph Domke's new horse, Prince, shot to death. Being open range, apparently Prince reached over the fence to nibble grass, thus annoying Mr. Thompson. The court found him guilty and required him to pay for the horse.

Mr. Thompson became quite ill in 1949 and through 1950, going to Vancouver several times for treatment. Then in November 1950, Maggie, Jimmy and Chrissie moved to Vancouver to be with him. He died in Vancouver August 17, 1951 at age 67 years.

Ben Domke and Lena Kaduhr state that Jimmy later joined the army and visited them in person and by phone. Despite his abusive childhood, he developed into a fine young man.

TOWNSEND

Elsie Ruth Kulchyski finished Grade 13 in Meadow Lake, Saskatchewan in 1947 and entered Normal School that fall in Saskatoon, Saskatchewan. In 1948 she and her family moved to Nelson, B.C. She began teaching that September at Johnson's Landing, B.C. and at Bonnington Falls the following year. During the summers she took summer school classes until she received her degree in education.

While teaching in Nelson during 1951-52 she met and married Art Townsend and they moved to Revelstoke where he was employed by Canadian Pacific Express. Ruth taught at Arrowhead Superior School in 1952-53 and the following year, 1953-54, at Twelve Mile School.

Ruth Townsend on left, with her students at the Twelve-Mile-Sid-Arrowhead field day at Mackey's field in Sidmouth, 1954. Back: Ruth Townsend, Sergei Astrahantseff, Emily Rauchert, Helen Nipper, Herb Domke, Gloria Kaduhr, Ada Domke, Susy Podzun, Russell Gowanlock.
Front: Genny, Kathy, Larry and Carolyn Rauchert.
Sitting on Left: Kellina Domke and Nettie Nipper.
(Townsend family photo)

The daily car trip in rough gravel, mud, ice and snow from Revelstoke to Twelve Mile did not stop her determination to give the 13 students her best. The older girls were especially fascinated by her beautiful clothes and new hairdos! She formed her students into a team complete with "Twelve Mile" embroidered on the backs of yellow shirts. They competed in games and races against Sidmouth and Arrowhead during the spring picnic held on Bill Mackey's field.

After her year in Twelve Mile, she taught in Revelstoke until 1967. She moved to Castlegar, B.C., continued teaching, and retired there. She was actively involved in volunteer work with the P.C. party; hospital auxiliary; baseball, hockey and ballet clubs.

Arthur and Ruth's children are: Valerie, a registered nurse, currently with the Salmon Arm Hospital; Donna, a cashier with Extra Foods in North Vancouver; and Jeffrey, a civil engineer for B.C. Forest Service.

Ruth passed away in Castlegar in 2001, and Art passed away in Burton, B.C. in 2004.

ULLMAN (ALMEN?)

John Ullman (Almen?) was a bachelor from Germany and the only one in his family to emigrate to Canada.

He purchased Mike and Mary Petrashuk's second 40 acres on Drimmie Creek where he built a log cabin next to the creek.

Mary was known for her delicious cooking, so John boarded there. Rose Petrashuk-Dedosenco remembers the day John failed to show up for supper at their place. Mary sent her son, Jack, to look for him. He found John buried under a pile of fresh snow where he had died.

His homestead was later purchased by Cecil and Lucy Banks, then by the Kaduhrs and Gowanlocks.

VIGUE

When Arnold Vigue and Sophie Shamon married in 1947, they bought Sophie's parents' farm in Eight Mile and were neighbors of the Myers. Arnold's father, Lawrence Vigue, drowned in 1939 when booming logs between Ten and Twelve Mile South. Sophie's parents, Steve and Pearl (Polly) Shamon, homesteaded their 40-acre farm around 1914.

Arnold was a foreman for Celgar and Sophie ran the farm and raised their children. During busy times, she hired some of the older girls from the Rauchert and Schmidt families of Twelve Mile to help with cooking and childcare.

When the school district began bus service to Twelve Mile in the fall of 1959, the four older Vigue children were transferred from the Selkirk School in Revelstoke and bussed to Twelve Mile. Valerie remembers having to live with her grandmother Shamon in Revelstoke the first year or two before going to Twelve Mile. After grade seven, Valerie, Lawrence and Carl were bussed to Revelstoke. Rick continued on at Twelve Mile until grade four. Their three younger children, Gladys, Tom and Dolly, weren't yet old enough for school.

The family's farm was bought out by BC Hydro in 1968. They moved to the Big Eddy area of Revelstoke and the three younger children began their schooling there.

Arnold died in 1977 and Sophie passed away in 2006.

Lawrence and Lorraine live in

Vigue family. Back: Val, Lawrence, Carl and Rick. Front: Gladys, Sophie, Toni, Arnold and Dolly. (V. Vigue photo)

Salmon Arm and have two children, Brad and Anna. He and his wife own a daycare center and he also works in Canoe's plywood mill. Brad is a chef in Vancouver and Anna is a speech therapist in Vancouver.

Valerie (Val) and Larry Schmidt of Twelve Mile were married from 1970-1986 and have two daughters, Laurie Lynn and Dawn Marie, and three grandchildren. Val owned the Perogie Shack restaurant in Revelstoke from 1986-1987 but had to close it due to illness. She remarried to Barrie Fitzgerald from 1991-2003. Then in 2004 she suffered a massive heart attack. Val continues to reside in Revelstoke. Laurie and Ken May live in Maple Ridge and have a son, Ethan, and daughter, Brylin. Dawn and Jason live in Revelstoke and have one son, Paden.

Carl and Mila live in Castlegar and have two sons, Derek and Dustin. Carl operates big machinery.

Richard (Rick) and Carol live in Revelstoke and have two children, Matthew and Amanda (Mandy) and three grandchildren. Rick is a butcher at Cooper's grocery.

Gladys and Chris Pylatuk live in Revelstoke and have two sons, Scott and Justin. Chris operates a tugboat at Mica.

Thomas (Tom) and Tiffany live in the Big Eddy area. He has three children, Abbi, Cole and Hailey, and one stepdaughter, Richalle.

Dolores (Dolly) Tomlenovich has two sons, Kyle and Brandon. She now volunteers at Community Connections in Revelstoke.

WALTERS

Ernestena Walters was one of the teachers at Twelve Mile School during the school year 1941-43. No further information is available.

WESTON

Gordon Percival Weston and Sophie Margarite Nipper met in Revelstoke when Sophie was working the desk at the King Edward Hotel and Gordon was visiting from Vancouver. Sophie moved to Vancouver and became a sewing instructor for the Singer Company. Gordon was a Royal Canadian Mounted Police at the time. His parents were Percy Frank Weston and Grace Adela Lowman.

Gordon Weston, RCMP, circa 1956. (Weston family photo)

After their first daughter, Kelly, was born, Gordon gave up his Mountie position and they moved to Twelve Mile in August, 1955. Their first home was the small cabin next to the log cabin of Sophie's parents, the Nippers.

On February 8, 1956, tragedy struck the little family and almost all their worldly possessions were destroyed in a fire. Gordon and Sophie rebuilt a larger house on the property further from the river. After Jack Nipper died in 1956, they took over the Nipper property. Gordon logged for various operations and installed and ran his own shingle mill near their house. It was powered by a heavy-duty electrical plant that Gordon built. He harnassed the fast-flowing water of Mulvehill Creek that passed through their farm. Gordon and a friend lugged, with the help of pulleys, the huge intake pipes up through the trees on the mountainside to build the plant. The Westons sold the lower portion of their property to BC Hydro and moved their house to higher land that Sophie's father had owned. They eventually had access to proposed Highway 23 via the abandoned Celgar road near the log dump in the curve of the river. They were very self-sufficient with their own power and indoor plumbing, sturdy bridge that Gordon built across the creek, and a huge vegetable garden cared for by Sophie's expertise. Sophie canned and froze all their fruit and vegetables for the long winter months. She also had time to grow beautiful begonias under the shady eaves of their house. In the winter she caught up on her sewing and needlework.

The Westons had four children: Elizabeth Grace (Kelly), Beverly, Janet, and Jeffery. They all attended Twelve Mile School until it closed in 1967. Beverly remembers their schooling after the school closed:

> In 1967 we had to stay at Pearl Myers' at Eight Mile because they flooded the valley. There was no more schoolhouse, and Dad was building our new home. It wasn't finished and we couldn't live in it. We couldn't travel from there to Revelstoke because they hadn't made access for us on the new highway. So for that first year we used to take a boat across the lake from our place to Pearl's. We were bussed to school in Revelstoke from her home. It was just a little tin motorboat-- that's all we could afford. It was scary a lot of times because of rough waters. We stayed at Pearl's until our house was livable. I don't remember the pre-flooding. I just remember when the water came sky high in 1967. Dad finished the house that summer. Then the bus would drive out to where our road went down to our property. The bus would pick us up on the highway. It was a one-mile walk to the bus that we walked in the dark in the winter.

As the children became more independent, Sophie enjoyed designing floral arrangements for Creative Flowers, owned by her friend, Pearl Myers.

In 1990 Gordon died in an accident when he lost control of his truck on the snowy road on his way home from Revelstoke. Sophie tried to hold the farm together but maintenance was high in that isolated location. It was difficult for her to leave her beautiful, modern home in its park-like setting. So in September 1993 she sold out and bought a

Weston family. Left to right: Janet, Beverly, Sophie, Gordon, Jeff, Kelly. Under her birthday cake is Sophie's mother, Nettie Nipper. (Weston family photo)

house in Revelstoke. She was diagnosed with breast cancer in the summer of 1992 and passed away February 2, 1994. The Weston home is now known as the Mulvehill Creek Wilderness Retreat.

Kelly is an insurance agent living in Marietta, Georgia and has two children.

Beverly is an accountant/supervisor and lives in Revelstoke.

Janet is a homemaker living in Abbotsford and has two children.

Jeff is a business owner and CPR employee living in Revelstoke and has three children.

WHEATON

James (Jimmy) and Jeanette Wheaton and their three children moved to Twelve Mile from Beaton in 1953. Jimmy was born in Pedicodiac, New Brunswick in 1903, the youngest of 11 children; and Jeanette was born in New Glasgow, Nova Scotia.

Sandra and Diane Wheaton, 1955. (A. Domke family photo)

Since Jimmy followed the logging jobs, he worked in Beaton and the Columbia Valley with one of his brothers. When Charlie Sartorous moved his sawmill from Beaton to Twelve Mile, establishing it on the south bank of Blanket Creek, he brought Jimmy along as manager.

The Wheatons rented Asaph Domke's log cabin a half mile south of the mill. Diane, their oldest daughter, attended first grade at Twelve Mile School in 1954-55. She usually walked the two and a half miles to school, sometimes accompanied by Ada Domke who pushed her bike along side Diane. Daughter Sandra had fun visiting with the Domke ladies and especially bonded with Helen who entertained her with her guitar playing and singing, and she spent hours playing in Ada's doll house tucked in the trees next to the cabin. Gary was just a toddler and baby Karen died at birth in 1955.

The family moved to Revelstoke in 1955 when Jimmy began working for Parks Canada. One of his jobs was with Ben Domke to bring a caterpillar down from Mt. Revelstoke to be repaired at Domke's Machine Shop. Since the tracks fell off in Forward gear but stayed on in Reverse, they drove it all the way down in Reverse. This is when Jimmy first felt ill and they couldn't repair the cat because it turned out to be the first of four heart attacks that he suffered that year. He died in 1957 at the age of 54.

Jeanette was left with three young children. She was in and out of the hospital with chronic asthma, leaving her children to the care of social services. Those years were extremely stressful and unhappy ones for the children, but they all completed high school in Revelstoke.

Jeanette moved back to Ontario in the 1970s to be near her family. She remarried and after several other moves, ended up in Revelstoke, where she passed away in 2001.

Diane (Jack O'Brien) continues to live in Revelstoke where she works for Revelstoke Community Forest Corporation. She is involved in several of Revelstoke's civic activities including Revelstoke Hospice Society and Homecoming Committee. She has one grown son, James.

Sandra (Gerry Cowley) has three children: Dawn, Heather and Jason. Gerry works for Revelstoke Equipment Rental. When Dawn was a baby, they lived two doors down from Helen and Oscar Domke on Douglas Street. This suited Helen just fine for she loved to play, sing and joke with Sandra and Dawn and bake for them. Sandra feels attached to Blanket Creek, remembering it as a happy place in her life, so she and Gerry are regular campers at the campground.

Gary is a bachelor living in Revelstoke and working for Powder Springs Resort.

WHYTE

Edna Whyte was hired to finish out Twelve Mile's school year from November 1945 through June 1946, the year consolidation was attempted and failed. Her school-aged daughter, Phyllis, helped boost the school's enrollment.

WRAIGHT

Stanley (Stan) and Florence (Vigue) Wraight lived in Arrowhead before moving to Twelve Mile where he operated the ferry from 1954-56. They lived in the ferry house with their family.

Their daughter, Wendy, and husband, John Walker, live in the Big Eddy area of Revelstoke. They have two children, Billy and Eugen.

Both Stan and Florence have passed away.

YINGLING

Marjorie Yingling taught at the new Twelve Mile School from 1931-35. Sharry Kelly remembers that "she managed all the grades in one room very well. I loved listening to all of the other classes doing their lessons. When I tried to get involved in their work, she was so patient and allowed me to read to them."

ZIBULAK

Fred Zibulak first emigrated from Ukraine to Canada and homesteaded before World War I, about 1908-10. In 1914 he returned to Ukraine, fought in the war, and married Katherine. They had two daughters: Joanna, born in 1924; and Annie, born in 1925. When the war was over, Fred returned to Canada in 1926 to prepare a home for his family in Twelve Mile.

Fred Zibulak in Ukraine before emigrating to Canada. (Makarewicz family photo)

Fred homesteaded 40 acres south of the train station and also purchased the land south of Walter Miller's place and across the tracks on the east side. He later purchased Miller's farm in approximately 1940 and also Andrew Hulyd's place that bordered on their property.

He cut the charred, cedar stumps with a crosscut saw. The story is that he cut wood into the night and in the morning delivered it with his team of horses and wagon to the brewery in Revelstoke. He turned the team around and they found their way home while he slept in the wagon. In this manner he earned enough cash to send for his family from the Ukraine (now Poland). Before his family arrived, however, Fred's house burned down at the hands of an apparent arsonist. Being resourceful he rebuilt, using lumber from the Chinese stores being torn down across from the old Civic building in Revelstoke. Katherine and her daughters arrived Halloween eve in 1938. On the way to their new home in Twelve Mile, the girls wondered what kind of country they had come to as they passed by all the Halloween pranks along the way that night. Sadly, Annie had contracted tuberculosis on their ship voyage, and passed away in 1942.

Fred and Katherine were hard working farmers. He even grew his own tobacco that he called what sounded like "tu tune." Evelyn Domke remembers Katherine working in the fields and gardens in her long dress and boots. They raised cows, horses, pigs, geese and chickens. Katherine taught Joanna the art of tasty Ukrainian cooking and how to grow beautiful flowers and vegetables. Gloria Kaduhr remembers Mrs. Zibulak walking on the railroad tracks to bring fresh cream to "fatten up Gloria."

They didn't have a motor vehicle for transportation but used a wagon and team of horses in the summer. Fred wrapped the iron rims of the wagon wheels with wire to make them last longer. In the winter, his team pulled a sleigh with hay for the passengers' warmth. On their way to town they passed Camozzi's farm at Montana Lake. In the early 1940s, Asaph and Kellina Domke of Twelve Mile were renting Camozzi's farm for a couple of years. Their impish goat, Alexander, jumped onto the back of Zibulak's sleigh and chomped on the hay all the way to town and back.

Joanna attended school at Twelve Mile from 1939-41. Since she didn't know English, the Kozek children translated for her and the teacher, but they didn't translate very accurately and thought it fun to teach her "every bad word in the book!"

Joanna worked on the farm along side her parents. When she asked for a bicycle, her parents made a deal with her. If she raised roosters, butchered and plucked them, she could have all the money that Beech's Butcher Shop in Revelstoke paid for the fresh poultry. In 1942 she was the proud owner of her first bike. The family socialized with those in Twelve Mile, but also with the Eight Mile families where there were more young people for Joanna to associate with. She was talented in needlecrafts, at times designing her own work that she embroidered or cross stitched. She often shared her finished artwork with her friends and neighbors. When the May Day (May 24) celebrations were revived in 1946 in Revelstoke, she was one of the beauties on one of the floats.

In 1946 or 47 she began working for Queen Victoria Hospital in Revelstoke alongside Maris Gawiuk and Alli Graham. They lived on the second floor of the nurses' residence. Joanna's work ethic learned from her parents, stood her in good stead for she was required to dust, scrub, polish, set up and deliver food trays, and wash dishes (without a dishwasher).

When the Columbia River overflowed its banks in the historic flood of June 1948,

Joanna Zibulak, the beauty on the May Day Float, Revelstoke, 1946. (Makarewicz family photo)

Katherine and Annie Zibulak. Note the split cedar picket fence. (Makarewicz family photo)

their farm was entirely flooded and they moved in with the John Raucherts until it was safe to return home. The children in Twelve Mile had fun swimming in the floodwaters at their farm.

In 1953 while Fred was haying, the horses were spooked by something that sent them flying. Fred was thrown off the hay rake, was dragged and badly injured by the tines. Joanna found him lying in the field unable to move. She rushed to Kaduhrs for help and called the Revelstoke ambulance. It was an old bread wagon that Ronnie and Albert Dedosenco remember having to push in order to get it started. As it bumped along, Joanna and Lena Kaduhr hung onto Fred but they were unable to prevent the makeshift stretcher from sliding under the front seat where a screw cut open Fred's forehead. Lena asked the driver to stop in order to try to control the bleeding. Unfortunately he died of blood loss and a broken neck soon after arriving at the hospital. The neighbors were invited to the funeral held at the house where he lay on a bed in the room off the kitchen. In keeping with their custom, he was to stay there for three days. He was then placed in a coffin box and transported by horse and wagon to the Mt. Cartier cemetary. Along the way, people placed irises (flags) on his coffin as it passed their farms.

Then in 1955 Joanna again ran frantically to Kaduhrs, "Come quick, Mom's sick!" Lena found Katherine sitting at the kitchen table with her arm around the burning kerosene lamp, just ready to pull it over. She had her lie down, had someone call the ambulance to take her to the hospital but it was too late. She was also buried in the Mt. Cartier cemetery.

Joanna first met Nick Makarewicz while at a dance in Revelstoke. Later when Nick was cutting wood for the Kaduhrs in Twelve Mile, they re-met and began dating. About six to eight months later, they married on May 16, 1953. They took up farming on the Zibulak farm where they raised their seven children.

Chapter 2

RAILWAY, HIGHWAY AND FERRY

Where's the bridge?

RAILWAY

The CPR's Arrowhead branch-line that opened in 1895 provided transportation for passengers as well as mail and freight to the homesteaders, loggers and miners along the way. The rail yard in Twelve Mile was kept busy with poles, logs and produce waiting to be transported. There were set rates for hay and potatoes by the ton, milk by the quart or can, butter by the pound and eggs by the dozen. The CPR built a small, one-room "station" at Twelve Mile with a potbellied stove in the middle so people could keep warm while waiting for the train. It didn't have an attendant or ticket agent. Originally, the train ran south on Sunday, Wednesday and Friday, and returned the day following. It later returned the same day.

Train days were always exciting. People went to the station to wait for the mixed train out of Revelstoke pulled by steam locomotive No. 443 or 444, as it *chug chugged* into Twelve Mile with their mail, supplies and friends. Homesteaders who could afford the train ride, rode the 15 miles to Arrowhead for supplies, returning the same day. Those who could not, walked the tracks to shop in Arrowhead or Revelstoke. On the day the first diesel locomotive went through, students were dismissed from class to witness the event.

First highway bridge over Blanket Creek looking downstream from Sutherland Falls. (W. Kozek photo)

HIGHWAY

As more settlers began moving to the area south of Revelstoke, it became necessary to provide a road for motor vehicles. In 1922, the highway south of Revelstoke was completed to Eight Mile, and in 1923 it joined up with the road at Sidmouth with free ferry crossings at Sidmouth and Twelve Mile. The highway was just roughed out of the wilderness with a lot of blasting through the rock cuts. Fiorino Perosso died from a premature blasting powder explosion while building the road at Twelve Mile. Harold Catherwood, who lived at Sixteen Mile, described the road in 1933 as being "just a trail with grass growing in the middle." It was ungraded, unmaintained and not plowed regularly in the winter. Wagons, trucks and cars rattled and shook as they traversed

Truck stranded in Drimmie Creek flood. (O. Astra photo)

the potholes, washboard and rocks. And during spring thaw it was not unusual for farmers to use their horses to pull vehicles out of the gumbo. Boards and branches were placed over the muddy areas to help buoy up the vehicles from the mud. It was big news, making newspaper headlines, when the road was graveled to reduce mud holes. Traffic was also interrupted by flooding when the river spilled over or when creeks overflowed, blocking culverts with debris. The avalanche at Greenslide off Mt. Cartier managed to block the highway almost every spring. When plowed in the winter, the highway was probably at its smoothest.

Slushy spring road conditions. (A. Domke photo)

Avalanche off Mt. Cartier at Greenslide, blocking traffic. (Makarewicz family photo)

In 1933, Proctor Stage began running a bus for Greyhound Lines from Revelstoke to Arrowhead and back on the same day. In the 1940s, small companies out of Revelstoke began offering bus and freight truck service to the south valley. Some of these were F. W. Waby, Craig Rutherford's Coach Lines and Austin Bailey's Rocky Mountain Freight Lines. Gib Lyons ran a taxi service out of Arrowhead, and Jimmy Cancelliere's car taxi ran Monday, Wednesday and Saturday out of Revelstoke

FERRY

Twelve Mile ferry looking toward the west bank. Note the Millar/Demers/Podzun barn on left, and cable tower and Nipper's house on right. (W. Kozek photo)

Jim Millar, Ferry Operator, 1930. (Millar family photo)

Allan Kelly, ferry operator, 1930. (Kelly family photo)

Before the south highway was completed from Revelstoke to Arrowhead, there already was a ferry connecting Arrowhead with Hall's Landing, docking at Sidmouth on the west side of the Columbia River. When the new highway opened and another crossing was established at Twelve Mile in 1923, Sidmouth's tiny wooden ferry was moved to Twelve Mile, and Sidmouth received a larger, powered six-car replacement ferry. Twelve Mile's first ferry was current driven and operated only during the daytime. The ferry landing on the west bank was just south of Mulvehill Creek, and the one on the east side was south of Drimmie Creek. Wooden planked wharfs connected the landing sites with the riverbanks and highway. Vehicles were required to line up to wait a short distance above the wharfs. When a vehicle drove to the approach, the ferryman would come for it or motion for it to drive onto the ferry if it was already on that side. Depending on the ferryman, foot passengers sometimes were made to wait until a vehicle arrived. When this happened to the school children, they were late for school.

Eventually a comfortable frame home was provided on the east bank for "ferrymen." On the west bank, ferry fuel and supplies were stored in a small building, and its outside wall supported a telephone for ferry and public use. The telephone was the wooden type with a bell-shaped earpiece and a crank handle to ring the operator in Revelstoke (one long, two shorts, then state the number to be called). There was another phone like it on the east side at the ferry house.

Car off east wharf. (Kaduhr family photo)

A ferry operator was a Federal Government position and was a steady job. Edward Mulvehill was its first operator. Over the years there were many more ferrymen. Some were already established residents of Twelve Mile; others were transferred there and given the ferry house to live in. At times, the Public Works Department cooperated with the school district and moved in ferrymen who had several children in order to keep up the school's enrollment.

Tragedy struck on an early Sunday morning, October 1, 1934 when a 24-year-old woman drowned after the car she rode in went into the river. It was foggy and visibility was extremely poor. The ferry was on the far side of the river. Unaware that he was approaching the river, the driver, Mr. G. W. Churton of Vancouver, drove into the water. Churton and two other passengers were able to get free of the car and swim to safety, but Mrs. Jean McEwan was unable to save herself. Her body still had not been recovered five days later when the incident was reported in the October 6 *Revelstoke Review*. There were many other incidents of vehicles ending up in the river at the ferry crossing.

Ferry hung up on log bundle, circa 1959. (E. Rauchert photo, RMA)

The ferry was an important part of the community. Ferrymen kept a log of all vehicles and passengers who crossed, including the direction of travel and time of day. They seemed to know everything about everybody. The ferry was unscheduled, operated from 6:00 a.m. until 10:00 p.m. on weekdays and until midnight on Saturday nights. Those who arrived after it closed either had to wait until opening time in the morning or pay a ferryman one dollar to get out of bed and take them across. Allan Kelly installed a spring-loaded gong on a post by the ferry house so travelers could pull the chain to alert him during the night. In 1945 a formal request was filed for 24-hour ferry service at Twelve Mile and Sidmouth, without any action being taken to do so.

Sandbars in the river in the Twelve Mile area plagued the earlier sternwheelers that plied the Columbia and Arrow Lakes regions. This fact encouraged the CPR to complete its branch line from Revelstoke to Arrowhead and these sandbars presented problems for the ferry as well. Since the first two ferries were on a cable, they depended on the river current. The ferry operator turned the pilot wheel attached to the cable, thus angling it into the current that pushed it across the river. It was landed with a winch. During slow-flowing low water in the late summer and fall, the ferry scraped on the sandbars and got stranded. When that happened, ferrymen either pushed it across with pike poles or rowed foot passengers across in a small boat.

When the river ran fast and high, the operators exercised their skill in dodging logs, uprooted trees and ice floes while the cable towers creaked and the cables sang. It was not unusual for the water to rise two feet in a week following the melting of even a first snow on mountains. On several occasions the cable snapped during rushing high water, sending the ferry downstream

East cable tower down, 1933. (Kelly family photo

East side cable tower down, dislodging "deadman," 1933. (Kelly family photo)

several miles. Sharry Kelly remembers a frightening experience her ferryman dad had in the summer of 1933.

. . . when the river was extremely high water and dangerous, a couple of government employees insisted they had to cross to go south to the Arrow Lakes. They had a caterpillar tractor with several connected units that weighed a great deal. In the middle of the river, they nearly capsized with such a heavy load. The tower on the east side was pulled off its concrete base. Mother had to phone Revelstoke for help as the ferry was unable to move to either side and there were at least four men aboard, including Dad and Mr. Jim Millar, his assistant. Many officials drove down to look at the catastrophe and finally Paul DePietro of Revelstoke took an axe and chopped the steel cable through. This released the ferry entirely and with the high-water river filled with logs and debris from flooding above, the ferry went down the river. It was finally tied up at Wigwam.

In addition to the wooden tower being pulled over, its concrete *deadman* was also dislodged. A gas-powered ferryboat was put to use temporarily.

Ada Domke remembers the time she and her family were waiting to cross on their return home from Revelstoke with groceries when the cable broke, sending the ferry adrift. It caught against the bank a short distance down river. Luckily it was "train day" so they left their pickup at the train station and rode the train to Sidmouth. There, they happened to meet Billy Mackey who drove them to their home at Fourteen Mile. Others have had similar experiences over the years when cables broke.

Hickie Kaduhr, ferry operator, on new steel ferry. (Kaduhr family photo)

During especially cold winters, the river froze over and a channel for the ferry had to be blasted. In December 1946, the *Revelstoke Review* reported that the ferry was closed down for repairs and then froze in, resulting in the children from the west side missing school for a week. When a channel couldn't be cleared, residents needing supplies from town walked across the river on the ice, and the school children were guided across the ice by a ferrymen. Asaph Domke, like some others, looped a rope over the overhead cable and hooked it to himself to avoid breaking through the slush into the frigid river water.

Ferry channel between ice and snow, 1955-56. (Weston family photo)

In December 1949, Mrs. English and her pupils had completed weeks of rehearsing and were ready to perform a two-hour Christmas concert at the school. However, it was not to be. As the December 22, 1949 *Revelstoke Review* article put it:

The ferry chose that day to freeze in all the slush coming down the river, with the major part of our actors on the far side. We've stood for a lot from that ferry, but that is the crowning indignity. We are all in favor of a bridge—and soon. That was Tuesday, the last day of school and we had no guarantee the river would be passable even the next day.

1949 was also the winter that the *Minto* became ice bound in the Arrow Lakes, cutting off food supplies to Halcyon and St. Leon. When they radioed for help, the RCAF from Vancouver made a food drop to them.

In January 1950, temperatures reached minus 40 degrees Fahrenheit with food freezing in cellars and homes, and even reports of frozen hot water bottles. The ferry froze in and the road crew worked on it all day. A slide in the "rock cut" (a narrowing of the highway along the river) further south had to be cleared, delaying the bus going to Arrowhead. The Sidmouth ferry was also iced in.

In February 1950, the newspaper reported that "O. Domke, Evelyn and Ben left their truck on the east side and walked across the ice to get home," and the "Sidmouth ferry sunk due to a hole punctured by ice." With their ferry out of service, the Sidmouth people rode a sleigh to Twelve Mile, walked across the ice and rode to Revelstoke by a called taxi or in a friend's car that could be started despite the cold weather. Train service was also off schedule by a full day. When clearing ice off the wharfs, the caterpillar chewed up the planks, which then had to be replaced in March. By April most of the ice had moved out and it was time for the highway crew to repair the towers and cables in time for the anticipated high water in May and June.

East ferry wharf covered by high water, 1947. (Weston family photo)

With all of these inconveniences caused by having to rely on a ferry, the residents always entertained the hope of having a bridge, or a road on the west side all the way to Revelstoke. On May 19, 1949, the *Revelstoke Review* said that it wouldn't "be too long before the road is completed all the way to Revelstoke...now that (CRT) have (sic) constructed five miles or so of it," on the way to its timber limit on Mt. Begbie.

Short of having a bridge or a through-road on the west side of the river, the community longed for 24-hour ferry service rather than the 6:00 a.m. to 10:00 p.m. schedule, but this did not happen either.

As the logging trucks got bigger, a larger ferry was needed to accommodate them. In 1947 Columbia River Timbers (CRT) was taking out 75-foot poles, but the ferry wasn't long enough to take them across the river. That year a "Ten Ton Limit" sign was posted, and the grade on the east side was cut down to accommodate disembarking heavy loads of logs and poles.

Bill Mackey's truckload of cedar poles, offloading the ferry. (W. Kozek photo)

In 1948 Hon. E. C. Carson, Minister of Public Works, announced that Western Bridge and Steel Fabricators, Ltd. of Vancouver was contracted to build a new steel scow for Twelve Mile for $24,480, according to the May 27, 1948 *Revelstoke Review*. It was designed to carry up to

12 cars or a total of 50 tons. Its fabrication began in May. Workers spent three weeks welding the plates together. They built it on greased skids on the northeast bank of the river. The school children walked down to the river to get in on the excitement of the launching. A bulldozer pushed it down the greased rollers and it struck the water with a resounding splash! The community was so thankful for the hard work by the builders, they put on a dance at the school in their honour and the proceeds benefited the Christmas Tree Fund. There was still a lot of work to be done before the new ferry was operational, however.

By November the heated pilothouse was completed but the aprons had not yet been built by Pete Lonzo's road crew. In December when huge masses of ice came down the river, it became apparent that the motor was not strong enough for the large ferry, and the cables kept slipping. So it was closed for two days while new cables and new machinery were installed.

FERRY TALES

Many colorful tales can be told about the ferry and its operators. Emil Rauchert was known for wearing his captain's hat while singing, "Cruising down the river on a Sunday afternoon." He truly seemed to enjoy his ferryman job.

An event that must have given ferryman Hickey Kaduhr quite a scare involved his car. He parked it at the top of the east wharf, facing down hill. The heat from its motor gradually melted the snow and he helplessly watched his car roll into the river with a splash. The next morning Mike Kozek winched out the car and towed it to Revelstoke for repairs.

During the 1945-46 school year, ferryman Alec Michels was assigned to drive the students to the Greenslide School when Twelve Mile School was closed.

In June 1948 the river was at one of its all-time highs and the ferry closed because it couldn't land. The water was waist-deep at the phone on the west side. So Public Works

Emil Rauchert, ferry operator, at the controls in pilot house, circa late 1950s. (E. Rauchert photo)

put the ferrymen to work in the south valley. They rowed folks across the flooded area at the Mt. Cartier and Six Mile areas, taking about 20 people per boatload.

A ferryman's work was not only interesting and varied, it was also dangerous. In 1948 Hickey Kaduhr injured his back when he slipped on the wharf while carrying a plank. In 1949 Alec Michels sustained an arm injury requiring several months of treatment. Also in 1949 ferryman Ross Howard's hand was crushed in the cable while trying to remove some ice. He was rushed to Queen Victoria Hospital by Dan Crawford of Arrowhead who was waiting to cross. It took him two and one-half months to recuperate, per the *Revelstoke Review* of February 3, 1949.

The ferry also caught fire several times, causing some delays to traffic.

Ben Domke recalls a joke he and Jim Cwikula played on

Eric Kramer, ferry operator, with passengers. (A. Domke photo)

the ferry operator one day. Jim had obtained the innovative, amphibious Amphicar that doubled as a boat. The pair approached the ferry landing and waited. Eric Kramer, the ferry operator, started across for them. While the ferry was still a distance away, the fellows began driving towards the water. Fearing another tourist was about to drown, Eric hysterically waved at them to halt. To his amazement, they drove the Amphicar into the water and right past the ferry waving to Eric as he watched dumbfounded.

Nick Makarewicz, ferry operator. (Makarewicz family photo)

Another time, Rod Luschnat, a logger in the area, had to take his caterpillar across the river to his next job. The river was running high and the ferry was docking on the bank past the wharf. On this particular occasion, it couldn't dock completely, leaving a space of several feet between the apron and the bank. With a job waiting across the river, Rod gunned his cat, jumped it across the gap of water and successfully landed onto the ferry's apron.

Following is a near-complete list of ferrymen from 1923 to 1969 when it closed and was moved to Needles-Fauquier: Edward Mulvehill, Allan Kelly, James Millar, Bill Mobley, Alec Michels, Jules Fiset, Ross Howard, Percy Demers, John Rauchert, Emil Rauchert, Brooks Gowanlock, Hickey Kaduhr, Ed Sharp, Stan Wraight, Mr. Peterman, Nick Makarewicz, Eric Kramer.

Ferry operator's residence in background, cable tower, Kelly's goat shed in foreground, Circa 1930. (S. Kelly photo)

Truckload of logs in river, 1957. (Weston family photo)

New steel ferry in high water,1949. (Kaduhr family photo)

Ferry fire on east side of river. (Weston family photo)

Ferry fire, pilot house burned. Note cars waiting to cross. Circa 1966. (Weston family photo)

Ferry channel in winter. Note the frozen-in channel to the left.

Chapter 3

THE LAST COUNTRY SCHOOL OF DISTRICT #19

A teacher takes a hand,
Opens a mind,
And touches a heart.

PRE-SCHOOL TIMES

When settlers first moved to the Twelve Mile area, there was no road and no school for the children to attend. Prior to 1930, students were either home schooled, or sent away for their education. Walter Kozek remembers being sent to his uncle's in Drumheller, Alberta at age five for grades one and two. The Mazar family left their Twelve Mile home for two years so their children could attend school in Drumheller, Alberta. The three Petrashuk children were mostly self-taught using their father's books, and Rose didn't start school until she was 12 years old.

SCHOOL ESTABLISHED

When the Kelly family moved to Twelve Mile in 1929 with five of their older children being of school age, Marjorie Kelly began a successful campaign for a school building. J. Middleton & Sons began building the new school in the late summer of 1930 between the road and the CPR station. A 1918 Department of the Interior map indicates the property was likely that of Mike Hewko's.

In 1930 Vivian L. Gardiner, a rookie teacher, was hired to start the Twelve Mile School before the new building was completed. For the first couple of months the students met in a log shack that had belonged to Andrew Hulyd. The students had to walk south on the railway tracks, around the corner and past Miller's place to get there. For the next few months, they

1932-33 School year. Back: Dorothy Mazar, Jack Petrashuk, Douglas Kelly, Walter Kozek, Kenneth Kelly. Front: Christian Kelly, Rose Petrashuk, Nordy Kelly, Sharry Kelly, Betty Petrashuk, Steve Kozek, Joe Kozek, Mack Mazar, Joan Kelly. (Kelly photo)

crossed the river by ferry and had class in the living room of William Thompson's log cabin which was just south of the ferry on the west side.

The new school opened in the winter of 1930 with Marjorie Kelly being its first trustee. Mr. A. E. Miller was the Inspector of Public Schools for the Revelstoke area at the time.

Unfortunately, the school burned down in 1935 of suspected arson, and the community pitched in to rebuild it. The rebuilt second school functioned as a school until 1956, then as a community hall and as a gym for physical education classes on foul-weather days until 1967.

A modern modular third school was moved onto the property and operated from the fall of 1956 until 1967. Each school had a teacherage but the third one also had electricity. The teacherage was equipped with a bathroom, but the students had to continue using the outhouses. When it closed, the building was moved by Oscar Knoblauch on Kozek's truck to an area next to the Revelstoke airport for the Flying Club's clubhouse.

1948-49 School children and friends. Back row: Helen Mobley, Mildred Kozek, Lena Kaduhr. Second row: Helen Domke, Lil Gowanlock, Evelyn Domke, Marie Astrahantseff, Maggie Thompson. Third row: Sergei Astrahantseff, Eugen Domke, Olympe Astrahantseff, Mary Nipper, Kellina Domke. Front row: Helen Nipper, Ada Domke, Herb Domke, Alyce Mobley, Gloria Kaduhr, Jimmy Thompson. (A. Domke photo)

Third school. A modular building, 1956-67. (Makarewicz family photo)

First school, 1930-35. (Kelly family photo)

Second and third schools. (O. Astra photo)

Modular school being moved in 1967. (W. Kozek photo)

GETTING TO SCHOOL

Students walked, rode bicycles or rode horses to school. Ben and Evelyn Domke rode in a cutter (sleigh) in the winter and stabled their horse at Emil Rauchert's during the school day. They "got the dickens" from their dad when he found out they dragged their feet off the back of the cutter causing

Ben and Evelyn Domke ready to ride to school in their cutter.
(O. Domke family photo)

the horse to work even harder through the deep snow. When the snow began melting in the spring, there was more mud than snow on the road. It was a challenge for the students to manoeuvre through this mess as they tried jumping from side to side, over and around all the slush, mud and puddles.

Eugen and Ada Domke biking home from school. (A. Domke family photo)

SCHOOL DAYS

Over the years the school was known by various names: Twelve Mile Ferry School, Twelve Mile School and Twelve Mile South School. For the first few years, grades one through nine were taught, and then one through eight. After completing those grades the students either quit school, or boarded away from home for high school. A few years before it closed, kindergarten was also offered. Enrollment varied, but reached a high of 21 in 1957-58.

Like other country schools at the time, the schoolhouse became the community centre. Classes were cancelled so it could be used for political elections. It was also used as the "post office," for social events and sometimes church-affiliated programs.

The second schoolhouse was faced with shiplap and had a pitched shingle roof. It consisted of a small cloakroom at the entrance, one classroom with a row of four windows on the north, a two-room teacherage in the back with an attached woodshed. The boys' and girls' outhouses were two-holers in the trees behind the woodshed. A well with wooden cribbing and hand pump was added in about 1936 on the south side. Before that, drinking water was carried to school from neighbors' homes.

The classroom entrance was through the cloakroom. Along its north wall was a long bench with hooks above. Each hook was labeled so the students knew to hang their jackets and place their lunches and boots in their sections. Since it was unheated, wet jackets and boots froze unless their teacher took pity on the students and brought their clothes inside to dry out. With most winter clothing being woolen in those days, the classroom smelled like a corral. There was a row of unlocked pigeonholes on the south wall called the "post office" with a mail-sorting table under them.

School urn for drinking water. (A. Jarvis photo)

Once inside, the entrance was deemed the back and the front of the classroom was straight ahead. Two rows of desks with iron scrolled sides were on each side of the room facing the teacher's desk at the front. Each desk had an attached seat and the slanted desktop hinged open to the bin for books and supplies. An inkwell and pencil groove were included at the top. Desks were hand-me-downs from other schools, well worn with students' names carved here and there. As the younger students advanced, they looked forward to getting dibs on a desk next to the row of windows on the north wall. They had "arrived" with a window desk!

To the right of the entrance was a tall cupboard with supplies of paper, textbooks, hectograph, extra chalk, and bottles of white paste that smelled like wintergreen. A few low shelves were tucked into the southeast corner that housed the "library" of hand-me-down magazines and later books from the lending library in Victoria. Students always anticipated the boxes of different books that were shipped a couple of times a year that they could check out. Next to the library stood a low, large table with six small chairs for the first graders. This is where they learned to read about "Dick, Jane, Sally, Spot and Puff." On the left back wall was a table, later replaced by a counter, with a bucket and later a crockery urn for drinking water. A sink was added in 1948 that drained into a gravel leaching bed of its own. Finding places under the counter were sports and science equipment, the total inventory consisting of one old softball and bat, Bunsen burner and some bottles of chemicals for science experiments

There were no copy machines or typewriters to aid the teachers for many years. They wrote lessons on the blackboards along the east and south walls. The closest gadget to a copier machine was a hectograph. There were three or four of these glycerin-coated sheets of gelatin (8 ½" x 13") with a distinctive chemical scent. Teachers wrote tests or drew pictures to color on paper with an indelible purple pencil. After the gelatin pad was dampened with a squeegee, the original document was pressed face down onto the hectograph pad that picked up single images of the original. About 12 to 15 copies could be made before fading. Pitting of the jelly occurred after repeated use, so it was not unusual to have parts of words or pictures missing on the copies. When the bus linked up to the Twelve Mile School, the teachers prepared their lessons at least two days in advance. These were taken to the district office by the bus driver to be copied and returned.

Inside classroom, 1952-53. (E. Norris photo)

The chalkboards were topped with large maps on spring rollers that seemed to be used more for covering tests written on the boards ahead of time, than for teaching geography. There was also a row of upper and lower case alphabet letters above one board. The lower grades figured their math on the chalkboard on their side of the room so teacher could instruct them while teaching the higher grades. The flag, first the Union Jack, was displayed above the front board next to the watchful royal eyes of the reigning king or queen. When Eric Norris began teaching in 1952, he installed the school's first flagpole next to the cloakroom.

In 1948 Helen Domke donated her old pump organ to be used for music class. Mrs. English played it as the students learned the songs she wrote out on the blackboard: "Shortnin' Bread," "The Teddy Bears Picnic," "The Maple Leaf Forever," "When Johnny Comes Marching Home," "Ye Banks and Braes," to name a few. Dave Story was an accomplished musician and conducted some fun music classes. Other teachers who did not know how to play used records with which to conduct sing-alongs.

In the center of the room stood a heater. The first was a pot-bellied wood stove. It was replaced by a coal-burning heater with the tin pipes held up by haywire as

Inside classroom, 1952. Note long stove pipe.
(E. Norris photo)

they traversed the ceiling to the chimney on the wall of the teacherage. The third school was efficiently heated by an oil space heater.

The first schoolyard was full of big stumps and there were no walkways to the entrance or outhouses. In the winter, students just tramped down trails, since none were shoveled. Those were the days when the government extolled the virtues of manual labor. When teacher asked the school board to clear the land so the children could at least have room to play ball, Ken Millar remembers their response:

> What they did was send us a big rope, two shovels and an axe. Thanks to the big Kozek boys we had a field in a couple of seasons. We dug down to the roots, chopped them off and dragged them away with the rope. After we had this done the teacher bought us a ball and bat out of her own earnings and we were in business. We sure didn't need a gymnasium to keep in shape.

It wasn't until 1949 and 1950 that the playground got a good upgrading, with swings and teeter totters built by the parents.

Some teachers got creative during foul weather and taught the students folk dances indoors requiring minimal space. Still being in close quarters, even with desks pushed aside, students had to dodge the hot stove in the center of the room. There were also regular hikes to Twelve Mile Falls on Drimmie Creek, to Mulvehill Falls across the river, to Echo Lake that the students renamed "Orchid Lake," and along the railway tracks. Students were encouraged to collect and identify nature items they found, and sometimes they enjoyed a good snowball fight in May.

Students enjoying teeter totters, 1953-54. Left TT: Herb Domke, Ronnie Dedosenco, Sergei Astrahantseff, Helen Nipper, Ada Domke, Emily Rauchert, Susy Podzun. Right TT:Albert Dedosenco, Caolyn Rauchert, Larry Rauchert, Kathy Rauchert, Gloria Kaduhr, Genny Rauchert. (Ruth Townsend photo)

Students usually arrived in plenty of time, anxious to play a good game of "scrub" softball before classes started at nine o'clock. Scrub continued during the morning recess, lunch hour, and into the afternoon recess. It was always coed.

In 1946 with the implementation of the New School Act, the Twelve Mile School fell under the jurisdiction of Revelstoke School District No. 19. Parents were shocked and chagrined to learn that their beloved school was to be consolidated into the larger ones. In Revelstoke, the Selkirk School added rooms in anticipation of students to be bussed from Mt. Cartier, Greenslide and Twelve Mile. Twelve Mile School was closed from September through November 1945 and students were driven to Greenslide School by Alex Michels and Bill Mobley, ferry operators. Parents organized and fought consolidation. The parents were successful in keeping their school open and Edna Whyte was hired to finish out the school year. She brought along her school-aged daughter, Phyllis, to boost the enrollment. Twelve Mile School remained one of the last one-room country schools in the district until it closed in 1967. The negotiating experience that Oscar Domke and John Rauchert obtained from this incident encouraged them to continue being actively involved on the Board of Trustees for the school district in the ensuing years.

The school received minimal upkeep until after it came under the jurisdiction of School District No. 19. When the district noted in 1947 that its rural schools were in need of extensive repairs, Twelve Mile School received a new cement foundation and birch floor. Re-cribbing the well and leveling the playground was also scheduled. The following summer Tony Ambil and Ben Domke installed imitation red brick insulated siding. A sink with drain pipe to a cesspool, new cupboards, teacher's desk, chair, dresser and pump organ were also added that summer. After that, repairs and improvements continued more regularly.

In 1949 the Parent Teacher Association (PTA) was also formed. Twenty-six people attended the organizational meeting that was conducted by J. Hammond, J. M. Cameron and R. H. Mann of the Revelstoke School Board. They elected Lillian Gowanlock as President; Kellina Domke, Vice-President; Ruth Rauchert, Secretary-Treasurer; and Irene English, Corresponding Secretary. The Membership committee were Helen Domke and Brooks Gowanlock; Program Committee: Emil Rauchert, Asaph Domke, Percy Demers; Social Committee: Lena Kaduhr. At that first meeting, $50 were collected for Twelve Mile's share in a traveling movie projector, screen and generator so films could be shown at the school every five weeks. The meeting closed with a vote of thanks to Irene English for the refreshments, and with the singing of "God Save the King."

A hot soup and cocoa program was instituted for the students by the PTA that winter. Parents took turns donating the vegetables and soup bones and teacher Irene English cooked huge pots full in her teacherage kitchen. Each child was served hot soup and cocoa in green Fire King cups. Evelyn Domke recalls "the soup tasted great on Monday, but as water was added daily to make it last, by Friday it was pretty flat!" Prior to this hot lunch program, lunches forgotten in the cloakroom during winter months froze. Ken Millar remembers retrieving his lunch from the "frozen food section" and thawing it over the big old wood stove in the classroom.

Ball game in progress, front school yard, 1952. (E. Norris photo)

With the new PTA in effect, the community became involved in a more organized manner in maintaining its school. The floors were varnished by Brooks Gowanlock and newly-enameled stove and pipes were installed. Using Shiell's bulldozer, Ernie Funk leveled the playground for a better ball field. John Rauchert donated fence posts and wandering cows were finally fenced out of the school grounds with wire fencing. The school district freshly kalsomined the walls and equipped the school with fire extinguishers. The following year at a work bee, parents planted trees and shrubs, and a garden plot was prepared by Percy Demers and Emil Rauchert. In the winter the PTA cleared the snow off the roof and shoveled paths from the road to the entrance, to the pump and to the outhouses.

To keep up with important current affairs, students gathered around a battery-operated radio. They listened to the live broadcast of General Douglas MacArthur's famous "Old Soldiers Never Die" speech in 1951 and Queen Elizabeth II's coronation on June 2, 1953.

Lunch time, June 1952. Florence and Della McLeod, Helen Nipper, Albert Dedosenco, Herb Domke, Olympe Astrahantseff. Note outhouse in background. (E. Norris photo)

One of the advantages of a one-room school was that the students "heard" everything at least six or seven times, especially when work was done orally. Teachers reminded students to "do your own work" when this happened. Teaching eight grades in one room was compared to tutoring by teacher Mary Hashimoto. Each week monitors were chosen for certain chores. The worst one was cleaning the chalkboards and felt chalk erasers. Each had his own way of doing it that included banging the erasers on the outside walls of the school leaving white geometric designs, or beating them together in front of their faces while trying to avoid choking on the clouds of chalk dust. Other jobs included filling the water bucket or urn, bringing in the stove wood or coal, and replenishing the newspapers, catalogues or toilet paper in the outhouses. Olympe Astrahantseff remembers one of his teachers bringing old magazines and newspapers to school for the students to cut into four-inch squares to spear onto nails in the outhouses for toilet paper. When no janitor was available, they even swept the floor with an oily green sawdust material to keep down the dust. Sometimes the monitor rang the hand-held bell summoning the students into class following recess. In later years, local people such as Rose Dedosenco and Ruth Rauchert were hired as janitors.

School days began with respect, standing at attention while singing "O Canada" and facing the flag and portrait of the King or Queen. One of the older students was chosen to read a few verses from the Bible, followed by everyone repeating the Lord's Prayer while standing. Teacher read off the names of students and those present answered, "Here" or "Present." Then there was health inspection that consisted of a chosen student from each row of desks examining each student's hands and fingernails. They also checked off on a chart the possession of a hanky and morning teeth brushing. Then it was time to illustrate the day's weather on a special weather calendar.

It is interesting to note the various means of discipline used. With a room full of students from ages five or six through 14 or sometimes 15, teachers certainly had their hands full. One prank that came to Evelyn Domke's mind had to do with ink bottles, pens with nibs and ink blotters that fourth- or fifth-graders began using in place of pencils. Boys flicked ink on the backs of girls' blouses, but they soon found out the girls could take care of themselves, thank you. Some teachers had the student stay "after school" and do class work, or write repeatedly a certain sentence on the board such as, "I will not talk during class." Students living on the west side of the river were seldom kept after school because it would mean an extra trip for the ferry. One of Olympe Astrahantseff's teachers left a lasting impression on him.

"She whacked me every time I went by. She turned me against school early on! I was strapped by her many times with a stick or with her hand."

Another teacher became so frustrated trying to control a room full, that she threw chalk board erasers and chalk across the room and the shot was a ringer for those who failed to duck in time. Some got her thick yardstick across their backs. Sergei Astrahantseff was a favourite recipient of this treatment when he fumbled with his math problems at the chalkboard.

Public speaking and critical thinking were taught using debate teams. Evelyn also remembers that "city living" always won over "country living."

The rule in school was "English only" even though some students came from homes where parents were still learning English as their second (or third, or fourth) language.

Teacher Gowan started holding Open House in 1955 and invited parents to come and discuss student problems, observe a debate, listen to their reading skills and enjoy displays of art work, sewing and woodwork. Displays included Plasticine models, a scene in the sand table of camping, and a miniature town built to teach citizenship and cooperation. Mrs. Gowan told the parents it was important for them to observe how their tax money was being spent and how their children were progressing.

HOLIDAY CELEBRATIONS

As far back as can be recalled, teachers did an outstanding job in developing Christmas concerts to which the local and outlying communities were invited. After weeks of preparation, memorizing and practicing parts, the children were ready to take center stage.

There were always huge Halloween parties at school complete with prizes for original costumes created by parents and children—no bought stuff here. In 1950 the winners were: Gloria Kaduhr, witch; and Russell Gowanlock, headless man. Little Richard Demers was so scared by the witch, he needed to be taken home. Apples were floated in tubs of water so children could bob and catch them with their teeth. Another favourite was a race to see who could finish eating an apple hanging on a string from a line stretched across the room. Other games were musical chairs, Bingo, popcorn-eating contest, and wink 'em. In the evening everyone surrounded a big bonfire built on the school grounds, firecrackers were exploded by the older students, and sparklers waved around by the younger ones. There was no such thing as "trick or treat" out in the countryside where homes were spread out. When Ada moved to the United States, she was surprised that fireworks were set off on the fourth of July instead of Halloween! The outhouses were prime targets for pranks.

Valentine parties also included the community. Students exchanged cards that they constructed at school and at home with the help of their parents. They decorated them with silver paper saved from candy bar wrappers or colorful Christmas wrap.

SCHOOL PICNICS AND SPORTS DAYS

Spring school picnics were organized by the teachers and parents for the entire community. They included potlucks with soda pop, hot dogs and sometimes even ice cream. Races and games were organized at the school, at Williamson Lake near Revelstoke, or at Bill Mackey's field in Sidmouth. In June 1950 the winners were:

Race for 5 years and less – Jenny and Kitty Rauchert

Race 6-9 years – Ada and Herb Domke

Race 9-14 years – Mary and Pauline Nipper

Race for ladies – Joanna Zibulak and Helen Domke

Sack race for designated ages – Ada and Herb Domke, Russell Gowanlock, Pauline Nipper

Potato race – Herb and Ada Domke

Three-legged race for designated ages – Gloria and Lena Kaduhr, Pauline Nipper, Russell and Lil Gowanlock, Sergei Astrahantseff, Helen Domke, Joanna Zibulak

Wheelbarrow race – Russell Gowanlock, Sergei Astrahantseff, Pauline Nipper, Herb Domke

Nail driving – Sergei Astrahantseff, Eugen Domke, Pauline Nipper

Teacher Elsie Ruth Townsend got into the team spirit and had all her students dress in yellow shirts with "Twelve Mile" hand embroidered on the backs, so they could compete in the Sid-Arrow-Twelve Mile ball game and races in May 1954. Mackey's field in Sidmouth became the most popular venue for these combined sports days. Students were given four free tickets to start the day: Green for ice cream; Orange for a hot dog; Black for pop; and Brown for choice of pop or ice cream.

"Twelve Mile" special shirts for sports day. (A. Jarvis photo)

Ribbons awarded at Arrow-Sid-12 Mile picnics. (A. Jarvis photo)

Williamson Lake. Back: Ann and Mary Nipper, Marie Astrahantseff. Front: Larry Rauchert, Genny Rauchert(?), Herb Domke, Olympe Astrahantseff, Eugen Domke, Helen Nipper, Ada Domke, Jackie Morton, Russell Gowanlock, Allan Morton, Emily Rauchert. (A. Domke family photo)

School picnic at Williamson Lake near Revelstoke, circa 1949. (A. Domke family photo)

THE TEACHERS

The salary scale for teachers was never great. In 1966 an elementary teacher with a one-year basic certificate received $4,230 per year and the Teachers Association requested it be raised to $5,290 per year.

In the early years, teachers lived in the teacherage. Not having cars, they occasionally caught rides to town on the weekends. Walter Kozek remembers having to go to town with horse and wagon to pick up Teacher Yingling. Because he was one of her students, his father sternly warned that he wasn't allowed to initiate any conversation with her. He found the trip totally boring. She paid him five dollars that he had to turn over to his father. As more teachers acquired cars, they daily tackled the 12 miles of dusty, gravel washboard from Revelstoke. When bus service began in 1958, the teachers could choose to ride the daily school bus.

The children of Twelve Mile were blessed by the dedicated lives of the many teachers who did their best to motivate these young minds to learn despite primitive conditions. Many formed lifelong friendships with parents and students. They were:

1930-31	Vivian L. Gardiner	Fall 1951	D. C. Story
1931-35	Marjorie Yingling	Spring 1952	W. Eric Norris
1935-36	David Mitchell	1952-53	W. Eric Norris
1936-37	Ruth Lindsey	1953-54	Elsie Ruth Townsend
1937-40	Marjorie Johnstone	1954-57	Mrs. P. B. Gowan
1940-41	Mabel Horsley	1957-58	Newton Minion
1941-42	Ernestena Walters	1958-59	Audrey Deverall
	Mary Fulton	1959-60	Eileen Kernaghan
1942-43	Olga Shamon	1960-61	D. McIntosh
	Rose Slym		
	Mrs. Mais Moffat (?)	1961-62	Vernon A. Fischer
1943-45	Margaret MacRae	1962-65	Nellie McKay
Fall 1945	School closed	Fall 1965	Nellie McKay
Spring 1946	Edna Whyte	Spring 1966	Mary Hashimoto
1946-50	Irene English	Fall 1966	Ted DeVolder
1949	Marjorie Smith (practice)	Spring 1967	James Floyd
1950-51	William L. McLeod		

THE LAST YEARS

Things began changing in the 1958-59 school year when grades eight through 12 were bussed to Revelstoke. As people started leaving the Arrowhead and Sidmouth areas, their school enrollments dropped. By the 1965-66 school year, students from Arrowhead in grades seven through 12 were bussed to Twelve Mile where they joined students in the same grades there, and boarded another bus to Revelstoke. Some of the teachers such as James Floyd and Mary Hashimoto from Revelstoke rode the bus back and forth. The bus also transported some elementary-age students still living in the Six Mile and Eight Mile areas to the Twelve Mile School on its way to pick up the older students to be taken to Revelstoke. This was a creative way to assure all students still living in the soon-to-be-flooded valley could continue their education.

HIGH SCHOOL THE HARD WAY

Before 1958 when students finished eighth grade at Twelve Mile School, they were forced to find places that would room and board a high school student. Some students were fortunate enough to have relatives in town to live with. Bruce and Gloria Kaduhr had the Gowanlocks. Annie Nipper had relatives in Shoreacres and attended high school for a couple of years in Castlegar. Della and Florence McLeod and their mother, of Wigwam, moved to Kamloops for their first two years of high school. Eugen Domke attended Canadian Union College boarding academy in Alberta. Pat Shiell boarded in town and came home weekends, as did Evelyn Domke. Emily Rauchert had to catch daily rides to meet the school bus at Six Mile. Sometimes she rode with Olympe Astrahantseff in his small army Jeep. Sometimes she walked. Whenever he could, her dad, John, took her in his logging truck. On cold winter days, they had to first warm up the motor by placing a can of burning oil under the motor.

Ada Domke searched for a family in Revelstoke that would take her and finally found Mrs. Elizabeth Pilkey who had run a boarding house in Sidmouth before moving to a house on First Street. James (Jim) Mackey of Sidmouth found her also. By this time in 1955, Mrs. Pilkey had lived a full life and was up in years. She definitely filled a need for these two highschoolers.

Her home was three to four small buildings strung together in a long row. Ada settled into the tiny room off the living room and had a street-side window. Jim's room was at the tail end of the train-like structure, past the indoor woodshed. Tacked into the woodshed was the bathroom with a toilet, a ceramic washbasin and pitcher on a washstand, and a portable kerosene heater—which was off limits to the young tenants. The narrow connector portion between the living room and woodshed housed the kitchen. On opposite sides were the sink and tiny table and a stove jammed against the east wall. Mrs. Pilkey's bedroom was between the kitchen and woodshed room. Not surprisingly, there was no such thing as central heat, nor any heaters in the tenants' bedrooms.

Elizabeth Pilkey, 80th birthday, 1955.
(E. Pilkey photo)

In order to reduce expenses, the Domkes brought fresh beef and vegetables to Mrs. Pilkey from their farm. When those ran out, the meals were meager. For supper one evening, Jim and Ada took their seats at opposite ends of the tiny kitchen table and they were served a large boiled onion in the center of their plates; no side dishes were offered. For a special treat one evening, Mrs. Pilkey very excitedly announced several times that there would be ice cream for dessert. The students couldn't wait. Excitement ran high! But wait-- there was a catch. At dessert time, Jim was asked to get the ice cream, so he obediently went into the woodshed room that also housed the tiny tabletop refrigerator. However, in frugality it was turned off and empty. "Oh, Jimmy, you must go to Sally Ann's ice cream parlor to get it. It's already paid for." Nothing was far in Revelstoke, so 20 minutes later dessert was served with a flourish.

Helen Domke, Ada's aunt, paid her a visit one winter evening. Their family had moved from Twelve Mile to the Big Eddy area where they lived in their partially-completed new house. She took one look at Ada's bed stacked high with her winter coat and other clothing.

"Why don't you hang up your clothes, Ada?"

"It's so cold in here, I have to pile everything on my bed." Then she further described the food situation, and how the light bulb hanging from the ceiling cord in the dining area had to be removed and screwed into the socket hanging in the entrance before answering the door; and how her friend had to wait outside or write chalk messages on the sidewalk because she was prohibited from knocking on the door to pick her up on the way to school.

After listening carefully, Helen announced, "That's it! You're coming to live with us after Christmas. We'll find a spot for you in our unfinished house." Needless to say, the rest of that school year was a lot more fun!

Once in town, Ada was finally able to take piano lessons, taught by Sharon O'Rourke, a high school student. A few doors down the street lived Mrs. Hall who generously offered her piano for practise.

Ada rode the bus from Six Mile on Monday mornings and back on Friday afternoons. Between Twelve Mile and Six Mile she caught rides with others who had vehicles, such as Podzuns or Olympe in his small army Jeep.

With transportation, room and board difficulties, it's no wonder many students dropped out of school before finishing high school, or in some cases before even starting.

REPORT CARDS

On the last day of school, the eighth-graders were given the contents of their "cumulative file" which included samples of their art and schoolwork saved for them through the years. As the report cards were handed out, friends cautiously asked each other, "Did you pass?" The newspaper always posted the promotions for all the district schools.

1930-31 Report Card . (A. Jarvis photo)

Days absent	0	2	0	—				—
Times tardy	0	0	0	0				1
Reading, Oral	70		C	75				70
Reading, Silent	40		B	60				B
Writing				C				B
Spelling	92		B	66	96			82
Hand-work								
Arithmetic	58		B⁺	55	56			61
Drawing	80			B				85
Language				56				
Literature								
Grammar								
Composition								
History, British				60				
History, Canadian								
Geography								
Nature Study								
Hygiene								
Music								
Manual Training								
Domestic Science								
				372				
	390			62				
Standing in class	1		B	2	2			2
Number in the class	2	2	2	3				3

A signifies Excellent; B, Good; C, Very Fair; D, Fair; E, Poor.

Progress			B		B
Attitude to work			C	B	B
Preparation of lessons			B	B	B⁺
Care of school property			B	C	B
School spirit			B	B⁺	B

N.B.— In filling in the foregoing columns use A for Excellent; B, Good; C, Fair; D, Poor.

OTHER REMARKS: *Promoted to Grade 4.*

Chapter 4

THE FARMS

*I hauled the cream cans in a wheelbarrow
or wagon to the Twelve Mile
train station and waited for the train
coming back from Arrowhead.*

A common misconception held by people today is that rural life in the past was simple. It certainly was not. It is amazing what people had to know about animal husbandry, and raising and preserving foods for their families and animals when living in the country.

PRODUCE

When the industrious settlers cleared the rich soil of the Columbia Valley in Twelve Mile, it brought forth abundant crops, and frequent rains provided enough water without the necessity to irrigate. Everyone, it seemed, had a small orchard of apples (Yellow Transparent, Winter Banana, Wealthy, and small rosy crab apples), cherries and plums. Honey bees were kept for pollinating the orchards and the bonus was delicious honey. Loads of potatoes, carrots, sugar beets, mangels, raspberries and strawberries were shipped to markets, mostly by rail.

In 1954 Revelstoke Canning Co. Ltd. was established by Mr. Ohlhausen in the Big Eddy area of Revelstoke. That year, the Asaph Domkes raised a huge field of beautiful Blue Lake beans for the cannery. However, the first season's frost came the night before the first picking was due, and that was the end of the bean venture!

FARM ANIMALS

Cows and horses went on sampling tours in open range and found lush grasses especially in the slough areas along the river. At times they even crossed the water to the river islands. This left the fields for hay and grain crops that were fenced in with split cedar rail or barbed wire, from the animals. In the winter, their foods were hay, carrots and mangels. Cows weren't fed turnips because they produced strong-flavored milk.

Cows wore bells around their necks so they could be easily located and were identifiable by the specific bell sound. Many stories could be told of going to the slough after the cows for their milking. Evelyn Domke was always frightened to go to the slough. There were so many animal tracks and strange sounds. But out of respect for her mother she did go. Once when following a cow trail, she encountered a huge snake coiled up on a log across the

Olga Kramer with Blackie. (Kramer family photo)

trail. That was enough to send her running lickety split all the way home without the cows. At other times there was plenty of "bear sign" and huge paw prints on the muddy shores of the slough, but she does not recall ever encountering one. Sometimes she couldn't find the cows and they returned on their own but in the morning with overfull udders. The brush often ripped their udders that had to be treated with generous amounts of Rawleigh's carbolic salve.

Hans Podzun's Hereford cattle returning home. (S. Podzun photo)

Farm animals occasionally needed medical attention. Cows were prone to bloating when they indulged in the new spring grasses after a winter diet of dry hay. Evelyn remembers putting "burlap gunny sacks over their bellies. We kept them cool by pouring cold water over them. Then Mother walked to Herrmann's in Sidmouth for help. He came and poked a hole in the cow's gut with a sharp pick to release the gas." Men and women assisted cows and horses with difficult birthing, always hoping the young were born at home and not in the field or bush where coyotes were on stand-by for an easy meal. In the late 1940s government inspectors began testing all cattle for tuberculosis. Before the farmers began raising curly white-faced Herefords for beef, cows were mainly kept for milking so the calves were weaned soon after birth. To teach them to drink from a bucket, someone (often a child) placed fingers into the milk for the calf to suck on, thus teaching them to drink from a bucket.

Mike Kozek's work horses, resting. (W. Kozek photo)

To change a potential bull into a steer or horse into a gelding, there was a simple neutering procedure done by tightening a silk thread around the stalk of the scrotum. This restricted the blood flow causing the tissue to die. Horns were discouraged from developing by rubbing caustic blue stone on the horn roots of calves and sheep.

Large workhorses were important for farm work, logging and transportation. Before farmers could afford motor vehicles, they used teams of horses to haul supplies or people in wagons and sleighs, and to pull farm implements.   Olympe Astrahantseff recounts one of his exciting horse stories:

My father always trusted me with horses—I was a teamster, hauling stuff as truck drivers do today. Once when returning from delivering a load to the Twelve Mile train station, I stopped in the bush next to the school to check on something. I tied the reins to the wheel of the wagon, but when the horses started moving a bit, the reins tightened around the wheels. So they backed up until something snapped, they panicked and took off—a runaway team of horses and broken wagon! By the time they got home, all that was left was a wagon tongue and a few harness straps. The rear axle had fallen off and boards were strewn all the way down the road. It took us the rest of the day to pick up all that stuff. Needless to say, there were some questions to be answered. We had other runaway horses and it was always exciting.

One day Mike Kozek was cleaning the horse barn when one of his horses kicked him so hard that Steve had to take him to the hospital for X-rays. Annie Nipper witnessed the incident and helped Joe find Mike's dentures in the barn.

The Emil Raucherts and Kellys kept milk goats. Joan Kelly couldn't tolerate cow's milk as a baby, so they got a few goats. When they moved back to their Revelstoke farm, the children carried the kid goats in their arms as they herded the adult goats the 14-15 miles on the road.

After lambs were several weeks old, their tails were cropped with a sizzling hot tool that looked like a large wire cutter. Shearing the wool in the spring required special tools and training. The knots and dirt were carded out of the wool and spun into yarn or stuffed into fluffy quilts.

Children loved cuddling and feeding the new lambs when their mothers were unable to. They usually attached a long lamb nipple to a pop (soda) or beer bottle.

In addition to the larger farm animals, some homesteaders also raised geese and ducks. Helen Domke's geese strutted from the house to the barn and back like a row of

Hans Podzun taking his newly-acquired flock of sheep home from Domkes. (A. Domke photo)

penguins. They acted as watch dogs becoming noisier if anyone came over. Their feathers were choice for pillows and feather bed quilts.

Farmers were always on the alert for a clucking setting hen in the springtime. Once found, she was resettled on a nest of eight to 12 fertile eggs in a quiet spot until the chicks hatched out in three weeks. Sometimes hens hid nests in the hayloft or in a hollow stump and surprised everyone with a new family of fluffy, yellow chicks. Children enjoyed watching the metamorphosis of an egg being pecked open by an emerging wet, scraggly chick, and within minutes

Katherine Zibulak with her geese. (Makarewicz family photo)

looking like a fluffy white or yellow tennis ball on the move. If it was too cold outside, they were kept warm by the kitchen stove in a little pen with a jar of warm water slipped into a woolen sock. They instinctively knew how to peck at the tiny morsels of boiled egg and water siphoned into a saucer from an upside down jar. Baby geese and ducks were similarly cared for. Sometimes chicks were ordered by mail and delivered by train or freight truck in a cardboard box with air holes and lots of peeping.

Chickens scratched for insects and worms, but still had to be fed wheat, oats and vegetables. During winter, they enjoyed a warm mix of cooked potatoes, vegetable peels and ground grain that was cooked on the kitchen stove. Oooh, that chicken mash aroma! They also needed oyster shells to produce strong egg shells.

It was necessary to pen up chickens in coyote-proof fences, pickets even dug into the ground. At night, they were secured in a hen house with a ladder-like roost made from tree limbs or poles. There were straw-filled nesting boxes for their morning egg laying. If any small door was not carefully latched, a nocturnal weasel on the hunt could destroy the entire flock, sucking the blood and leaving the carcasses.

Helen Domke's first chicken coop. Evelyn attending the chickens. (O. Domke family photo)

Dogs and cats were important to every farm and logging camp, but weren't generally allowed in the house. Dogs were not only pets but protected the property and farm animals from predators. Cats could be prolific propagators. The excess kittens that weren't choked by the tomcat in the area often disappeared with a bunch of rocks in a gunnysack tossed into the river. A few farm cats were always saved to control rodent and squirrel populations.

Pigs were not picky eaters and in the days before garbage disposals, this was an important feature. However, in cold winter months, farmers cooked up huge kettles of potatoes and added excess skimmed milk to give them warm food

Several farmers kept honeybees: the Astrahantseffs, Robert Brinkman and Oscar Domke, to name a few. They used a honey extractor that was a special large tub. The steam from a pan of boiling water on the stove was routed through a hose to a special knife. The hot knife was slid over the honeycombs to melt the top layer of wax. The honeycombs were fastened inside the extractor and when the handle was turned, centrifugal force released the honey. Honey pails and jars were filled from a tap at the bottom. It was a sweet and fascinating operation to say the least.

Oscar Domke tending his bee hives. (O. Domke family photo)

RAMMED

"Why dad bought the flock of sheep, I'll never know. Maybe it was because the lambs were so cute. They got into everything and refused to be fenced. One thing they did do is clean up the underbrush on the mountain behind our house," sighed Ada Domke as she relived her adventure. She didn't think keeping the sheep were worth the damage done to flowers and vegetable gardens when they broke through fences.

Only one of the sheep had a name. Gordon. The bully ragging ram. The white of his snout and forehead stood out in contrast to the rest of his grayish wool coat. He left no doubts as to who ruled the barnyard as well as anyone entering therein.

One winter the barnyard was packed in three feet of snow with narrow paths tramped or shoveled allowing only a single file of cows and sheep to walk in them. Not being her favourite place to go--ever, much less in the winter, Ada conned eight-year-old cousin, Helga Mantei, into accompanying her to the hen house to gather eggs. She took a broom for protection just in case Gordon appeared. He was nowhere to be seen—the coast was clear right into the smelly chicken coop. The girls held their noses and quickly gathered the eggs into a small bucket. But they weren't fast enough. They were met at the door by Mr. Barnyard Bully himself. He stood guard, immobilizing the girls as they tried to exit the door. Every time they opened the door a crack, he moved in for the kill. Ada still vividly remembers the event:

Being 12, I felt responsible for Helga. I wasn't sure if we were turning blue from the cold or from trying to hold our breath in that smelly coop. I finally talked her into running for dear life as I took the broom after Gordon. I backed him into a side snow channel while Helga made it safely to the barn. But the fun had just begun for Gordon. As I backed on the trails toward the barn, he kept raring up on his hind legs, lowering his head, then ramming me with his steel-strong forehead. The broom absorbed some of the impact as I fought for my life. This happened over and over. I thought he would never stop. Both of my snow boots and socks had fallen off in the melee by the time I finally ducked into the barn door to safety. Here we were trapped again, with him butting the door at intervals, making sure we knew he was still on his watch.

Helga and I pounded and yelled for help from the inside of our prison, hoping a passerby on the gravel road in front would hear our cries. Finally, the loggers renting our log cabin across from the barn, drove in from work and heard the

Gordon, the ram, being subdued by Eugen Domke. (A. Domke family photo)

commotion. They came running over, picked up Gordon by his front legs and walked him backwards on his hind legs, then tossed him into a snow bank, while we girls made a run for it. Whew! What an adrenalin rush. What happened to the eggs, I'll never know.

That was the last straw for Gordon and his harem. A neighbor, lucky fellow, bought the whole flock and they never saw Gordon again.

DAIRY FARMING

In addition to domestic use of dairy and poultry products, many farmers shipped milk and cream to Armstrong, and sold meat, eggs, cream, cheese and butter to stores and individuals in Revelstoke and the area. Cream was shipped in cans by Cancelleri's taxi for about 25 cents each, by Rocky Mountain Freight, or by train. The CPR picked up cream cans from Sidmouth to Revelstoke and transferred them onto a station wagon that took them to a big tank of ice water. The cream waited in the ice until the train left for the creamery on the Okanagan train. Empty cans were returned the following week with a slip inside each indicating the butterfat content and whether the cream arrived "sweet" or "sour."

Walter Kozek tells about hauling their cream cans in a wheelbarrow or wagon to the train station where he waited for the return train from Arrowhead:

> When he came around the corner, I'd keep waving my hand until the engineer blew the whistle indicating he saw me. When he stopped, I lifted up the five-gallon cans and he bent down and pulled them onto the train by the lid handle (the lid was wired to the can). Cream was 29 percent butterfat for butter. The biggest check we got in a month from cream from 15 cows was $45.

The North Okanagan Co-Operative Creamery Association (NOCA) provided helpful dairy information via *The Cream Collector* publication, and purchased milk and cream shipped in metal cans by the farmers by rail or freight truck. Successor to NOCA was the amalgamation of area creameries into the Shushwap-Okanagan Dairy Industries Cooperative Association. When dairy prices began dropping in the 1950s, farmers resorted to raising beef cattle, especially Herefords.

Galvanized two-gallon milk pails were sterilized on the wood-burning stove, with boiling water and/or by setting out in the sun after each morning and evening milking. Today, many people wonder why public health authorities warn against the use of unpasteurized milk when it was commonplace to do so in the past on small farms. It is because people using milk regularly from the same cow herd build up an intestinal immunity to its bacteria. The same does not occur when buying raw milk on the open market.

Cream can with Vernon Creamery address. (A. Domke family photo)

Separating the milk was a laborious and daily chore. The milk separator (DeLaval was the make most commonly used) had a large collecting basin at the top onto which was clipped a cloth to strain out foreign materials. When the handle was manually turned, a series of 35 discs separated the cream from the milk and ran out of two separate spouts into milk and cream cans. The handle had to be turned at just the right speed and the little bell changed it's little "ding, ding" tune when the speed was correct for the amount of butterfat desired. Children groaned and complained when it was their turn to wash the separator. Not only did it have a sour smell, there were numerous parts to be cleaned and sterilized.

Butter churn. (A. Jarvis photo)

Every child had plenty of milk to drink. Calves, hogs, dogs and cats got the leftover skimmed milk, and some was used to make delicious cottage cheese. Extra cream was used in cooking and for churning into butter. Buttermilk was also a special beverage treat and used in baking. Walter Kozek says,

"It's okay to drink sour, whole milk when it's not pasteurized. Just break up the clabbered milk and drink it. It's especially good on a hot day."

Those making butter used manual churns, either wooden homemade ones or crockery purchased ones. Both types had wooden plungers. For "pin money" some ladies formed butter into pounds using special wooden butter forms. It sold from 15 cents to 25 cents a pound.

HAYING

Brooks Gowanlock and Hickie Kaduhr hitching their team of horses to the disc. (Kaduhr family photo)

Haying started in late June and early July, always with fingers crossed to beat the rain that could easily spoil a mowed crop drying in the fields. A team of horses pulled a riding mower through the hay fields and then pulled a riding rake that flipped it into windrows to dry. Farmers turned the windrows once by pitchforks, then stacked it into small mounds to be pitched onto a wagon or truck to be hauled to the hay barn. Children or ladies usually got the job of arranging the tossed hay on top of the load. Except for being stabbed by thistles, it was better than pitching from the dusty ground below. Carolyn Rauchert remembers haying as always being a great time:

We liked to help Grandpa (Ferdinand) Rauchert and Uncle Emil bring in the hay. The hay would be piled up in mounds and we would ride around and pick it up. The kids' job was to jump up and down on the hay to pack it down in the hay wagon. Kathy, Larry and I were really good at this! Grandpa could pick up an entire mound. He would lift it high over his head and carry it to the hay wagon like a huge, brown umbrella. He worked all day in the fields dressed in a three-piece blue wool suit!

Hay balers were a real boon to the process when they appeared in later years. They used either baling twine or baling wire to hold the bales together. Once in the hayloft, children enjoyed the scent of Timothy, clover and alfalfa as they slid, napped, built tunnels and played hide and seek in it. Mother cats also found the hayloft a safe and private place to bear and raise their kittens, not far from some tasty morsels of mice also hiding out. The hay barn also served as overflow sleeping accommodations when visitors arrived.

Jim Millar and Dan Crawford hitching a sloup behind Jim's team. (Millar family photo)

Leo Rohde raking hay with horse, Billy. (Rohde family photo)

Valentin, Nelli and Rosa Rohde truck haying. (Rohde family photo)

Haying with truck. Evelyn Domke on load and Ben below. Note hay mounds in background and to right. (O. Domke family photo)

PRODUCE

Creeks, wells, root cellars and basements kept produce and dairy adequately cool even without mechanical refrigeration. Some farmers took ice from the river or piles of snow and insulated it in straw or sawdust for summer use. Evelyn Domke can chuckle now when thinking about those days:

> Mom would send me to the root cellar for food. I'd sink in the snow up to my hips and scrape out the snow from the door and take out cabbage and root veggies. Then I'd back out and close the door behind. Pile

Nick Makarewicz and his children with hay baler. (Makarewicz family photo)

the snow against the door to seal it up again. Dad set aside a calf to feed and then butcher in the winter. He'd hang it in a sheltered place outside to keep it frozen. We'd go out there and cut off pieces when we needed some meat.

Various methods were used to can, salt, smoke and pickle vegetables, fruits and meats as well as make wine. Butchering larger animals was generally a man's job, but the chickens, geese and ducks seemed to be left to the women. When Jim Wakita opened his frozen food lockers on Second Street in Revelstoke in 1951, farmers found it more convenient to package and freeze their meats.

FORAGING

Children and adults joined together on mountain outings to pick wild huckleberries and blueberries that were baked into delicious pies and preserved as fruits, jams and wines. They also were keen observers of wild mushrooms—where they grew and which were safe to eat. "Mom used to put a silver coin in the pan of mushrooms. If it turned black it meant the mushrooms were poisonous," remembers Evelyn Domke. (Caution: this folk practice is not a universally reliable way to test mushroom toxicity.)

FALL FAIRS

In September 1950, several Twelve Milers began participating in the Junior Fall Fair at the Civic Center in Revelstoke. For a small community, they took a record number of ribbons that year and more in the coming years. Olympe and Ada remember the arduous task of digging, washing and sorting blue-ribbon fresh vegetables, and artistically arranging every piece of fruit or vegetable in canning jars. Netted Gem potatoes had to be oblong but wider at one end than the other to be a perfect shape. Winners that year were:

Netted Gem potatoes – Eugen Domke

Turnips – Herb Domke

Carrots, long – Eugen Domke

Carrots, short – Olympe Astrahantseff

Beans, green – Olympe Astrahantseff

Onions – Evelyn Domke

Citron – Ada Domke

Celery – Herb Domke

Mangels – Eugen Domke

Snapdragons – Evelyn Domke

Gladiolas – Ada Domke, Olympe and

Sergei Astrahantseff

Cosmos – Russell Gowanlock

White bread loaf – Evelyn Domke

Bran muffins – Evelyn Domke

Canned fruit – Ada and Eugen Domke

Apple pie – Evelyn Domke

Lemon meringue pie – Evelyn Domke

The school class display of crafts received

Second Prize

REVELSTOKE AND DISTRICT
AGRICULTURAL ASSOCIATION
ANNUAL FALL FAIR
Revelstoke, B.C.
195....
Div............, Class..*1*...., Enrty. No. *35*
Article *Stamp Album*
Variety ....
FIRST PRIZE
NOT TO BE OPENED UNTIL JUDGING COMPLETED
Name *Mrs Ada Domke*
Address *12 Mile*

Fall Fair awards. (A. Jarvis photo)

October was always potato-harvest month. They grew exceptionally well in the fertile soil deposited by the Columbia River's swollen waters each spring. Farmers shipped railcar loads every year and took prizes at the fairs for their high quality potatoes.

SEEDS

Without television to consume the long winter evenings, men and women poured over Buckerfields seed catalogues planning their summer flower and vegetable gardens. New seeds would be added to those they had already harvested from certain plants and those traded with neighbors. Special seeds and potato starts were brought from "the old country", and some plants were kept over the winter in the house or basement. They placed their seed orders by mail or through the Farmers' Institute. They developed seedlings in indoor window boxes, to be transplanted after the last spring frost. And there was plenty of fertilizer from the manure pile waiting by the barn.

FARMERS' INSTITUTE

The Farmers' Institute promoted productive farming and provided a platform from which its members could present their various needs to the government. Its official organ was *Country Life in B.C.* and an agriculturist was on staff. During the 1930s and 1940s, H. E. Waby was the agriculturist for the district and Henry Popplewell its secretary. Henry and Clara Popplewell were an older couple who were very helpful and loved by the farmers. Representatives were chosen from Twelve Mile and other areas in the district south of Revelstoke. The Institute also sponsored an experimental farm that was Rolly Hold's (Hulyd) in Six Mile.

The Institute provided a stable for horses in Revelstoke when farmers did their business in town. It was near the Columbia River where the Recreation Center now stands. At meetings, farmers were taught rodent control, soil care and ways to increase crops. It sold certified seeds and dynamite for land clearing, provided farm tools for borrowing, a certified bull for breeding, and veterinarian equipment to borrow for inoculating and castrating. In 1932 and 1933 the Institute lobbied the Province for cheaper blasting powder much needed for land clearing, for reduced freight rates on seed grain ordered, and for electrification and mosquito control of the rural areas. When necessary, Henry Popplewell oversaw the loading of produce in boxcars to be shipped from Twelve Mile to Vancouver. The Institute also organized banquets, meetings and field days with sports and races. In July 1938 Twelve Milers Tom Mazar and Steve Kozek were race winners.

COUNTRY BOYS' PRANK

It was during one of those "Indian Summer" days that Bruce Kaduhr and his buddies, Olympe and Sergei Astrahantseff, perspired in the potato field near the one-room school they attended during the week. It was where they learned many valuable life skills in addition to some reading, writing and arithmetic. They learned to load the pot-bellied heater with wood from the back shed to keep warm. They also learned to be sure there was always a supply of catalogues or newspapers in the "two-holer" out back. One of the most important tasks that each pupil learned well by repeated trials was how to prime the water pump and refill the water crock on the counter in the classroom.

On one particular day, the boys engaged in an unsavory prank.

"Boy, am I ever exhausted and thirsty," 12-year-old Bruce announced after tying off the top of his twelfth gunnysack full of Russets.

"Yea, I can't dig another hill without a good, cold drink," chimed in Sergei.

Olympe, being the practical one of the three, suggested they all go to the water pump on the windowless side of the school. The pump handle screeched and squawked dryly as they took turns pumping the iron handle up and down, becoming even sweatier than ever. It soon became obvious that there would be no water without a good priming. But how? The blue enamel dipper hung on the pump waiting to do its job. During school hours, priming water was dipped from the crock inside the school and poured down the pump shaft as the handle was vigorously pushed and pulled by another student.

Water pump. (A. Jarvis photo)

"The school is locked," moaned Sergei. "Where can we get the priming water?"

Being a resourceful lad, Bruce came up with a solution. Since boys will be boys, he didn't need to beg for 100 percent cooperation. Each jubilantly contributed some of his own "liquid" until the dipper overflowed. Voila! the pump was primed successfully. But wait—how long would it take now to get to the safe drinking water?

"Keep pumping."

"Keep pumping."

"I can't wait, give me the dipper."

And so the potato farmers got their fill of refreshing water. They also learned another life lesson the next day when Mrs. English learned about the nature of the liquid the boys had used to prime the pump. No one was ever going to drink from the contaminated dipper again. She required them to each pitch in some of their hard-earned potato-digging money to buy a new dipper for the school. Who was the mystery tattler?

Chapter 5

LOGGING

Oh Stranger, ponder well, what breed of men were these
Cruisers, Fallers, Skinners, Ox, Horse, and "Cat"
Chokersetters and the rest who used these tools.
No summer's searing dust could parch their souls,
Nor bitter breath of winter chill their hearts.
'Twas never said "They worked for pay alone"
Tho it was good and always freely spent.
Tough jobs to lick they welcomed with each day,
"We'll bury that old mill in logs," their boast,
Such men as these have made this country great.
Beyond the grasp of smaller, meaner men.
Pray God, Oh Stranger, others yet be born
Worthy as they to wear a Logger's Boots.

"Ode to the Loggers," by Nelson Reed

EARLY LOGGING

The area along the Columbia River between Carnes Creek (north of Revelstoke) and the Sproat area (north of Arrowhead) was designated the "Railway Belt." This was a strip of land granted by the Federal government to the CPR for its timber needs. Enterprising folks easily took advantage of the Crown Timber's lack of supervision and tax collecting in this and other established railway belts when they did their initial logging. Timber along the river was taken first because it could easily be skidded by horses to the water for transport south. Some people's sole purpose for obtaining a homestead along the Columbia River where huge virgin timber abounded, was to log off the timber and then let the property revert back to the Crown. Logging companies even made attractive offers to buy timber from those who obtained homesteads for that purpose. This appears to have happened in Twelve Mile based on early land records. In the 1890s, the Genelle family's sawmill at Nakusp depended on timber floated down the Columbia

By 1897 Crown Timber finally realized the amount of revenue it was missing out on and began trying to control timber stealing. A method of bidding on Timber Limits was established which included registered timber marks and collection of royalties. It wasn't until 1927 that Land Act Amendments were instituted to control abuse of pre-empted land. It granted "only land suitable for agricultural purposes, and which is not timberland, i.e., carrying over 5,000 board feet per acre west of the Coast Range and 8,000 feet per acre east of the Range," according to an article in a 1927 *Revelstoke Review*.

Over the years, many individuals and larger companies came and went as they logged and poled in the Twelve Mile area, and a few stayed and established their homes there.

TWELVE MILE TIMBERMEN

Even though most Twelve Milers had small farms, the men usually worked in the timber industry as well. The moist, mild western slope climate enabled second growth timber to reach marketable size in just a few years, replacing the huge virgin cedars over 10 feet in diameter that had been logged off before the settlers came.

A. J. Waskett had a logging camp on the property that straddled the railway tracks along the river by the 11-mile eddy near Islands No. 6 and No. 2. He was also one of the first to contract for cedar to be made into shingles at his Arrowhead mill.

John Rauchert with his first logging truck, circa 1947. (J. Rauchert Family photo)

Before 1920, John and Meta Dedosenco and Thomas McCormick operated a sawmill four miles north of Twelve Mile that depended heavily on its timber. Mike Hewko also had a mill early on in the area. Dick Sawyer and Maknamura-Ogawa had mills later near Revelstoke to which Twelve Mile timber was taken.

Notices of regular timber sales were placed in the newspapers. Its publication was held in the office of the Revelstoke Forest Ranger. When a person or company was issued a license to log, they were given a large hammer with a royalty stamp embossed in its head. Each log or pole was required to be stamped with the specific identification so its source could be determined.

Mike Kozek obtained his first timber sale on Mt. Cartier that he horse logged to get enough timber for his farm buildings. Then he got an old relic bulldozer and logged with John Rauchert for a while. John's first timber rights were also on Mt. Cartier where he repaired an old, previously used five-mile road. He took out logs and poles.

At first logs were taken out by horses. They could work in the snow easier than motorized vehicles. Loggers took their sandwiches in three- or five-pound Shamrock Lard pails, built a fire and boiled water in the pail for tea. Walter Kozek claimed that sparks from fir and spruce needles gave their tea an extra zing!

Many loggers stayed in small cabins for a week at a time, packing their weekly supplies on a packboard. It was fairly common for them to return after a weekend away, to a cabin that had been ransacked by a bear.

During the boom years after WWII when highways and the building of cities, hotels, industries and mines increased, the need for forest products rose and more modern equipment was introduced. Some of the individual timber brokers in the area in the post WWII era were Sandy and Meta Toma, Bill Mackey,

Loggers' tools: packboard, lunch kit, crosscut saw. Eugen Domke reminisces with his father's early logging equipment. (A. Jarvis photo)

Oscar and Ben Domke, John Rauchert, Mike, Walter, Steve and Joe Kozek.

To reduce hauling expenses, small, portable sawmills called "gypo" mills were moved onto timber limits. War surplus vehicles were put to use in these small camps because they were built for rugged terrain and were readily available. Many small operators owned gypo mills and a few of those mill owners continue to exist today on a larger scale. Joe Kozek Sawmills, Ltd. is still in operation on Camozzi Road in Revelstoke, and Ivan Graham operates a mill south of Revelstoke. The lumber was hauled away and piles of slabs and sawdust were left on the sites when the mill was moved to the next timber limit. Loggers were transported to and from their work site with "crummies," (old four-wheel-drive vehicles, such as Bradshaw's Landrover), to spare them the necessity of living in a camp cabin for a week or more at a time.

Relatively small logging truck typical of small operators. (O. Domke family photo)

Small operators frequently had difficulty maintaining equipment as well as paying employees. When that happened, the individual employee and his family paid the price. Asaph Domke worked hard to pay tuition from his meager income as a logger so his children could get a good education. His children, Eugen and Ada, attended boarding school since they were unable to get transportation to Revelstoke High School at that time. This is the letter he wrote to his son in 1958:

> Here is some bad news for you. Mama went last Monday to cash my cheques and you know, they bounced. So Mama did not know what to do. And I was not home all week. She just told me last night. And I won't be able to see _____ till Monday 1 Oct. And then I don't know when we will be able to cash the cheques. And I have not enough money to send the payment away.

Ben Domke cat skidding poles, with Oscar Domke in driver's seat. (O. Domke family photo)

Some local operators never did make good on wages owed loggers like Asaph.

In 1947 Columbia River Timbers (CRT) built a modern camp near Mulvehill Falls, complete with running water and electricity. They extended the logging road about five miles north of the camp. When they discovered their 75-foot poles were too long to take across the ferry, they built a large raft near the ferry and hauled their poles and rough lumber to the

Twelve Mile CPR station for shipping.

Walter Shiell and William (Sandy) Robson moved with their families from Nakusp and logged in Twelve Mile from 1948-50. Their specialty was cottonwood that they logged off the islands and shipped from the Twelve Mile rail yard to Vernon. Where the islands were close to shore, they hoisted the logs out with a donkey engine. (It was called a donkey because the motor was too small to be called a horse and its line ran to a spar tree. A high climber with spiked boots climbed a tree, cut off the top and fastened a pulley for the spar tree line.) They had to time their operations between the ice leaving the river and arrival of high waters. When the bottom dropped out of the cottonwood market, Shiell and Robson logged birch. In May, 1949 they hired every truck available to haul their poles boomed by the ferry to the CPR yards in Twelve Mile to beat the rising water.

In 1953 Charlie Sartorous moved his sawmill from Beaton to the south bank of Blanket Creek. He set up a large camp including cook and bunkhouses. Jimmy Wheaton managed it all. Asaph Domke was the sawyer. Joe and Walter Kozek, Ben Domke and Eddie Ott were some of the suppliers of logs that they hauled from the Cranberry area. Ben also cut and hauled logs to the mill with an arch truck from above Blanket Creek. Ben and Oscar used the lumber from those logs to build their new machine shop in Revelstoke.

ORIGINAL   CERTIFICATE

TIMBER MARK   № 47022

THE GOVERNMENT OF
THE PROVINCE OF BRITISH COLUMBIA

FOREST SERVICE,

Victoria, B.C.,   JULY 14th   , 19 59

Issued to

, a Timber Mark as shown below, registered under the provisions of Part IX of the " Forest Act " and amendments thereof; said Timber Mark to be used exclusively on the tract of land described as:

Fr. L.S. 4,5 of Sec. 8, Tp. 22,

R. 1, lying S. of Columbia River

STUMPAGE RESERVATIONS
Sawlogs

			Cedar Poles and Piling	Per l.f.
Cedar	$ 3.90 per M b.m.			
Hemlock	2.00 " " "		Under 30'	½¢
Other Species	2.20 " " "		30' and over but less than 35'	1¢
Cordwood	30¢ per cd.		35' and over but less than 55'	4¢
Cedar Shakes	$ 1.20 per cd.		55' and over	9¢

Situated   10 MI. S.E. OF REVELSTOKE, B.C.

Land District W. OF 6TH M.   Forest District   NELSON

Acquired   Crown Granted

TIMBER-MARK DESIGNATION

Class 1—Old Crown Grants ....

Class 2—Crown Grants, 1887–1906 ....

Class 3—Crown Grants, 1906–1914 ....

Class 4—Full Royalty ....

Class 5—Special 13SR

This certificate does not constitute any acknowledgment that the above lands are owned by party to whom this mark is issued or that the said party has any rights to the said lands or the timber thereon.

R.G. McKEE,
Deputy Minister of Forests

F.S. 163—2.500 (25)-557-7956 (2)

TYPES OF TREES LOGGED

Huge, charred cedar stumps filled the valley. They were grubbed out and often harvested for "brewery wood." Oscar and Helen Domke pose before grubbing out this stump. (O. Domke family photo)

Spruce, hemlock, fir and pine were harvested for lumber. Cottonwood and birch were used to make airplanes by the National Defense Department during World War II.

The most valued and main timber logged in the Twelve Mile area, however, was cedar. Dried and charred cedar butts and stumps were used for shingles, shakes and brewery wood. Gordon Weston built up a large shingle mill powered by the electricity he generated from nearby Mulvehill Creek. Cedar can be either sawed or split and has many uses. It can be straight-split into boards, fence rails, fence posts, shakes and shingles. Clear cedar lumber has been and still is in demand for building homes and ships.

Cedar, however, was most commonly cut, peeled and trimmed into telephone and power poles. The Cranberry Creek area was considered to have the best stand of pole timber in the Province. Poles had to be treated with a preservative before going on market. Arrowhead Wood Preservers (AWP) had a plant at the Arrowhead pole yard that was used by CRT. In 1946 AWP opened up a new wood treatment plant in Revelstoke. The January 30, 1947 *Revelstoke Review* summarized manager of AWP, Wallace Johnston's, interesting description of the plant as follows:

Load of cord wood, ready for market. (O. Domke family photo)

Revelstoke has the only wood treating plant in Canada using the solution known as pentichloral phenol…the facility being the most modern yet developed for wood preserving purposes. Poles treated that way were first used in swampy ground in Florida, have withstood the bacteria without any signs of deterioration. There are only five plants in the United States and the one in Revelstoke is the only one of its kind in Canada . . . there are seventy different sizes in piles in the yard. Each pole is branded with the name of the concern purchasing it as well as with the stamp of Arrowhead Wood Preservers, Ltd. A large perforating machine similar to a six-cylinder motor without the crank case goes into operation before the poles are bundled and lifted by a huge crane into the steel treating tank which is eight feet deep, eighty-five feet long and eleven feet wide. Oil burners are used to heat the six furnaces used and ducts lead to the fans. Two storage tanks for the raw oil are also located on the premises. When the poles are hot, cold oil is poured into the tank, contracting the wood cells and drawing in the oil. Only an eighth of an inch penetration is necessary to enable the oil to gradually seep through the wood. Only a small trace is needed to provide immunity to bacteria. During the first three weeks in January, the plant treated thirty carloads of poles.

Ruth and John Rauchert by their first logging truck and Essex car, soon after arriving at their new Twelve Mile home. (J. Rauchert family photo)

Load of poles heading down hill. (O. Astra photo)

Truck load of poles, crossing on ferry going east, 1967. (Weston family photo)

Load of logs crossing Mulvehill Creek on Weston's steel-girded bridge. (Weston family photo)

WEATHER DEPENDENT

The logistics of the timber industry is weather dependent, and was especially so before the advent of modern equipment. When the snowfall reaches building eaves, it takes time and ingenuity to move equipment to a work site. Rod Luschnat experienced this when he tried to move his caterpillar out of Oscar Domke's shed. But first he had to start it. So he could plow the snow and get to his job, for several days he and the boys put a pan of lighted diesel under the motor and cranked the flywheel a quarter turn at a time, went to lunch, returned and cranked some more. This went on for what seemed like days before the cat started. It wasn't unusual for logging camps to close for the winter, leaving employees without work for several months, and in dry autumn seasons, the woods were closed to logging to prevent forest fires.

HAZARDS

The timber industry is hazardous. When a loose branch hangs up in a tree, it is known as a "widow maker" for it can become dislodged and crash onto a faller's head. Asaph Domke escaped at least one of these events and came home with bruises on his head. He also suffered broken ribs when a log rolled over him. John Rauchert and Joe Kozek each landed in Queen Victoria Hospital with back injuries.

Another time Joe's truck caught on a tree, and when he bent over to remove it a chain reaction trapped him under a larger tree.

When Ronnie Dedosenco was just 16 years old he was driving one of W. Durrant's heavily-loaded logging trucks on the Big Bend highway. On October 21, 1957, the *Revelstoke Review* reported his accident:

[It] failed to make the turn and plunged through the wooden guard rail into the gorge 100 feet below.

The driver was pinned inside the cab, which was completely covered by logs. The cab was squashed practically together and it seemed impossible that the occupant could still be alive.

It went on to tell how a tourist who was a nurse crawled under the logs and administered "K" (potassium). Then a nurse from Revelstoke arrived with morphine,

> . . . as hours must elapse before Dedosenco could be freed. . . . She crawled down a bank and walked over the logs to administer drugs to the unconscious driver. The difficulties encountered were accentuated by the darkness and in a heavy downpour of cold rain.

Lorance Toebosch* came from 29 Mile with a power saw when it was discovered the logs would have to be cut into smaller lengths to facilitate their removal. The wrecker pulled the logs off the cab...

Then hacksaw and crowbar were necessary to free Dedosenco from the wreckage. It was a tedious, painstaking task as the man had his arm through the steering wheel and could not move. When the steering wheel was cut away it was found his leg could not be freed so his shoe was cut off. But finally he was removed, miraculously alive, and rushed to Queen Victoria Hospital.

The following day he was in "fairly good condition."

*Coincidentally, Larry Toebosch was Helen Mobley's husband.

By the early 1950s, hard hats became required safety equipment and were introduced by Celgar.

Sergei Astrahantseff hauled logs for Walter Kozek and one morning he couldn't start the loader because a porcupine ate off the fuel lines. Walter tells more porcupine stories:

> He ate the fan belts off the bulldozer, chewed the wiring, copper, the seats, just the nails left. Hirum Creek up the Jordan. We had guards around the cat. We got an electric fencer, put chicken wire on the road, dry gravel, so no shock, put old rubber truck tires over the wire and drive the cat on the tires. Then hooked a live wire from the cat batteries to the electric fencer sitting on the seat. So when the porcupine touched the cat he was grounded, kept them away. But once Sergei got up there after the weekend, someone stole the fencer and drove the cat up the road a couple of miles, the porcupine ate the fan belts. You have to move the radiator, take the hydraulic pump off, disconnect all the oil lines, then put the belts in. But they aren't available, had to order them and wait.

Ben Domke, Oscar Knoblauch and Dick Renneberg logged together. Once when they had to move their cat across the river from above Mulvehill Falls but couldn't cross the corner of Nipper's property to get to the ferry, they improvised. Luckily the water was low that winter so they boated across first and tested the depth with a stake. (It wasn't customary to use life jackets in those days). As he drove the cat across the river, Ben says he

> . . . stood on the seat steering the thing. The air intake was high. I put the cat in high gear and squared the blade against the water. That left kind of a space around the motor. When I got to the deep spot, I gunned it and the water was swirling. I think I turned too fast and it made me dizzy. I made it across and met Oscar and Dick who had already crossed in the boat. We had to get a fire going right away to warm up and dry out.

FINAL DAYS

When BC Hydro contracted with Celgar to clear the reservoir of timber before building Mica Dam, the river waters in Twelve Mile buzzed with activity as log booms were towed to Castlegar. At times it was tricky for the ferry to time its crossing to avoid the bundles and booms of logs tugged and towed by tugboats and river boats.

New Highway 23 built high above the river on the west side in the late 1960s after the Twelve Milers moved out, now makes access to modern logging roads a breeze compared to "the old days."

Chapter 6

UTILITIES

*Recycling was a necessary
way of life.*

In modern times utility services are conveniences taken for granted, but in the early days country folk had to provide for their own utility needs.

THE MAIL

Mail delivery was provided by the CPR under contract from the government. The mail came one to three times a week, depending on the train schedule. A tall hook was installed between the railway tracks and the tiny station. Incoming and outgoing mail in canvas bags was placed and picked up there by the conductor. It was John Kelly's job around 1930 to leave and pick up the mail. In 1945 the train delivered mail Wednesdays and Saturdays but on Mondays James Cancelliere's bus carried it. It was sorted into named, unlocked, open pigeon-holes in the school's cloakroom. Since the pigeon - holes were not secure and mail was highly valued, the Domkes and a few others chose to rent postal boxes in Revelstoke and pick up their mail whenever they went to town. In 1945 Twelve Milers petitioned the Director of Postal Services for a post office, stating it would be justified since it was an important community on the CPR branch-line to Arrowhead. Nothing ever came of their request.

WATER

When settlers built their homes, they wanted them as close to a creek as safely possible. Otherwise, they had to dig a well that was no easy feat without modern equipment. With homes located deep in the valley, there was not enough wind on a regular basis to make use of windmills, so water had to be drawn or pumped up from wells, or carried from creeks. Eventually, some folks plumbed their homes with gravity-fed systems, and a few homes had hand pumps inside their kitchens.

ELECTRICITY

One of the objectives of the BC Power Commission in Victoria was to facilitate rural electrification throughout the province. As early as 1941, the Farmers' Institute requested electricity for its members south of Revelstoke. When Revelstoke began its Walter Hardman dam project south of Twelve Mile, taking water from Cranberry Creek, the Farmers' Institute in 1950 again requested that power be provided to residents from Revelstoke to Twelve Mile. After numerous meetings and letters between the City and the Commission over a two-year period, an agreement was not reached. The Commission offered to pay for the construction of the power line and lease it to the City. The City was to maintain it, read meters and receive all revenues from the sale of the energy, but it did not feel it was economically feasible to do this. Neither did the Commission want to take it on, feeling it would be a financial risk.

The power line right-of-way was slashed through private properties along the way. The settlers could only look resentfully at the power lines passing their homes while lighting their kerosene and Aladdan gas lamps with fragile mantels, and foregoing all the other conveniences electricity could have provided. Helen Domke, Lena Kaduhr and Tiny Rauchert eventually got propane stoves—a real step up for the ladies. A few folks put in their own power generators.

RUBBISH

Since most foods were canned in reusable glass jars and most people used fresh milk, there were very few food containers to dispose of. Food bought in cans was necessary, however, to backpack or transport to logging camps. That is where most of the garbage dumps were formed. Anyone with animals had ready-made disposals for food scraps.

RECYCLING

Recycling could have been invented in places such as Twelve Mile. Being short of cash and transportation, people frugally saved anything that could be put to use in the future. Enamel cookware easily chipped and then started leaking, so even those were repaired with metal rivets or rag plugs. Gift wrap and ribbon was easily ironed and reused; rags were braided or crocheted into rugs or sewn into quilts; calendar pictures and metallic candy bar wrappers were incorporated into custom-made greeting cards; flour sacks were sewn into dresses, aprons, tea towels, or underwear; hay wire, rope and twine were the "duck tape" of their day. Salvaged windows, doors and lumber were purchased from Needham's to build homes. The Arrowhead Hotel discarded dishes that ended up in kitchens. Bent nails were straightened and reused. Bones from butchered animals were made into headcheese and soap. Rubber boots and tire inner tubes were patched with special kits. Hand-me-down clothing was altered and re-worn, sewn into blankets, and woven into rugs.

TELEPHONE

Telephones were a boon to isolated communities. The first phones in Twelve Mile were not in people's homes. The government initially installed three wooden wall telephones, one inside the ferry house, one on its porch and the third on the west bank supply shed. That was just about the time B.C. Telephone and the Alberta government established an all-Canadian telephone system in 1928 between Vancouver and Calgary without going through the United States. Repeating stations were at Kamloops and Glacier.

In 1951 Okanagan Telephone Company provided radio dial phone service through Twelve Mile to Arrowhead. It was the first company to install rotary phones in the province. The caller dialed the operator who answered, "Central," and asked for the name or number with which to be connected. Being a "party line," conversations were never private. News traveled fast that way!

Wall telephone with bell earpiece. (A. Jarvis photo)

BATHROOM

Without indoor plumbing, galvanized washtubs were useful items, not only for laundry and steam baths, but also for weekly family bathing. A few families had separate bathhouses behind the house, but most used the kitchen, next to the stove where the water was heated in large buckets or boilers. During the rest of the week, one took "sponge baths" at the enamel basin on the washstand in the kitchen or on the porch. There were always "thunder buckets" next to the beds for nighttime and cold weather emergencies. No one wanted the job of emptying "the pot" in the morning. Outhouse lore and legends abound. Everybody had a little trail to a one- or two-holer out back that had to be used regardless of the weather. Evelyn Domke reminisces about this topic:

Our "john" was a two-holer on the end of the woodshed. In the winter we used a long stick to knock down the frozen "material" in the "hole". The paper was courtesy of *T. Eatons, Simpsons* and the *Free Press Weekly and Prairie Farmer* newspaper. Or sometimes we recycled the tissue paper that Mandarin oranges came wrapped in. We "sweetened" it up a bit by tossing some chloride of lime down the hole and we hung up one of those sticky fly strips by the window.

Her brother, Ben Domke, continues: "Every spring it was my job to clean it out. I opened up the back and dragged out the full box and dumped it in the bush. One time the horses pulled it too fast and over the bumpy ground the box fell apart. The contents went flying everywhere!"

THE HOUSE BEHIND THE HOUSE

One of my fondest memories
As I recall the days of yore
Was the little house, behind the house,
With the crescent o'er the door.

'Twas a place to sit and ponder
With your head all bowed down low;
Knowing that you wouldn't be there,
If you didn't have to go.

Ours was a multi-holer, three,
With a size for every one.
You left there feeling better,
After your job was done.

You had to make those frequent trips
In snow, rain, sleet, or fog—
To that little house where you usually
Found the Sears-Roebuck catalog.

Oft times in dead of winter,
The seat was spread with snow.
'Twas then with much reluctance,
To that little house you'd go.

With a swish you'd clear that wooden seat,
Bend low, with dreadful fear
You'd shut your eyes and grit your teeth
As you settled on your rear.

I recall the day Ol' Granddad,
Who stayed with us one summer,
Made a trip out to that little house
Which proved to be a bummer.

'Twas the same day that my Dad had
Finished painting the kitchen green.
He'd just cleaned up the mess he'd made
With rags and gasoline.

He tossed the rags down in the hole
Went on his usual way
Not knowing that by doing so
He'd eventually rue the day.

Now Granddad had an urgent call!
I never will forget!
This trip he made to the little house
Stays in my memory yet.

He sat down on the wooden seat,
With both feet on the floor.
He filled his pipe and tapped it down
And struck a match on the outhouse door.

He lit the pipe and sure enough,
It soon began to glow.
He slowly raised his rear a bit
And tossed the flaming match below.

The Blast that followed, I am told
Was heard for miles around;
And there was poor ol' Granddad
Sprawled out there on the ground.

The smoldering pipe still in his mouth,
His eyes were shut real tight;
The celebrated three-holer
Was blown clear out of sight.

We asked him what had happened,
What he said I'll ne'er forget.
He said he thought it must have been
The pinto beans he et!

Next day we had a new one
Dad put it up with ease.
But this one had a door sign
That read: No Smoking, Please!

Now that's the story's end my friend,
Of memories long ago,
When we went to the house behind the house,
Because we had to go.

--Author Unknow

Chapter 7

HOUSEKEEPING

A man's work goes from sun to sun,
But a woman's work is never done.

Tough determination is what it took to keep a country household running. Chores were many and varied, indoors and out, and the amount of skill, knowledge and time management necessary is incomprehensible by today's standards. Domestic engineer, homemaker, or call her what you will, the lady of the house wore many hats: wife, mother, housekeeper, child care provider, janitor, gardener, milk maid, tutor, wood cutter, seamstress, barber, beautician, laundress, photographer, secretary, snow shoveler, animal husbandman, butcher, painter, nurse. She knew how to cook, bake, can and dry foods. She made cheeses and churned butter. She carried water from the creek, pump or well to keep her household running.

There were no ATMs on the way to the store—there were no stores in Twelve Mile. A homemaker had to plan ahead, order supplies from catalogues and from town (Revelstoke or Arrowhead). Sometimes she didn't get to town for weeks, and when she did, her list was frugally made and the supplies "charged" at the store and paid for whenever the family got some money.

A woman's day began at dawn or before. She started the fire in the kitchen wood stove and put the water kettle on to heat. A quick brush through her hair and sponge bath at the washstand, and she was off to milk the cows and feed the other animals. Then the milk had to be separated into cream and skimmed milk and the utensils sterilized. Now it was time to cook breakfast: a large pot of oatmeal (porridge) served with fresh cream or milk, bacon and eggs, toast from homemade bread, pancakes, and coffee or tea. Pancake syrup was easily made by boiling together brown sugar, butter and water until syrupy.

Helen Domke cutting firewood with chain saw. (O. Domke family photo)

No automatic dishwashers here! Everyone used a dishpan, placed on the oilcloth –covered kitchen table, where the dishes were washed, dried and put away in the small dish cupboard. Nearby flowers were watered with the dishwater, or sometimes the pigs were lucky enough to get it mixed with their food.

Only winter gave a reprieve from gardening. Planting, weeding, harvesting and preserving kept everyone busy—adults and children alike. Sorry the lady who hadn't planned ahead to buy enough sugar, salt, jar lids or rubber rings for canning.

Canning during summer was an ongoing job as fruits and vegetables matured. Shelling peas and cutting corn off cobs became time-consuming family affairs in preparation for canning. It took about three hours to process peas, green beans and corn in large oblong brass or copper boilers.

Conversation among the ladies always included the number of jars of fruits, jams, vegetables and meats they had "put up." They proudly showed off their shelves of colorful strawberries, raspberries, plums, applesauce, gooseberries, rhubarb, beans, peas, corn, beef, pork, poultry, and dill and sweet pickles. Large pottery crocks were full of preserved kraut.

Cabbage slicer for making sauerkraut. (A. Jarvis photo)

Foods were also preserved by smoking and drying. Apples were peeled and strung on strong string (from flour sacks) and hung behind the wood stove to dry. In the winter they could be eaten dry or cooked into applesauce. Homemade sausages were strung up in the smokehouse to cure.

Without electricity there were no vacuum cleaners, so brooms and mops did the job. Rugs had to be shaken outside.

In the spring, many ladies applied a fresh layer of paint or light green or white kalsomine to the inside walls, and had the boys mix up a vat of whitewash to paint on the inside of the henhouse as well as fruit tree trunks.

During her "spare" time, the homemaker polished the heater and stove with black stove polish; knitted, mended and sewed clothing and blankets for her family; helped with the haying and homework.

She did some fun things like crocheting and embroidering doilies, pillow cases and dresser scarves. She included the family in making homemade root beer, ice cream or candy. An easy treat was homemade fudge made out of brown sugar cooked with fresh cream.

If the family did not have a hand-turned ice cream maker, they improvised. They placed a bowl with ingredients into a shallow hole in the snow and packed coarse salt and snow

Kellina Domke checking her crock of sauerkraut. (E. Domke photo)

around it. Then they spent a lot of time whipping it with a hand-turned egg beater until thickened. Children had fun taking turns beating it, all the while thinking of the yummy end results.

When haying on hot summer days, the farmers looked forward to breaks with homemade root beer that was chilled in the creek or cool milk room. Making root beer was a summer tradition for some families. It could be capped in bottles or stored in fruit jars. The containers had to be positioned horizontally in a warm place for a few days to begin "working." When the handiest warm area was behind the stove or under the bed and a weak seal broke, the explosion was quite a syrupy mess to clean up! After it began to get fizzy, the bottles were stored in a cool place. The joke was, if it was really strong, it must have come from "way up the creek."

Polly Astrahantseff weaving rag rug on hand-made loom. (Astrahantseff family photo)

The ladies were barbers and even gave each other and their daughters home permanents, like "Toni."

LAUNDRY DAY

Lucky the lady who had a gas-powered washing machine. The Beatty had a pedal on the side. With a few quick, firm steps onto the pedal, the motor started with a putt-putt and the fun began.

In preparation for washday, whether done by machine, or by hand with a washboard and galvanized tub, most people hauled water in buckets from a pump or creek to be heated in large pots either on the kitchen stove or over outdoor wood fires.

Laundry soap was purchased in bars or soap flakes, or homemade. Soap was made out of tallow and lye or wood ash. Those who could afford it, bought lye in a can such as Gillett's Flake Lye with full instructions for soap making. When the lye was poured into the vat of tallow, it bubbled up like a geyser. After it was boiled down to a thick paste, it was poured into flat pans,

Polly Astrahantseff with team of horses ready for field work.(Astrahantseff family photo)

hardened, then cut into hand-sized bars. Carolyn Rauchert recalls the time she and her sister, Kathy, discovered laundry soap in the making at Polly Astrahantseff's. When taking a break from picking raspberries, they explored the farm yard and "if we were really lucky, we would come across a fire with a large vat of bones and fat rendering down for laundry soap. We would poke at it with sharp sticks."

Rubbing the clothing on a washboard was a real knuckle scraper. It is no wonder women had rheumatism early on, since the wash went on regardless of the weather. To keep whites really white, they were boiled in large pots, stirred and lifted out with a broom handle.

Rinsing the soap out was usually done in tepid or cold water to decrease the scum. Then the wringing began. Some folks had portable wringers that screwed onto the edge of the tub. These were made of two rubber rollers about three inches in diameter and about eighteen inches long, stacked together. When the edge of a piece of clothing was placed in the crack where the rollers met, a handle on the side was hand turned to feed the clothing through the wringers and drop into a tub on the other side. The motorized washing machines came with the wringers already attached and could be activated with a switch. Wringing was a two-step operation, one to squeeze out the suds, and the second to squeeze out the rinse water. Almost everyone knew of someone who had fingers or even a hand squeezed through the wringer. Evelyn Domke caught her hand in their Beatty wringer, but luckily she quickly found and hit the lever at the end of the wringers to release

Washday at the Domkes, with Mt. Cartier in background. Ben Domke stirring up a batch of whitewash to paint the walls inside the hen house. (O. Domke family photo)

it. Sometimes bluing was added to the rinse water of whites. It came in bottles or little cakes twisted and tied in a piece of cloth to be swished around in the rinse water.

Clotheslines were about as varied as the laundry they held. The simplest was a rail or picket fence, usually used to dry work pants on. Some lines were galvanized wires strung between two posts. The more elaborate ones were made of two pulleys mounted on tall posts quite a distance apart, with clothesline wire strung through in a continuous piece. As the clothes were fastened on with wooden clothespins, the top wire was pulled, thus sending the filled bottom line toward the opposite post. There is nothing like the scent of breeze-dried clothing, notwithstanding the abrasive nature of sun-dried towels. Weather isn't controllable, so on rainy or snowy days, the ladies had to come up with creative drying methods. It could be hung in small batches on lines strung across the porch or inside the house. Some even had large wooden frames strung with about five lines that could be pulled up to the ceiling on small pulleys. The children had fun using the sheets hung from these ceiling lines for theater drapes as they performed ad lib. In the winter, it was common for the laundry to freeze on the line. This was indeed the early form of freeze-drying. Frozen shirts looked like headless men as they were taken into the house.

Wrinkle-free wasn't in the vocabulary in those days. Irons were lined up on the wood-burning stove like docked boats preparing to sail. When hot enough, a wooden handle was clipped onto the first one and ironing began. Some homes had real ironing boards while others improvised with a pad of sheets over the kitchen table. If starch had been used, the irons had to be just the right temperature to prevent scorching and sticking. It took experience and coordination to keep the stove stoked so the irons stayed hot enough to do their job, and not too hot which could scorch fabrics.

One anonymous country woman described her washday as follows:

Bild fire in backyard to heet kettle of rane water.
Set tubs so smoak won't blow in eyes if wind is pert.
Shave one hole cake lie sope in bilin water.
Sort things. Make 3 piles. 1 pile white, 1 pile cullerd, 1 pile werk britches and rags.
Stur flowr in cold water to smooth, then thin down with bilin water.
Rub durty spots on bored, scrub hard. Then bile. Rub cullered but don't bile, Just rench and starch.
Take white things out of kettle with broom handle. Rench, blew and starch.
Spred tee towels on grass.
Hang old rags on fence.
Pore rench water in flower bed.
Scrub porch with hot, sopey water.
Turn tubs upside down.
Go put on cleen dress…smooth hair with side combs. Brew cup of tee. Set and rest and rock a spell and COUNT BLESSINGS.

And those are called "the good old days!"

COOKING AND BAKING

Wood stoves had to be stoked to just the right temperatures necessary for cooking and baking. A large teakettle full of hot or boiling water was kept on each stove, always handy for any recipe, for dishwashing, or hand washing.

The lack of electrical appliances didn't stop the ladies from putting together some great recipes. Imagine the energy it took to whip cream or egg whites for angel food cake or divinity fudge, with only a manual eggbeater.

Unfortunately for their surviving families, many favourite recipes were stored in the cooks' heads and not on recipe cards. Therefore, some are lost forever. Polly Astrahantseff was an excellent cook, but none were preserved.

Included below are a few family recipes that did survive on paper or from memory.

DILL PICKLES

8 cups	cool water
2 ½ cups	vinegar
½ cup	salt
½ cup	sugar
5 heads	fresh dill
15 cloves	garlic

Boil the water, vinegar, salt and sugar. Arrange washed cucumbers in sterilized jars, placing a head of dill and about three cloves of garlic in each jar. Pour boiling brine over cukes in jars. To seal, place jars in a boiler of boiling water, but remove from heat (don't boil jars). Let stand until cukes turn yellow in jars. Watch closely. Above brine makes 5 quarts of dills.

--Joanna Zibulak-Makarewicz

--Olga Kramer-Bernard

SWEET PICKLES

3 quarts	small cucumbers, scrubbed, thinly sliced
3 cups	onions, thinly sliced
2 medium	green peppers, sliced
1 sweet	red pepper, sliced (can substitute cauliflower for peppers)
½ cup	coarse pickling salt
4 cups	white sugar
4 cups	white vinegar
2 tsp	turmeric
2 tsp	mustard seed
1 tsp	celery seed

Combine cucumbers, onions, peppers and salt. Cover and let stand 12 hours (or add 2 trays ice cubes and let stand 3 hours). Drain well. Combine the remainder of ingredients in large saucepan, bring to boil. Add drained vegetables to liquid and return to full boil. Pack vegetables into hot sterilized jars and cover with hot brine. Seal. Yields 6 pints.

--Ruth Rauchert

SAUERKRAUT

Finely shred fresh cabbage. Thoroughly mix with salt. Fill large crock with mixture and pound down well with a tamper (large wooden spoon) until brine surfaces. Be sure cabbage is completely submerged in its own juices. Cover with piece of floursack or cheesecloth. Add a china plate and weigh it down with a heavy stone. Allow to ripen in a cool area for about three to four weeks. Optional: Intersperse apples into the cabbage after pounding kraut. Sour apples are a gourmet treat in the middle of the winter.

--Evelyn Domke-Riegert

DILLY GREEN BEANS

2 ½ cups	water
2 ½ cups	vinegar
¼ cup	coarse salt

Bring brine to boil. Sterilize jars and lids and fill with green beans, add to each jar

1 toe	garlic
1 head	dill
¼ tsp	cayenne pepper (or 1 ½ hot peppers from dry spices)

Pour boiling brine into each jar and seal tight. Put jars in hot water bath and bring to simmer for 10 minutes.

--Mabel Horsley

POTATO PANCAKES

4 large	potatoes
1 small	yellow onion
1 large	egg
2 Tbsp	flour
1 tsp	salt
¼ tsp	pepper
vegetable oil	
sour cream	

Peel and coarsely grate potatoes and onion. Stir in egg, flour, salt and pepper. Drop batter by spoonful into hot oil and fry until golden brown on each side, about 12 minutes. Drain well and serve warm with salted sour cream. (Hint: a bit of lemon juice on the grated potatoes will keep them from discolouring.)

--Ruth Rauchert

RUSSIAN BORSCH

3 large	beets with tops
1 large	potato, diced
2 medium	carrots, chopped
½ large head	cabbage, shredded
1 large	onion, chopped
1 can	butter beans
3-4 toes	garlic
2-3 heads	fresh dill, or 2 Tbsp dill seed, wrapped in cheese cloth
1 quart	canned tomatoes, chopped
butter	
salt, pepper	

Wash, trim and cube beets. Wash green tops and finely chop. In skillet, sauté in butter the onions, beets, garlic and tomatoes. Boil potatoes, carrots, cabbage, butter beans, salt and pepper in about 8 quarts water. Add the skillet mixture and the dill. Cook until all vegetables are tender. Remove dill. This soup always tastes better after it seasons for several hours or over night. Part of the liquid used can be turkey stock. Serve with a dollop of sour cream in each bowl.

(I constructed this recipe based on memory of my mother, *Kellina Domke*'s, borsch since her recipe was not written down. —*Ada Domke Jarvis*)

VARENIKI

4 cups	flour
1 Tbsp	shortening or oil
1 large	egg
cool water	
¼ tsp	baking powder
1 tsp	salt

Mix together the flour, baking powder and salt in large bowl and make a well in its center. Drop the egg and shortening into well. Stir with fork or hands, pulling flour in from sides. Gradually stir in cool water. Knead dough into medium firm ball. Let dough rest for one hour. Begin heating large kettle of water while forming vareniki.

Roll out dough about ¼ inch thick. Cut into 4-inch squares. In center of each square, place 2-3 tablespoons of filling. Fold over corner-to-corner forming triangles and pinch edges well. Use a bit of water if necessary to make the edges stick together. Drop carefully into boiling water. Bring to full boil, stir gently. When they float, remove with slotted spoon and drain in colander. Rinse with cold water to prevent sticking. Serve warm with sour or sweet cream.

Fillings:

Cottage Cheese. Wring out liquid or purchase dry cottage cheese to make 3 cups. Add 2 large eggs and salt. Mix well.

Sauerkraut. Drain, chop and sauté sauerkraut and chopped onions in butter or oil.

Potato. Peel, boil and mash potatoes. Add 1 egg, salt, pepper, minced garlic and sautéed onion.

Huckleberry. For each vareniki, use about 2 teaspoons berries, 1-2 tablespoons sugar and ½ teaspoon flour. Serve these with sweet cream.

--Helen Domke

BLINTZES

Pancakes:

2 large	eggs
1 cup	milk
salt	
¾ cup	flour

Beat together into a smooth batter. Pour about 1/4-1/2 cup batter into skillet of hot shortening. Brown both sides.

Filling:

2-3 cups	cottage cheese
1 large	egg
2 tsp	sugar
vanilla	

Mix filling ingredients together.

Spread filling over each pancake and roll up. Serve hot with sour cream. OR, place rolled pancakes in baking pan. Cover with sour cream and bake until sour cream bubbles and browns around edges.

--Kellina Domke

PADLIFKA

Saute´ chopped tomatoes and chopped onions. Add sour cream and flour. Heat until smooth, bubbly and thick. Serve warm as a sauce or dip.

--Gregory Astrahantseff (as remembered by Walter Kozek)

GOLUPTSY (PR. HOLOPSI) CABBAGE ROLLS

1 cup	uncooked rice
¼ cup	butter
Salt	to taste
Pepper	to taste
1 small-med.	head cabbage
1 cup	tomato juice or water
More	butter
3-4 quarts	boiling water in large kettle, kept at low boil

Cook rice until par done. Add and combine salt, pepper and butter. Set aside to cool.

Remove core from cabbage. Immerse whole head in boiling water for 2-3 minutes. Carefully remove into a sieve or pan. Remove blanched or wilted outer leaves until firm leaves are reached. Then repeat wilting process in boiling water until all cabbage leaves have been blanched. Trim thick part of large leaves to make flat. Place 2 tablespoons of seasoned rice into bottom of each cabbage leaf. Fold ends toward center, then roll up to top to make bundle. Place in small roasting pan or baking dish. Leaves from center of cabbage that are too small to roll can be placed in bottom of pan or reserved to cover top of cabbage rolls. Pour tomato juice or water over and dot with additional butter. Cover with lid.

Bake in hot oven (350° F.) about one hour. Test doneness with fork. Cabbage rolls should be soft but not overdone. Remove from oven and set cover ajar to let steam escape a bit to prevent development of a strong flavor.

Options: Many farm ladies added bacon, ground beef or sautéd onions to rice before rolling.

--Helen Domke (as remembered by daughter, Evelyn)

HEAD CHEESE (HOLODETS)

4 pork hocks, cleaned up. Boil about 1 hour. Remove from water and rinse. Wash pot. Return hocks to pot and cover with water. Boil about 2 ½ hours until meat starts flaking off bones. Remove bones.

To hot liquid, add 3 bay leaves, salt (a little extra to absorb into meat) and pepper. Sprinkle of chile pepper and 1 ½ head crushed garlic. Stir well.

Remove meat from bones. Grind or chop fine. Add to liquid. Cool in pot. Pour into flat cake pan. When it gels, cut into squares. Yields about 4-5 quarts.

--Sophie Shamon-Vigue and son Rick Vigue

CHEESE

1 gallon	whole or partially skimmed milk
½ cup	vinegar
1 tsp	salt

Heat milk to 190 °F (turn off heat before it boils). Add vinegar. Cool. It turns into curds and whey. Drain in cheese cloth. Place curds in bowl and salt it. This cheese is made without the usual Rennet, an enzyme that produces harder curds.

--Kellina Domke

POTATO SOUP

8 slices	bacon, diced
1 cup	onion, chopped
4 medium	potatoes, diced
2-3 cups	water
1 tsp	salt
1 tsp	pepper
10-oz can	cream of chicken soup
1 cup	sour cream
1 ½ cups	milk

Cook potatoes, water, salt and pepper. Fry bacon until brown. Add onion and sauté until tender. Drain fat. Add to potato mixture. When potatoes are cooked, reduce heat. Add chicken soup, sour cream and milk. Heat but don't boil. (Doesn't freeze well.)

--Helen Mobley-Toebosch

EASTER BREAD

2 pkg.	dry yeast
½ cup	lukewarm water
1 Tbsp	sugar
3 medium	eggs
touch of	salt
½ cup	butter, melted
½ cup	sugar
¾ cup	milk
¾ cup	water
6-7 cups	flour
2 cups	raisins

Dissolve yeast in ½ cup lukewarm water. Put raisins in bowl and cover with hot water.

For dough: Into yeast, stir in ¾ cup milk, ¾ cup water, sugar, salt, eggs and 3 cups flour. Add drained raisins and remaining flour to the mixture. Knead well. Let rise until double in size. Knead down once. Take one large piece of dough for bottom, medium piece for middle, small piece for top. Place in pie plate. Let it rise. Bake at 350° F. until done. After it is baked, spread melted butter over top.

--Tiny Ocepoff-Rauchert

LENA'S BREAD

When Hickie and Lena Kaduhr found it difficult to buy bread before 1941 during the Depression, he found a bread recipe in one of the Vancouver newspapers and clipped it out for Lena. Over the years, she modified it and shared it with friends. She continued to use the recipe until she passed away.

2 cups	scalded milk
¼ cup	sugar
2 Tbsp	salt
¼ cup	shortening
1 ½ cups	cold water
2 pkg	dehydrated yeast
½ cup	lukewarm water
11-12 cups	sifted all-purpose flour

Combine scalded milk, sugar, salt and shortening. Add 1 ½ cups cold water. Soften yeast in ½ cup lukewarm water in which 1 tsp has already been dissolved. When foamy, add to lukewarm water-milk mixture. Blend in flour. Knead until smooth. Place in greased bowl. Place in warm area covered with towel. Let rise until double in bulk, about 1 ½ hours. Punch dough down by plunging fist in center. Fold edges toward center and turn upside down in bowl. Cover and let rise ½ to ¾ hour. Place dough on floured board. Cut off pieces to fit loaf pans. Shape. Place in greased pans and let rise until pans fill. The dough may be formed into buns also.

Bake at 350° F. for about 45 minutes.

--Lena Kaduhr

EASTER EGGS

To dye Easter eggs with onion skins:

Boil brown or purple onion skins.

Boil eggs with onion skins.

Remove, drain and cool.

--Tiny Ocepoff-Rauchert

BOOLKA

One bread dough recipe.

Fillings: Sauerkraut sautéd with onions, salt and pepper; seasoned cooked rice; and seasoned cottage cheese.

Cut off pieces of bread dough and roll out to about three inches in diameter. Place prepared filling in center. Fold in half and double-pinch edges together. Place in large, greased baking pan with sealed edges down (12 to a pan). Let rise. Bake in hot oven until brown.

--Walter Kozek

BLONDE BROWNIES

1 c. + 2 Tbsp	flour
½ tsp	baking powder
1/8 tsp	baking soda
½ tsp	salt
1/3 cup	butter, melted
1 cup	brown sugar
1 tsp	vanilla
1 medium	egg, slightly beaten
½ cup	nuts
½ cup	chocolate chips

Sift together dry ingredients. Add the rest of the ingredients, except chocolate chips, and mix well. Spread in greased pan. Sprinkle chocolate chips over top and bake at 350° F. for about 30 minutes or lightly firm to touch. Do not overbake.

--Sophie Nipper-Weston

GERMAN CHEESE CAKE

Pastry:

3 ½ Tbsp	butter
4 Tbsp	sugar
1 cup	flour
1 medium	egg
2 tsp	baking powder

Sift together dry ingredients. Cut in butter and add egg. Roll out and line pie plate.

Filling:

1 ½ lb	cottage cheese, quite dry
1 cup	sugar
2 medium	eggs
1 Tbsp	flour
½ cup	raisins
sour cream	
vanilla or nutmeg	

Mash cottage cheese through sieve and moisten with sour cream. Add sugar and well beaten egg yolks, flour, flavoring and raisins. Beat egg whites until stiff and fold in gently. Pour into lined pie plate. Bake about 50 minutes at 350° F. or until firm.

--Kellina Domke

HUCKLEBERRY BREAKFAST PUFF

3 med.	eggs
1 cup	milk
1 cup	flour
½ tsp	salt
1/3 cup	butter
Sprinkle	powdered sugar
1-2 cups	fresh (or frozen) huckleberries
½ cup	sweet cream

Preheat oven to 425° F. Place butter in 11-inch iron skillet and melt in oven. Beat together eggs, milk, flour and salt. Pour batter into hot butter in skillet. Bake 30-35 minutes until puffed up and golden brown. May serve in skillet or remove puff onto round platter. Pour huckleberries into puff, sprinkle with powdered sugar. Serve with cream. (Serves 6).

Option: May substitute huckleberry sauce for fresh berries.

--Ada Domke Jarvis from her book, *Huckleberries for All*, 2nd ed, 2002. Available from Grizzly Books, Revelstoke, B.C., *grizzlybook@telus.net*.

HUCKLEBERRY SAUCE

4 cups	huckleberries* (fresh or frozen)
1 cup	water
¾ cup	granulated sugar
3 Tbsp	corn starch
1/3 cup	cold water

Cook huckleberries with one cup water until soft, but not mushy. Stir in sugar. Stir corn starch into 1/3 cup cold water. Add corn starch mix slowly to huckleberries, stirring and cooking until thick. Remove from heat. This may be served warm or cold over foods of choice, such as ice cream, in cobblers, as pie or puff fillings.

*If using canned berries, add 3-4 Tbsp corn starch to 1/3 cup cold berry juice, stir until smooth. Heat the remainder of the berries and juice and thicken with the corn starch mix.

--Ada Domke Jarvis

Chapter 8

WILD ANIMALS

For the song of bird and hum of bee,
For all things fair we hear or see,
Father in heaven, we thank thee.

Child's Prayer

The Columbia Valley in the Twelve Mile area was blessed with a variety of wild animals, but the most remembered were the bears.

Black bears were common and the fact that they seldom attacked cattle or people didn't make them less scary. Some years there were more than others, depending on the food supply in the mountains. However, black bears caused considerable damage when they climbed trees for fresh fruit, breaking limbs and ruining crops. They also loved clover, eating and rolling in it, thus making it impossible to mow for hay. Raspberry patches were also a favourite. Ada Domke remembers the cold chills in her spine when encountering a black bear head on in the berry patch. She steadily and slowly backed away while maintaining eye contact as it moved slowly toward her. When she felt she was at a safe distance, she turned and ran away, then realized the bear had done the same.

Loggers had to secure their cabins well, or they could come back to a ransacked mess. It was nothing for a bear to claw down the door or enter through the shake roof of a mountain cabin, take a bite out of every can of food, spread the flour, eat the honey, jam and shortening, tip over and smash all the furniture.

It was fairly common to see bears at a distance on the way to school, but one incident in particular was a heart stopper. Ada and Herb were zipping down the Gold Creek hill on their bikes to school when a bear ambled across the road in front of them as they turned the corner. Their only defense was a lot of shouting and fast peddling.

Black bears were trapped for their furs, meat and fat. The meat reportedly tastes like pork. Bear fat was rendered down and used as smelly water proofing on logging boots. Part of black bear lore is the story of trapper Harry Williams. One winter while stranded on his trapline near Jasper, Alberta, he saved his extremities from frostbite by massaging them with bear grease.

Lena Kaduhr feeding her pet bear cub.(Kaduhr family photo)

Having fruit trees and beehives with honey, Bob Brinkman's farm was bear paradise, and interesting stories flowed from Bob. One summer when a bear was feasting on his fruit every day, he set up a stand on the windowsill of his pantry, patiently sited his gun toward his orchard, and surprised Mr. Bear when he arrived. He had a huge bearskin rug on the floor of his upstairs bedroom. Ada was so awestruck by it, she used to sneak upstairs to take a peak at it.

Sometimes, wild animals and birds became family pets. The Kaduhrs raised orphaned twin black bear cubs as their pets. Bruce would take one to town perched on his shoulder. He found this to be quite helpful in attracting girls. It was a sad day when one of the cubs drowned in the barn during a flood and the game warden took the other one away.

Grizzly bears rarely ventured lower than about five thousand feet elevation in those days. John Rauchert had an encounter with a grizzly when logging on Mt. Cartier in 1948. Here is his story:

Hans Podzun with his pet dove.(H. Podzun family photo)

When I came across a grizzly bear, he saw me at once. I was talking to him. He came down on all four feet and down to the road in front of me. Slowly he crossed the road and walked into the bush as if he didn't see me at all. He walked about half a mile to where Astrahantseff was going to skid logs for me. There was a long windfall across the path that Gregory was trying to saw a hole through. He noticed the bear a long ways away. The next time he looked up the bear was on the windfall where he was sawing. He threw down his saw, asked me to bring his tools down the mountain, took his horses and left.

Another animal seldom seen but feared was the cougar. Lucy Banks shot one in 1945 to protect her family while her husband was away. The McLeod girls were warned by their father not to go out in the dark for fear of cougars. John Rauchert recounts the following experience he had with a cougar:

I was walking Twelve Mile Creek on snowshoes, looking for poles and finally I was too high up and there was no timber there so I walked back. I spotted cougar tracks and a place where he had eaten a porcupine, quills and all. It kind of scared me. I thought I had noticed something behind and I listened several times, but I couldn't hear anything. I decided to put a stop to this and made a big circle, coming around to my own tracks. Sure enough, there were cougar tracks on my tracks. I said to myself, If you like my tracks, I'll make lots of them. I watched the trees in front of me in case the cougar tried to head me off. But I never saw him, only the tracks. That was enough for me!

Porcupines generally kept their distance from the farms, but cows did come home with noses full of quills that had to be painfully removed with pliers. They also caused considerable damage to logging equipment left overnight in the bush because they liked to chew the fan belts, hoses and upholstery.

Squirrels and chipmunks were always in competition with humans over wild hazelnuts, mushrooms and berries. Hazelnuts are covered in prickly fur with a long tail. People don't pick them off the bushes until they start turning yellow or brown when the nuts are mature. But the little fellows like them soft, juicy and green, so guess who usually got most of them?

Mice and rats loved to munch on fresh and harvested vegetables, fruits and grains. Rats were easy to catch, however, with a gopher trap that was set below a low-hanging apple.

TRAPPING AND HUNTING

In 1922 the B.C. Legislature announced their pest control plan, offering to pay two cents a gopher tail for the first 250, and three cents for the next 250, according to the *Revelstoke Review* article in April 27, 1922. Some boys made their spending money by trapping or shooting gophers and turning in the tails to the government agent.

Trappers sold mink, marten, muskrat, ermine (weasel), beaver, otter and coyote pelts to fur dealers. Muskrat fur is especially adaptable to take almost any color of dye and is marketed as "Hudson seal," and "leopard skin."

Trappers had a choice of where to sell their pelts. F. B. Wells was a fur broker in Revelstoke's "Lower Town", as was Mackay and Dippie of Calgary. In 1922, A. B. Shubert, Limited

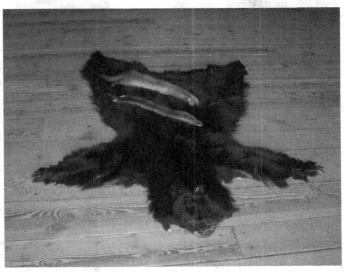

Mink and marten pelts on black bear pelt. (A. Jarvis photo)

of Vancouver that billed itself as "The largest house in the world dealing exclusively in North American raw furs" ran an ad in The *Revelstoke Review*, March 2, 1922 offering highest market value for muskrat and mink pelts. Depending on the time of year, size and color, they paid from $.50 to $5.50 for muskrat pelts, and from $1.75 to $25.00 for mink pelts. Trappers were to contact The Shubert Shipper for other fur prices.

In 1925 the British Columbia Game Board decided that trap lines should be registered in the trapper's name, giving him exclusive rights to certain areas. It was hoped that this system would inspire trappers "to preserve rather than deplete the fur bearing animals. . . and thus save the

River otter pelt. (A. Jarvis photo)

breeding animals." (*Revelstoke Review*, August 26, 1925).

Ed Mulvehill may have been Twelve Mile's first trapper. He sold his furs to F. B. Wells as early as 1914. Robert Brinkman was Twelve Mile's best-known trapper and hunter. He maintained his trap line on the west side of the river in the Cranberry area until he became ill and sold it to Ben Domke for $300. Cecil Banks was also a trapper and hunter. Fur trapping could be a complicated vocation, knowing when, where and how to set and bait specific traps for specific animals, and then knowing how to prepare the pelts for market. Trappers spent many weeks each winter living in little mountain cabins and tramping through the snow to check traps. Hunters and trappers also found a cozy shelter under the long boughs of spruce, hemlock and cedar trees where they could cook and warm up over a small fire. When Ada Domke was planning her wedding, she decided to make her own going-away

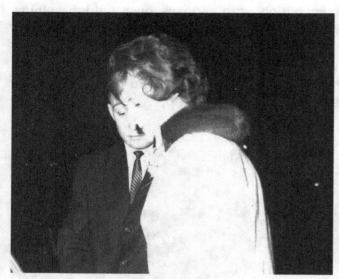

Ada Domke wearing marten collar from animals she and Herb Domke trapped. (A. Jarvis photo)

outfit with a fur collar. She traveled home to Twelve Mile that winter where her cousin, Herb Domke, met her and together they set traps on his brother, Ben's, trapline. They caught three tree martens and had them skinned, tanned and made into a fur collar. Her husband says that he knew he had chosen well when his bride-to-be got out the traps when she wanted fur.

Mountain goats have got to be one of the hardest animals to hunt. They find narrow ledges for their lookouts. It takes skill and time to find them. When Bob Brinkman got one above Blanket Creek in September 1947, it tumbled down a deep ravine, far too steep for Bob to pack it out alone. So he hiked all the way home and talked Asaph Domke into going back with him to help carry out the meat. Needless to say, the men arrived home very late in the dark, and were totally exhausted. In those days, hiking was not a sport but a necessity.

While on one of his hunting trips, Oscar Domke had a heart-stopping experience. He backed into a large, hollow cedar stump to eat his lunch out of the nasty weather. The leaves and moss he sat on began wiggling. He reached back and discovered two tiny bear cubs. Their squeals attracted the mother who came home on the run. Luckily, Oscar had backed into the stump with his rifle pointing outward. Had he not done so he would have been in real trouble because the gun was too long to turn around in the narrow enclosure. He had no choice but to shoot the mama bear that was on the attack. Sadly, he

Cecil Banks with daughter, Dorothy, and son Doug (on sled) with buck. (Banks family photo)

also was forced to dispatch the cubs because they could not survive without their mother.

Very few moose and deer inhabited the farming areas of Twelve Mile but were hunted in the mountains above, or more often in the Big Bend area north of Revelstoke. Hunters also hunted grouse — those the coyotes hadn't gotten.

FISHING

Fishing can conjure up many memories and ideas. As Izaak Walton put it,

Oh the brave Fishers life,
It is the best of any,
'Tis full of pleasure, void of strife,
And 'tis belov'd of many.

In Twelve Mile, the mountain streams flowed out of lakes, over waterfalls and into the Columbia River. That alone provided lake fishing and stream fishing with a pole and line. The river provided opportunities for deeper line fishing, off the banks or from small boats. The catch varied and included rainbow trout, dolly varden, kokanee, ling, carp, and white fish.

After the river floodwaters receded in late spring and early summer, backwaters were left enlarging the existing small, musty-smelling sloughs, and fish became trapped in them. Ambitious farmers and loggers tied strong lines with large hooks to the trees, roots or driftwood along the banks, leaving them overnight. In the morning it was exciting to check these nightlines for carp, white fish or ling. At times, the carp were so numerous in the shallow ponds, fishermen walked into the water with pitchforks and tossed their catch ashore. Gunnysacks were filled with the fish and carried home

Ben Domke with catch of "suckers."
(O. Domke family photo)

over their shoulders, or tossed into their pickups. The slough behind Astrahantseff's was a special fishing hole and playground for their boys and neighbors, Kozeks, Gowanlocks and Kaduhrs. Even the presence of huge bear paw prints left in the mud from an overnight fishing trip, didn't deter them. Twelve Mile Lake (today known as Echo Lake) on Mt. Cartier was a popular fishing spot for the people of Twelve Mile. They often got together with friends from Eight Mile for fishing outings.

When autumn arrived, the kokanee turned red. This species of land-locked salmon fought their way up the small streams in search of sandy spawning areas. Poachers played hide and seek with the game wardens and filled gunny sacks with their catch. This was also a great opportunity for bears to get their fill and put on fat before hibernating.

Eugen Domke trout fishing in Begbie
Lake off Celgar logging road.
(A. Domke family photo)

Blanket Creek was also a favourite fishing spot for locals and neighbors who bicycled across the ferry from Six Mile and Eight Mile. Herb and Ada Domke were five-year-old cousins who fished several times a week below Gold Creek Falls (Sutherland Falls). They cut willow poles with their jack knives and tied string to the ends. Sometimes the hooks were bent safety pins, but on lucky days they used real hooks snitched from their brothers. It was easy to find "rain worms" (earthworms) for bait under rocks and boards around their farm buildings, and they skewered them onto their hooks. Weeks of fishing without results didn't take away from the enjoyment and expectation experienced. Then, one Sunday an unmistakable jerk pulled the line in Herb's hand. Excitement was at an all-time high for the two towheads as they both began pulling in their catch. Wow, a real live rainbow! They landed it on the rocky shore and watched it flip around, fighting the hook and line. They had no clue how to subdue it, never having even watched a fish being caught before. As they held their breath they did it in with rocks, squinting to avoid the whole scene. But it was their first fish, and they proudly carried it home for all to see. To them, this single fish was more valuable than a sack full of kokanee or carp.

Chapter 9

MOSQUITOES

Annoying, whining, blood-sucking insects.

Spring floods assured the continual existence of riverside sloughs where mosquitoes bred and thrived. According to native lore, the Columbia Valley in British Columbia had so many mosquitoes that it was unfit for year-round habitation. The settlers discovered this for themselves and came up with various means of co-existing with the pesky insects. Mosquitoes were never mentioned, of course, in articles by promoters that extolled the attractive park-like resort area south of Revelstoke.

HOW BAD THEY WERE

Mosquitoes crowded on the inside windows, darkening the interiors of barns and other buildings. Their little lives could be snuffed out with oily DDT, sprayed from a hand-pumped can. Then the oil and layers of carcasses were wiped off the windows panes and sills.

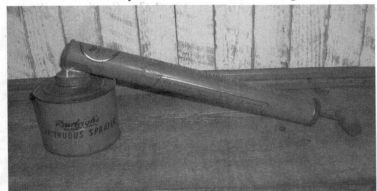

Rawleigh's hand-pumped insect sprayer. (A. Jarvis photo)

Typical mosquito garb. On left, facial net is on hat ready to be pulled over her face. (A. Domke family photo)

Outdoor workers wore neck scarves or bandanas for protection. They also wore long-sleeved shirts and tied their pant legs at their ankles. If the job permitted, netting was draped over hats and faces and tucked into collars. Raspberry and strawberry pickers often wore this special gear. In later years, repellants were available but they irritated skin when worn throughout the day.

Smudge pots gave farm animals some relief. Green grass or weeds were placed on a fire on the ground or in an old bucket to create smelly smoke. Cows and horses blackened by layers of mosquitoes and flies vied for positions near the smudge pots preferring the thick smoke to the dense layers of bugs. Ronnie Dedosenco remembers pouring diesel on the manifold of their truck that created smoke as they drove around the animals to drive away the mosquitoes. Some farmers alternated between swatting them off themselves and their animals with evergreen switches. Or if they brushed them off by hand, it dripped with blood.

To this day, Eugen vividly remembers running to the slough trying to ditch the mosquitoes on his way to fetch the cows for milking. A recurring thought of his was, "What if I fell over a snag and broke a leg. No one would know and when they found me, I would be dead in a shriveled heap with all my blood sucked out."

Mosquito garb while farming. (A. Domke family photo)

The early Twelve-Milers couldn't afford to spray the sloughs with thin fuel oil as volunteers in the Eagle Valley Mosquito League were doing, and the Provincial Government's priorities did not include trying to control the miserable pests. The Farmers' Institute made annual pleas for assistance to control the pests without much cooperation from the province. Finally, in 1948 following the large flood, the Public Works Department of the province began spraying standing water and sloughs on a limited basis. That year, new screens on doors and windows were also installed on the school. The spraying wasn't effective enough however, because the CRT camp at Twelve Mile had to temporarily close on account of mosquitoes. Early on, the Dominion Government Department of Agriculture advocated thoroughly rubbing liberal quantities of the following mixture over hands and face at least once every half hour. Their recipe appearing in the August 12, 1925 *Revelstoke Review* follows:

3 oz. oil of citronella
1 oz spirits of camphor
1 oz oil of tar
¼ oz oil of pennyroyal
4-6 oz castor oil

Those with 75 cents in 1936 could buy a pound of "Insect Powder" from C. R. Macdonald's drug store in Revelstoke. Other products advertised in the *Revelstoke Review* were: "Katol Sticks to burn, 50¢ per box; Katol Powder, 25¢; Skeeter Dig, 25¢ per bottle; Skeeter Fax, 35¢ a tube; Oil of Citronella, 25¢ a bottle." Large, empty baking powder tins with lids worked well as altars on which to burn the powder or sticks. Children took turns carrying the smoking tin from room to room before bedtime. The smoke ascended, effectively dropping its sacrifices and stopping the high-pitched whining. Only then could families crawl out from under their covers and get a decent night's sleep.

When BC Hydro Project cleaned out the valley, including the sloughs and backwaters in the 1960s, the mosquitoes' favorite breeding areas were destroyed which was one of the Project's blessings. For several years there was a noticeable reduction in the insects. But now with the raising and lowering of the reservoir, the pests seem to be returning.

Chapter 10

FIRE

Under control fire is
Our servant and comforter.
Out of control
It becomes our master and destroyer.

W. Jarvis

FOREST FIRES

A series of huge forest fires, from 1922 to 1925 started by loggers burning their rubbish, engulfed the Columbia Valley from north of Revelstoke into the Arrow Lakes area even threatening to wipe out the town of Arrowhead.

The Mike Kozek family took up their farm in Twelve Mile in the spring of 1922 and Walter remembers his parents telling him about an incident that occurred soon after their arrival. The air was filled with blue-grey smoke. It burned eyes, noses and lungs. As the wind came through the valley, it sent large sparks across the river starting a huge fire that burned down the south side of the river as well. Mike sent his wife, Nettie, pregnant with Walter, and 11-year-old daughter, Kate, to stay with a neighbor to the north. Mike stayed behind to protect his barn, but the pungent smoke got the best of him. In desperation, he climbed down the ladder to the bottom of their well. Here he could breathe and here he stayed for more than a day. The scent of the water bubbling up out of the earth against the wooden cribbing was healing to the rawness in his nose, throat and lungs. Afterwards, Nettie treated his burning eyes with tealeaf poultices but they took some time to heal.

Following the huge fire of 1922, the Dominion Forestry Service carved out a nine-mile trail to the top of Mt. Cartier from Eight Mile. A lookout tower was completed in 1923 on the pinnacle of the mountain. It was said to be the highest forestry station in Canada at the time. The viewpoint covered the area north into the Big Bend area and south through Twelve Mile and part way down the Arrow Lakes. It also had a view of the wooded areas east and west. Supplies were winched up with a windlass from the trail end to the cabin, according to a report in the July 5, 1922 *Revelstoke Review*. The trail was constructed well enough that by September 1924 four women hiked it in nine hours. They visited the lookout man, Sam Desimonés, and stayed overnight in the hut on the 9,000-foot mountain. The trail and lookout were well maintained until the Dominion Forestry Service folded about 1928. It then became overgrown and covered with windfalls, said the *Revelstoke Review* of September 19, 1940.

There were other large fires through the years. Most were started by lightning. The blaze on the west side of Blanket Creek above Sutherland Falls took 50 men to control in August 1934. There was another large fire in 1937 during which Ken Millar remembers ash fell like snow.

In those days, private citizens could be conscripted by the Forestry to fight forest fires and men were literally taken off the streets, from the bars and from their farms to do fire duty. Doug Mackey from neighboring Sidmouth remembers the conscripted men were given pack boards. Each included a paper sleeping bag, 3 x 6 canvas ground sheet, dried potatoes, meat, fruit, axe and shovel, totaling about 75 pounds. The men were taken as far as possible in a "crummy" (an enclosed panel truck), and then hiked or boated into the fire. He remembers receiving 25 cents per hour and being required to work from dawn to dark.

In 1945 young people could become Junior Fire Wardens appointed by the Canadian Forestry Association by receiving some training in forestry, signaling and fire reporting methods. Eleven-year-old Russell Gowanlock was appointed Junior Forest Warden for the district for 1951. Eugen Domke remembers taking his training by correspondence, writing a test and receiving his badge to become a Junior Forest Warden. To report fires, they called from the public phones on each side of the ferry.

ARSON

In addition to lightning strikes and out-of-control slash burnings, Twelve Mile had its fair share of arson. Arson is suspected when a number of fires of uncertain origin occur in a short period of time. Several such incidents were reported.

Early on Sunday morning, August 9, 1925, Petrashuk's home was burned. Mike was away fighting forest fires at Sidmouth at the time, and Mary was home with two of their children, escaping the fire with difficulty. The police suspected arson since the fire started outside, there were no fires in the stoves, and footprints were found around the house leading to the road. The family moved into a cabin nearby and the neighbors shared their supplies.

Then a few days later on August 23, 1925, also early on a Sunday morning, 10 carloads of fence posts were set ablaze by a "fire bug." The Hulyd brothers had them ready for shipping at the Twelve Mile railroad siding.

A third fire of suspicious origin that summer occurred the first week in September 1925, just a few miles north of Twelve Mile at neighboring Greenslide. The arsonist set fire to the lumberyard of McCormick and Dedosenco. They had just received an order for all of their lumber.

In the summer of 1935, Twelve Mile's precious new school burned to the ground one night. Although arson was suspected, nothing was ever proven. The school building was rebuilt that same year. Suspiciously about that same time, Fred Zibulak's home was also burned down.

ACCIDENTS

The frame and log homes of Twelve Mile were all equipped with wood-burning cook stoves and heaters fitted with metal stove pipes. Each house had a ladder to its roof so the commonly-occurring chimney fires could be squelched before the entire house went up in flames. Without running water, men or women quickly climbed the ladder with a bucket of water. Neighbours and those from nearby communities always pulled together during a crisis. This was always evident by the generous help offered when a family's home was destroyed by fire.

When Olympe Astrahantseff was about three years old, he tried adding wood to the kitchen stove while his mother was working outdoors. The piece was too large, so he quickly pulled it out of the fire and tossed it into the woodbox. Sad to say, it must have held some hot embers because their home caught fire and burned down. The family, with the help of a work bee from Twelve Mile and Eight Mile, soon rebuilt a larger, two-story log home in 1942.

Newlyweds Mr. And Mrs. Vincent Johnson moved into their tiny house in October 1949 when he took a job with Walter Shiell. But in January 1950 disaster struck. An overheated pipe burned down their log shack by the railroad crossing. Mary Petrashuk took them into her home and the neighbors donated supplies to help them set up housekeeping again. They were able to move to a house at Hewko's sawmill at Six Mile.

It was in 1952 or 1953 that Ule and Inge Podzun lost their home to fire. They were taken in by Asaph and Kellina Domke and made comfortable in their log cabin. Instead of rebuilding, the Podzuns moved to town.

The Gordon Westons experienced the same heartache on February 8, 1956 when fire consumed their home and possessions. Gordon was working in Sidmouth and Sophie had crossed on the ferry for the mail when the fire occurred. The snow was so deep that the fire couldn't be seen from the road. Sophie's father, Jack Nipper, was able to save a few things.

Not even the ferry was immune. The fire in 1966 burned its cabin.

FINAL FIRES

In the 1960s the Columbia Valley was again engulfed in smoke. This time it was from the burning trash and buildings when BC Hydro cleared the valley from Castlegar to Revelstoke, in preparation for its 150-mile-long reservoir Project.

Chapter 11

PLAY

*Play is often talked about as if it were a relief from
serious learning.
But for children play is serious learning.
Play is really the work of childhood.*

Fred Rogers

WINTER PLAY

When the weather turns cold, northern landscapes are transformed into great playgrounds. Fields of snow become ski and sled runs, and sloughs and ponds freeze over to become skating rinks.

Some, like John Rauchert, built their own rinks. They tramped down the snow and flooded it. The younger children wore bobskates that strapped onto their boots. They progressed to tube skates and figure skates. Emily remembers her white pair with fur around the ankles. Olympe Astrahantseff still winces when he recalls his feet hurting and freezing in an old pair of small skates he inherited from the Kozeks, but he wore them anyway so he could play hockey with his improvised hockey stick cut from a branch. One year John Rauchert formed a hockey team and, after weeks of practice, took on a team in Revelstoke, but it didn't go too well.

Florence and Della McLeod sliding down a snow bank. (McLeod family photo)

The snow was often wet and sticky and difficult to walk through. So when a crust formed on its surface during a cold spell, it was fun and easy to travel great distances to areas not otherwise accessible in the winter or summer. Sticky snow was also ideal for building igloos, forts and snowmen. Once Herb and Ada Domke built a huge snowman in the center of the Blanket Creek bridge, then hid behind a snow bank to enjoy the reaction of the next driver who came along! There were always lots of opportunities to play in snow and snow banks created by snowplows. Igloos, tunnels and forts were prevalent. The younger ones were always commandeered to make the snowballs for the older ones to lob at the opposing fort. After a fresh snowfall, "Cut the Pie" or "Fox and Goose" were popular games.

Few children owned toboggans, and sleds with skinny runners just sank into the deep, soft snow. So they improvised. Olympe Astrahantseff's eyes still sparkle as he remembers winter fun.

"After school in the winter (it seemed to be winter most of the time), we cut pieces from cardboard boxes and slid down the mountain side, dodging trees and rocks, getting soaking wet, but having a ball."

It was light and easy to carry up a snowy hill and held one or more riders. The front one held the cardboard between his/her legs, all leaning back and letting go. A piece of linoleum gave an even faster ride. During noon hour, school students walked the railway tracks to slide on Zibulak's hill and came back to class soaking wet. He went on,

"We skied around on skis purchased from the catalogue, but the snow was usually too soft or sticky for any fast downhill fun."

Emily Rauchert remembers when their ski tips flattened out, her dad soaked them in water, and clamped up the toes to restore the curl. Snowshoes were a mode of transportation and not usually used for sport in those days.

During winters of heavy snowfall, the snow either slid off roofs or was shoveled off, making tall piles next to the buildings, at times piling up above window tops. Children climbed the piles to get onto the roofs and then slid off the roofs and into or over the snow banks, hoping not to hook their pants on a roof nail.

It was great sport to chase a wandering pig through the narrow snow trails in the school yard since the banks along the pathways were too deep for the poor animal to escape.

It was fun to "go visiting" in the winter. The days were short and there wasn't as much outside work to do on the farms.

"My dad would harness up the horse, hook up the sleigh and take us visiting to the Domke homesteads. If it got too late to go home, we spent the night, horse and all, and left in time to get home to do the morning milking," recalls Olympe Astrahantseff.

Asaph Domke with winter toys.
(A. Domke family photo)

THE SNOW TUNNEL

It was 1949 and another one of those winters with a record snowfall. 1948 had registered 191 inches (486 centimeters), but this year the total tally would be 218 inches (555 centimeters). Some of the yellow government snowplows were graders converted in the winter with snowplow blades and huge side wings. There were also yellow government gravel trucks, weighted with sand, with a snowplow blade attached to the front. They were kept busy day and night. The highway between Revelstoke and Arrowhead was kept passable for the scheduled Rocky Mountain Freight truck, the residents and the occasional logging truck that ventured out during heavy snows. A priority was to keep the east and west ferry approaches scraped down to the planks if possible, so the vehicles wouldn't slip and skid off the sides into the river. The ferrymen took care of the snowfall on the ferry deck with snow shovels.

Ada, Eugen, Ben, Evelyn and Herb Domke all felt like they were in a snow tunnel when they walked the two and a half miles to school between narrow, towering walls of snow created by the plow. Evergreen trees along the road were plastered with clumps of snow hanging like huge marshmallows. The children headed for the snowbanks whenever the muffled *ching, ching, ching* of tire chains emerged around the corner.

This time, the plow hadn't yet come when it was time to leave for school so they stayed home rather than tackling the hike through the night's snowfall. Just as they were in the middle of sliding off the woodshed roof into the fluffy snow, the truck snowplow stopped by. It was Rollie Faucett plowing the road between Sidmouth and the Twelve Mile ferry. Everyone knew and liked Rollie.

"Hey kids," he called to them, "Want a ride to the ferry?"

"Sure, can you wait until we tell our moms?"

"Fine. Hop into the back."

Off they went with fluffy snow spraying up over the cab and into their faces as they stood leaning forward against the truck cab. The students dismounted at the ferry with encrusted faces and continued the last quarter mile to school on foot.

Most of the 15 students were present that day. They rarely skipped school and the school rarely closed for weather reasons. During the noon hour recess, construction began on the snow tunnel with the older students engineering, supervising and helping the younger ones dig out the snow. Tools were in short supply so the coal scoop from the shed, the dustpan and the snow shovel were all called upon for the job. The entrance was chosen in the deepest part of the snow bank. As the older students scooped the

Brian and Lillian Kramer heading for school through a snow channel. (Kramer family photo)

hard-packed snow, the younger ones loaded and slid it out in cardboard boxes. The relay work bee was truly teamwork.

Helga Mantei with skiis and sled. (A. Domke family photo)

Snow pants and mittens were soaked to the skin by the time the bell rang announcing the end of recess. Realizing the students had quite a walk ahead of them after school, the teacher arranged an area to hang up wet clothing by the heater to dry. Needless to say, the room smelled like wet sheep as the woolen clothing steamed beside the stove. That was Monday.

Tuesday came and more snow had piled up overnight. The tunnel entrance had to be cleared out so operations could continue. After determined hard work, in addition to a 20-foot tunnel, a large meeting room was cleared out under the snowfield over the playground. Granted, the ceiling integrity was a bit "iffy" with light filtering through, but the work was beautiful and satisfying to behold.

The bell rang at 1:00 p.m. Total silence, no one moved. *Clang, clang!* Teacher shook the bell even louder and faster. Still no response. After all this work, the fun was just beginning. Then, to their horror, 60-year-old Mrs. English came stomping onto the snow-covered playground, determinedly ringing the hand bell. *What if she broke through the ceiling!* The students could see her shadow above their heads as she continued to stomp and call to them to get out. Thoughts and fears swirled through the heads of some of the more conscientious students: What if teacher or someone else got hurt? The decision was finally made to exit the tunnel and take the consequences. As the saying goes, "It was all over but the shouting."

INDOOR PLAY

Just as winter weather turns the outdoors into a playground, shortened days turn the indoors into game and craft rooms. Darkness came early in winter—around 2:30-3:00 in the afternoon. One winter John Rauchert taught all the neighborhood young people to play poker. He said, "We would buy our money for five cents a hundred dollars and gather around the kitchen table to play all evening. Even the mumps didn't cancel the poker games."

One Christmas Ben Domke received a Chinese Checkers game at the concert. The board was the large, round metal type. (The family uses that board to this day.) He remembers that his

"Uncle Asaph was crazy about that game. We were the champions and spent hours during those long winter nights planning strategic moves. Sometimes it took half an hour to make a move. When Uncle would make a wrong move, he'd exclaim, 'Gunny Sacks!'"

In addition to games, there was plenty of time for reading books brought home from the school's traveling library. Parents taught their children the art of knitting, embroidery, crocheting, carving and other carpentry skills

When the weather was bad, there was always the hay barn to play in. It was easy sliding down the hay stacks, but sometimes one got wedged in a dusty hole between the hay and wall. The hay was too slippery to climb on to return to the top, so the children squeezed their way out along the barn wall.

SPRING PLAY

May Day seemed to be the magic day when feet held in bondage all winter were released. Bare feet ran around and experienced soft new grass, mud and water.

Every boy and even some girls carried jack knives wherever they went. They were important for whittling, carving initials in trees, cutting spruce gum off trees to chew, making whistles from spring willow branches, and slingshots from y-shaped branches and strips of old rubber inner tubes.

The closest things to swimming pools were the backwashes on the Columbia River or flooded hay fields in the late spring and early summer. Children taught each other the dog paddle and also how to build rafts from logs and old boards. They were regular Huck Finns as they maneuvered their rafts with long poles through channels between stumps and trees. Russell Gowanlock especially had fun playing in the slough with friends, tossing strings of slimy frogs' eggs at each other. The Rauchert girls tried crawling onto large log booms above the ferry wharf to dangle their feet in the river. However, Uncle Emil soon

Sergei Astrahantseff and Ronnie Dedosenco playing. (Dedosenco family photo)

put a stop to that when he spotted them. A licking from him and another from their dad ended that adventure on a sour note. On very rare spring picnic days, the school children were taken to Williamson Lake south of Revelstoke for a delightful day of water play on the slides and old inner tubes.

The playground at school was unlike the modern safety-engineered ones. It wasn't until 1949 and 1950 that swings and teeter-totters were built and the school grounds were fenced, protecting it from free-range cattle. The girls especially liked to sing this little ditty as they bounced up and down on the teeter-totters:

> *See saw, Marjorie Daw*
> *Jack shall have a new master.*
> *He shall get but a penny a day*
> *Because he can't work any faster.*

And a jump rope chant went something like:

> *Your mother, my mother*
> *Live by the lake.*
> *Every time they have a fight*
> *Listen what they say*
> *Acka backa, soda cracker*
> *I'll chase you out!*

Russell Gowanlock with his "toys." (Gowanlock family photo)

The ball diamond was marked off in front of the school with plates made of board scraps. The outfield extended to the lane going to the train station, and even the bush on the other side of the lane. Anyone coming to the school for their mail walked right through the middle of the diamond. There usually weren't enough children to have full teams for ball games, so they played "scrub" softball, and boys and girls of all ages played together. The game started in the morning before school and continued through the recesses and noon hour. Students called out, "I'm up," (there were usually two batters), "Pitcher," "First," "Second," "Third," "Catcher." As the batter up went out, everyone moved up a base, and whoever caught a fly ball automatically was "up."

The school had only one ball that made it very valuable and when its stitches broke, either the teacher or a student was responsible for sewing it back together. Olympe remembers stitching it at home with string. If it was hit out of the playground into the bush, the game stopped so everyone could look for it. It was the one and only ball they had. Once when Mrs. Townsend, the teacher, got word that the superintendent was to visit soon, she had the older boys squash the ball as flat as possible and left it on the back counter everyday with the old, beat-up bat, hoping the superintendent would take pity on the pupils and send out a new ball and bat. No one interviewed remembers if it was a successful ploy or not.

In 1954 John Rauchert organized a baseball team that the fellows called "The Twelve Mile River Rats." They didn't win many games, but sure had fun trying! Also during the 1950s the ball teams, "Loggers" and "Farmers," played other teams in the south valley and won several games.

In addition to softball, outside games included prisoners' base, auntie-I-over (throwing a ball over the school roof), and marbles. The "steelie" for marbles was usually a ball bearing from a truck or caterpillar and markers for hopscotch were broken pieces of china, glass or flat stones. Home made yoyos from large buttons and string emerged on the playground every spring.

Maple trees, hazelnut and other trees grew behind the school and the children often played there, during school or after school. It was a great area for hide-and-seek, tag, or making rooms for a pretend house. Some girls brought their dolls to school, and the boys built "furniture" for the outdoor rooms. Olympe Astrahantseff even turned a baking pan into a "kitchen sink" with a drain.

Across the road from the school was a forested area belonging to the Raucherts. During recesses, the older students built a two-story fort out of logs found lying around, with the younger children being their busy little helpers. The roof was never quite completed, but there were openings for a door and windows. After it partially burned, it continued to be a favourite hideout, but the children always left covered with telltale black charcoal.

School recesses were usually filled with a game of scrub softball. One day the girls were busy with their hopscotch game so there weren't enough players to fill all positions for a ball game. That left the boys to test each other by wrestling. The younger boys in the tiny Twelve Mile School looked up to the older ones who loved to demonstrate their moxie.

Benny in the eighth grade, and Bruce in the seventh, were two of the older boys in the one-room school. Ben had developed his strength from farming and logging. He loaded bales of hay, helped his dad cut logs with a crosscut saw and skid them out with their team of horses. Bruce on the other hand was a city boy and not used to hard, physical labor. His family had just moved from Vancouver the previous fall. The hardest work he had been exposed to at this point was carrying buckets of water from their creek (Drimmie Creek) that gurgled past their tiny home. His mom, Lena, needed plenty of water for cooking and cleaning. She was a stickler for a sparkling clean home, and for her two children taking daily sponge baths between their weekly tub baths. She also needed a dependable supply of firewood that Bruce had to chop and stack next to the kitchen stove.

On this particular spring day, several of the boys, including Ben, wrestled Bruce down. They removed his shoelaces and tied up his bib overalls at his ankles.

"Let's drag him closer to the road where the rocks are."

"Okay, I'll hold him down while you guys fill his overalls with these rocks."

As Bruce struggled to empty his pants, the baseball-sized rocks settled and packed in around his legs and torso and jabbed him with every twitch. At the sound of the bell, the boys scurried to the classroom with uncharacteristic speed, leaving Bruce to his own devices. No more overalls for him—his mom would buy him blue jeans from then on!

The following week, the spontaneous agenda again called for wrestling on the grassy playground next to the gravel highway. After a lively struggle for superiority, this time Bruce surprisingly got the best of Ben and held him in a head lock. He feared to lose his advantage lest the stronger Ben wrestle him down again. Just then Joe Kozek rumbled past with a truckload of logs heading for the flatcars at the train station behind the school. Still holding Ben down, Bruce flagged down Joe and pleaded with him for help.

"I'll be back after I dump this load of logs," promised Joe. Being a spirited young man himself, he couldn't resist the opportunity to be part of the fun.

True to his word, Joe did come back and lock down Ben while Bruce ran behind the school, hiding in the bushes until the bell rang. He felt pretty smart and lucky with his easy escape this time.

SUMMER AND FALL PLAY

In the summer, the children hiked to and precariously balanced on the edge of the falls at Mulvehill Creek and Sutherland Falls. It was traditional, if not mandatory, that they write their names on the Blanket Creek bridge. They could be gone for the entire day without any sense of worry on the part of their parents. Olympe Astrahantseff and others also remember building miniature ranches from twigs in sandy or mossy areas along the creeks.

Rosalie Rauchert remembers the fun she and other children had one summer playing their invented game:

> Several children got together and made a trail on my Aunt and Uncle's property. We had little animals and other things. We called it "Down Parsnip Road to Lovers Lane." The name came from the children involved. We used each letter of the group's first name. "D" was for Donna Rauchert, "P" for Pennie Banks, "R" was me, "L" was Lorna Rauchert and Larry Schmidt. The "T" was for Jackie Schmidt. We had to change his name to make it sound right. We charged everyone 10 cents to make the tour. We bought ourselves an ice cream treat at the end of the summer.

Herb, Eugen and Ada Domke by Ada's playhouse. (A. Domke family photo)

Homemade toys and games were common. Stilts were made from long poles with foot rests nailed on. It was a contest to see who could stay on them the longest, or walk the fastest. Competition was so keen that once Olympe had to climb onto the school roof to mount his. He survived his stilt walk without knee or elbow pads or helmet. Games such as "Waves" and "Colors" were also invented. It was easy to make boats to float in the creeks by scooping out old cucumbers and mounting sails on them.

Since the Revelstoke-Arrowhead train ran only two to three times a week, the tracks and Drimmie Creek bridge were interesting play areas. Some boys even made

their own firecrackers from blasting caps they found under the bridge, and it was always fun to watch pennies get flattened on the tracks by the huge steam locomotive wheels. They also had fun climbing into the open boxcars on the railway siding and exploring their contents.

Since play is a child's work, children mimicked their parents. Boys seemed to be born with the "logging gene." Ben Domke tied logs to the back of his five-year-old brother's trike and made him skid them out of the bush, under much protest by Herb. Albert and Ronnie

Ronnie and Albert Dedosenco's first "logging operation." (Dedosenco family photo)

Dedosenco also played logging by loading up their little wagon. Girls played house with their dolls or dressed up cats for more action.

The Makarewicz children lived a little distance from others their ages so had their own ways of entertaining themselves. The farm wagon that was usually hooked behind the tractor became a fun toy. After pulling it to the top of the hill, they all piled in, yanked up the latch with a rope and let it zoom down the hill. At the bottom of the hill, they threw down the latch and stopped with a jolt. They would also let loose down the hill on their bicycles.

Most families had cows, horses, pigs, dogs, cats and poultry, and some of these animals provided hours of fun for the children. The large workhorses were ridden bareback. They were led close to a stump or log so the young riders could mount. When finished, the riders just slid off. Some brave souls even attempted to ride steers, cows or calves, but that usually was disastrous, especially when thrown into a manure pile.

There were always plenty of alcoholic beverage bottles left lying around the schoolyard after each dance. Dogs were known to get drunk when the remains of these bottles were poured down their throats.

The Makarewicz children always enjoyed playing in the field with the newborn calves, laying on them and riding the older ones. One year their dad, Nick, chose a beautiful Hereford calf to be raised as the farm bull. He put the paste on the immature horns to retard their growth and he became the children's best friend. They continued to ride him into his adulthood. But one very hot day, he went berserk, snorting, kicking, pawing and ramming into the large tree in their yard. Joanna called the children into the house and the bull took off across the tracks to the other pastures. He was never to be trusted around children again.

Ada floating on air mattress in swimming pool constructed by her father, Asaph Domke.
(A. Domke family photo)

The McLeod sisters, Della and Florence, were isolated in Wigwam from other children and had to entertain themselves. They had about 40 pet bantum hens one year that built their nests in the hay. One time they were given a white male duck and brown female duck that produced eggs. Della and Florence switched the banty eggs with three duck eggs under each hen and ended up with about 20 ducks. "Dad was furious with us because he had to dodge all those duck droppings, so we built a pond for the ducks. That kept them away from the house!"

Since the Domke children were also separated from other children by a couple of miles, they made their own fun. Grade schoolers Herb and Ada built a one-room cabin on adjoining property from boards and nails found lying around. It was complete with an abandoned little stove, chimney, hand-made table and chairs, and flagstone walk. They nailed handles onto tin cans for their cooking utensils. When BC Hydro demolished it, they filed a claim but it was graciously turned down.

Chapter 12

HEALTH AND MEDICAL

For every ailment under the sun,
There is a remedy, or there is none.
If there be one, try to find it;
If there be none, never mind it.

Mother Goose Rhyme

British Columbia's Department of Health and Welfare did its best to take care of its citizens. They published articles in the papers explaining the importance of protecting food, water and family from contaminating germs. Of specific concern were poliomyelitis, typhoid fever, diarrhea, and dysentery.

PUBLIC HEALTH NURSES

Public health nurses were sent out routinely to outlying areas to check preschoolers in their homes and give immunizations. Most of the women in Twelve Mile did not drive cars, so these nurses with cars were always admired by the young people who couldn't wait for their independence when old enough to drive. Nurses also visited the school several times a year, giving immunizations, checking for lice and giving physicals. A doctor usually accompanied her for the annual physicals in the fall. In 1948 the team was Miss Neuman and Dr. Best. Per their report in the *Revelstoke Review*, September 23, 1948, "the school was above average for a rural school in equipment and sanitary conveniences." Miss Morrison was the nurse in 1949. When it came time for their annual medical examinations, students shyly entered the teacherage, knowing they would be asked to remove most clothing. These were probably the only regular physicals the children had.

EPIDEMICS

The community was not immune to epidemics of flu, measles, chicken pox, whooping cough, mumps and even polio. Sharry Kelly came down with scarlet fever in the winter of 1934-35. Mrs. Rutherford, Robert Logan's housekeeper, and Mrs. Kelly made large, hot poultices of cooked onions and placed them on her chest to try and break her fever. When this treatment was not working, in desperation Mrs. Kelly stopped the northbound train and took Sharry to Revelstoke. Dr. Strong met the train and drove them in his car to Queen Victoria Hospital where she recovered. The flu epidemic in the spring of 1951 put Larry Rauchert and Roger Dunn in the hospital and the school was closed for two days.

Poliomyelitis was still being studied in an attempt to locate the viruses attacking children. In 1947, a case was reported in Vernon, and two in 1948 in nearby Salmon Arm. In 1947, insurance companies were offering medical insurance especially for poliomyelitis in Canada and the USA. Then polio struck Twelve Mile in 1952. Ben Domke recounts his frightening experience as follows:

When I was 18 years old in 1952, I contracted polio. My brother, Herb, was quarantined from school and we were not allowed to visit anyone. I was clearing land on our farm and putting in a water line to the barn with the cat. Henry Bittner came to help hook up the line from the creek. That night I felt like I was getting the flu. Went to bed early. Pain developed in my cheeks, hips, legs and feet. I was in such pain that I grabbed the iron bedposts and pulled myself up to bump my head against the wall to deflect the pain. In the morning I was wobbly on my feet and could not urinate. Mother also thought I had the flu. This was Monday morning and I had another small job on the cat to finish. I got on the cat and as it bounced around, I was able to urinate, so I thought I was getting better. Tuesday morning I was still in severe pain and laid down in the living room, but refused to go to the doctor as my mother recommended. About 10 a.m. I finally fell asleep for a couple of hours. When I awoke the pain was gone but I still felt weak, so I drove myself to the Queen Victoria Hospital. Dr. Mackay did a spinal test and sent me into isolation immediately. To me this was total nonsense. About a week later, a Provincial doctor who specialized in polio, checked me and told me, "You're one hell of a lucky guy. You had one of the worst strains of polio but came out of it pretty good." Then Dr. Mackay told me, "Your strength will come back about the same speed as the hair grows on your head." Well, that never happened. I was given no type of treatment, but sent home. Mother put hot packs on my legs. As an adult I developed post polio syndrome. The pain I now have is in the overworked muscles in my left leg that were not affected by the polio.

Ben missed the polio vaccine by just three years. In 1955 all young people were administered the Salk vaccine injections.

HOME REMEDIES AND BIRTHS

The "Rawleigh Man" and "Watkins Man" peddled much-needed supplies at about two-month intervals. Children were fascinated by their satchels containing various bottles of liniment, salves, cough syrup, cod liver oil, tonics, vanilla and so forth. Strong, orange-colored carbolic salve in four-inch round, yellow tins was a must to soothe and heal rough skin and cuts on both humans and animals.

When colds and flu struck, not having ready access to medical care, families took matters in their own hands. Some had nurses training and others employed folk medicine learned in "the old country," or by other means. Those who could, always ministered to those in need.

Mustard plasters and hot and cold compresses were applied to chests to treat chest colds and coughs. A common treatment for a sore throat was to rub it with Mentholatum ointment, usually Rawleighs, then wrap and pin a wool sock around it. The salve had a fresh, minty scent and came in a round, blue and silver tin. It also worked wonders to clear stuffy heads and noses when inhaled. The ointment was added to a can of water and heated on the stove and the patient breathed the vapors through a paper cone. Sometimes the patient sat next to a tub, feet immersed in hot water and a cape draped over head and tub for a steam bath.

Stings from bees and wasps were treated with mudpacks or the application of a paste made from baking soda and water. Applying a cut, raw onion seemed to work for some stings.

Babies born during Twelve Mile's early days were delivered at home with the help of a neighbour midwife. Elizabeth Mazar midwifed in the 1920s and 1930s, delivering Walter Kozek and Jim Millar among others. In more recent years, a pregnant lady went to Revelstoke to stay with friends to be near Queen Victoria Hospital when labour began. There are some reports of babies being born in autos on the way to town. Florence McLeod has the distinction of being born in the Twelve Mile School teacherage during the Dec 17, 1939 Christmas concert.

DENTAL

Dental care was a luxury with limited availability. Evelyn Domke remembers catching rides with neighbours on her way to Revelstoke for dental work. She was only eight or nine years of age. When her dental fillings were completed, she began walking until someone came along to give her a ride home. At that time, she doesn't recall having to make a dental appointment before hand. As the dentist became busier, dental work had to be scheduled months in advance. In the early years, Dr. Moore was Revelstoke's overworked dentist.

ACCIDENTS

Rural living was dangerous and few families escaped the pain and anxiety of serious accidents. There were drownings, burns, broken bones, lacerations and head traumas. Transporting the injured to Revelstoke for medical attention was not simple, especially from remote areas.

Alec Michels and Nick Kupchenko used a railway hand speeder to bring Brooks Gowanlock from Wigwam when he broke his ankle in a caterpillar rut.

When Donna Rauchert took ill in March, 1956, on the way to the hospital they were stopped by a pile of rubble from a slide on the highway. Her father carried her over it and they were met on the other side by Mr. Westby who took them to the hospital.

Annie McLeod found Lena Kaduhr in serious condition when her gas refrigerator leaked and encompassed her with fumes. She massaged Lena's extremities while someone called the "ambulance" which was the taxi from Revelstoke.

Fred Zibulak suffered serious injuries when thrown from his hay rake and died soon after arriving at hospital in a makeshift bread wagon ambulance.

FAMILY ALLOWANCE

No one except railway employees had health insurance until into the 1940s. Family Allowance was passed in 1945 by the Department of National Health and Welfare in Ottawa, to help cover medical, dental and nursing, among other costs, to children up to 16 years of age. Children age six and over were required to be in regular school attendance to receive the payments. The checks were issued monthly to the children's mothers and banks were required to cash the checks without charge. For age five and under, the payment was $5; six to nine years, $6; 10-12 years, $7; and 13-15 years, $8.

Chapter 13

SPECIAL EVENTS

*Be glad of life because it gives
you the chance to love and to work
and to play and to look up at the stars.*

Henry Van Dyke

CHRISTMAS CONCERTS

As far back as can be recalled, teachers and students put together outstanding Christmas concerts at the school to which the local and outlying communities were invited. Practice of plays, music and skits began early, probably November.

Students designed advertising posters and distributed them to the surrounding communities. Admission was usually 50 cents. The older boys and fathers put together the stage up front, built of planks laid over low sawhorses. A heavy wire was strung across the room on which thick dark green drapes were hung. The years took their toll on them and one year the teacher turned the holes into part of the program. Jack Frost stuck his long, pointed nose through the holes randomly while children swatted at it with paper rolls.

Excitement ran high the day of the concert. Children were dismissed early so they could get into their best clothes and hairdos. Parents brought sandwiches, cakes and cookies for the reception and games afterward. Salmon and egg salad sandwiches were favourites and were always brought packed in a shoebox. Someone was in charge of filling gas lamps and stoking up the stove. Desks were stacked against side walls and benches made of long planks were set up. A large, freshly cut fir tree, carefully decorated by the students, stood guard over brown paper bags full of nuts, oranges and candy for every child in attendance.

Some of the men began "celebrating" early, before coming. This caused a bit of rowdiness, usually in the back of the room, or outside by the door and the row of side windows.

Performers waited in the teacherage until their turns came. Headlines in the *Revelstoke Review*, December 31, 1936 issue read, "Twelve Mile Ferry School Holds Happy Christmas Concert." Under the direction of teacher Ruth Lindsay recitations, songs, pantomimes and pageants were performed. The group sang, "The First Noel," "Gay La La," "I Saw Three Ships," "Uncle Ned," "I know a Little Pussy," and "O Christmas Tree." Minnie Kozek and Tommy Mazar sang a duet, "Lavender's Blue." The recitations included "Don't Sleep on the Floor" by Mack Mazar; "When Mother is Sick" by Dorothy Mazar; "The Baby Jesus and His Mother" and "Christmas Eve" by Betty Pytrashuk; "The Cherry Tree Carol" and "What Would You Say" by Rosy Kozek; "A Shock," by Joe Kozek; "He Could Help" by Steve Kozek; "Poor Dolly" by Minnie Kozek. There was a pantomime by Dorothy and Tommy Mazar, "Tommy Goes to a Christmas Party," and a pageant, "Christmas Far Away," by six pupils.

Every year after students playing to a packed house, Santa arrived, decked out in his traditional red and white, lugging a huge bag of gifts. Sometimes Santa's bag was the canvas Canadian Post Office mailbag. Who played Santa was always a huge secret and sometimes he dropped from the "sky" through the attic hatch in the ceiling. Brooks Gowanlock did the honors several times in his jolly manner. Kellina Domke has the distinction of being the first and only female Santa, fooling even her family. And one year Art Domke donned the red suit only to have his logging socks with the red stripe betray his secret to his daughter, Ada, as he dropped down from the attic.

Where did the gifts come from? Each year Twelve Mile dances were held at the school, live bands and all, to raise money for the Christmas fund. Students made up their "wish lists" from the Eaton's or Simpson's catalogues and the teachers (later with the help of the PTA) purchased and wrapped the gifts for each child for Santa to deliver.

Mrs. Irene English was famous for directing creative Christmas concerts. She accompanied the vocalists on the old pump organ. Her 1949 concert had to be changed at the last minute because the ferry froze in that day. Many of the concert participants were stranded on the west side of the river. The schoolhouse was packed with people who came from Twelve Mile to Revelstoke. They made the best of things and children from outside the community ad libbed several parts to add to those of the few school students. After the concert, while turning out the gas lamp, Mrs. English tripped and landed across the edge of the platform. Although she was bruised and shaken, she was ready to put on the entire concert when the ice moved out of the river and the rest of the performers could attend.

1964 Christmas concert with teacher, Eileen Kernaghan, and Santa with his bag of gifts. (B. Weston photo)

EATON'S
Mail Order
Christmas Tree
Shopping Service

This EATON Service offers a simple and easy plan for the handling of bulk orders of prizes, toys, novelties, etc. It is maintained to assist Institutions, Societies, Schools and other groups who have the pleasant duty of distributing large numbers of gifts at Christmas time.

NOW . . . While Our Stocks are Most Complete is the Time to Send in Your Orders.
LET US . . . Make Your Gift Selections!

Looking through our Fall and Winter Catalogue, you will find that many items are splendid for Christmas gifts. We will make up your order with suitable items when merchandise you desire is not available.

Simply tell us the ages and number of boys and girls you are providing for. Enclose with the list the amount of money you wish to spend, also the date you require them and we will choose suitable gifts. Parcels will be shipped in time for your entertainment.

Below is a list of typical items. We suggest that the average cost should not be less than the prices shown. By allowing a larger amount you can be sure of a much better selection.

Kindly put an X beside class of goods desired.

Item	Price	Fall and Winter Catalogue Pages
Toys	25c, 35c and up, charges extra	220, 316, 416, 417, 525-546
Books	25c and up, charges extra	416, 417, 419, 425-428
Games	25c, 35c and up, charges extra	316, 417, 419, 534-537
Combs	25c and up, price del.	218, 314, 317, 318, 325, 361, 367, 371, 373
Handkerchiefs	25c and up, price delivered	100, 101, 318
Gloves and Mitts	39c, 45c, 59c and up, price delivered	112-115, 119-122, 216, 219
Ties	29c, 35c, 50c and up, price delivered	100, 195, 283-285
Purses	45c, 59c and up, price delivered	385, 388, 389, 392
Stockings	39c, 49c, 55c and up, price del.	105-112, 116-118, 196, 215, 218, 557

See also pages 415 to 419, inclusive, and pages 548 to 557, inclusive.

Presents for older people should be separately selected from our General Catalogue if possible, using separate Order Form enclosed. When ordering, please use the reverse side of this letter; envelope is herewith enclosed. By using these they will bring your order direct to the Christmas Tree Shopping Service. Orders will be ready for shipping in time for your entertainment if you tell us the date required.

T. EATON C°. LIMITED

Catalogue order form for Christmas concert gifts. (Genny Rauchert photo)

OTHER EVENTS

The school served as the community hall for all group events. When it held events such as sports days, picnics and Halloween parties, parents and other community members were always invited.

After the PTA paid for its share of a projector and generator, the community gathered in the evenings to watch movies. The students were pretty excited when the large, flat, strapped, square boxes containing film reels arrived by train. They couldn't wait for Tony Ambil from the school district to come and operate the projector for their movies.

Someone was always organizing a dance or card party on Saturday nights. The classroom was decorated with crepe paper streamers for bridal and baby showers and receptions. At the May, 1955 dance, music was supplied by Johnny Story, Jim Holley and Andy Chiymadia. The proceeds benefited the new sports equipment fund.

In 1944 parades of motor boats began their annual traditional flotillas up the Columbia River from Grand Coulee Dam to Revelstoke. As they cruised through Twelve Mile, word spread and the community hurried down to the riverbank to wave them on. They always looked forward to this special event.

On rare occasions, Twelve Milers took advantage of special events in Revelstoke. In March 1949 many were fortunate enough to take part in the excitement of the huge ski jump tournament on the Nels Nelson Hill. That was the year the Mt. Revelstoke ski hill was named in the great champion's honor.

It was a new era when CPR's first diesel locomotive made its run from Revelstoke to Arrowhead. The students were dismissed from class to watch the historic event.

Chapter 14

BC HYDRO

*Shame on those who lie in bed planning evil and wicked deeds
and rise at daybreak to do them,
knowing that they have the power!
They covet land and take it by force;
if they want a house they seize it;
they rob a man of his home
and steal every man's inheritance.*

Micah 2:1-2 NEB

1964 was the pivotal year that finalized and set in motion the grand, international governmental plan that would usurp the smaller plans and dreams of the residents of Twelve Mile. Homesteading and the ability to buy affordable, rough lands suitable for development is the stuff of dreams for common folks.

A GRAND PLAN

Discussions began between the United States (US) and British Columbia (BC) governments on a cooperative scheme to provide more water storage capacity in BC that would increase the year-round power output of Grand Coulee Dam in Washington State soon after its completion in 1940. By January 1964, BC Premier W.A.C. Bennett and Canada's new federal liberal government wrapped up the Columbia River Treaty with the US, and the final approval was made in June of that year. The real bonus of the Project, according to the "Columbia Pact" article in the January 30, 1964 *Revelstoke Review*, was the payment by the US to BC of approximately $344,000,000 which could increase to $500,000,000 when invested prior to its use in building the three treaty dams: Hugh L. Keenleyside Dam, five miles west of Castlegar; Mica Creek Dam 90 miles north of Revelstoke; and Duncan River Dam north of its confluence with the Lardeau River.

BC Hydro (Hydro) was the entity responsible for carrying out the Treaty guidelines. Hydro promulgated all the benefits of the huge Project. Waterfront recreation facilities would be constructed with new highways connecting them resulting in increased tourism. There would be 15-20 years of construction jobs in the Columbia Valley as a result of building the dams, transmission lines, highways, bridges, parks, hospitals, airports and new communities. In addition, all standing timber in the reservoir would be removed, for which Celgar received the contract. The areas affected by the reservoir would be cleared of buildings, slash and timber waste. Most buildings would be destroyed and some moved.

URGENCY

Once the deal was done, the Project moved forward with great haste. Hugh L. Keenleyside, Chairman of British Columbia Hydro and Power Authority, explained the urgency for finishing it quickly in his *Statement for The External Affairs Committee of the House of Commons* in April 1964. He stated that,

> . . . the advent of nuclear energy is bringing a new element into all power calculations. . . . the cost of nuclear energy is likely to become so low as to make most other new power installations uneconomic. . . . it would be desirable to develop every hydro-electric project, for the output of which a profitable market could be found, just as rapidly as possible.

The new agreement seemed to ignore water use priorities of the BC Water Act of 1909. Donovan Clemson, in "Refugees from Arrow Dam," appearing in the January 27, 1966 issue of *The Western Producer*, reviewed them as follows: "1. Domestic purposes. 2. Municipal purposes. 3. Irrigation of land for agricultural and horticultural purposes. 4. Industrial purposes. 5. Power, including the use of water for generating *power for sale*." (Emphasis added.)

No reasonable person would argue that harnessing the hydroelectric potential of the Columbia River, controlling its damaging floods, clearing out its incredible mosquito-hatching swamps and improving its recreational features was not a great blessing to both nations. The problem was that the powerful government planners failed to appreciate the plight they would bring to the common people who had put their sweat and blood, hopes, dreams and aspirations into their homelands. The powerbrokers saw only backwoods people living in rough-hewn homes of little value in their urban world. They failed to see that these hardy folks were living good lives in a beautiful, irreplaceable wilderness. Had the planners fully appreciated the quality of life in this place, they would have seen to it that the displaced were resettled into some similar setting without regard to the market value of their lands.

SELLING THE PLAN

Because Columbia River had a history of springtime flooding low-lying farms in B.C. and Washington State, the politicians emphasized the flood-control aspect of the project. Ironically, to save relatively few farms from those periodic floods, the Columbia River Project rendered unusable 150 miles of the valley along with roads, railways, bridges, cemeteries, public facilities, recreation and tourist facilities, and displaced about 2,000 from their farms, communities and towns in the valley.

Caterpillar clearing reservoir for BC Hydro.
(Weston family photo)

CLEARING THE VALLEY

Land clearing began in September 1966 in Twelve Mile, even though all land deals had yet to be completed. Contracts were awarded for the removal and disposal of buildings. Workers were given explicit instructions that removal was to take place only after the removal of inhabitants, personal belongings, guns and ammunition. They were to be bulldozed down and buried. Since they were to do the job "quickly," it is no wonder many fires of mysterious origin began occurring, usually at night. St. Ann's Church at Mt. Cartier was shattered by dynamite one night in November 1966 during the negotiation period with Hydro. Before the Makarewiczes had a chance to move, and while Nick was still operating the ferry,

Hydro contractors started burning their tool garage. Joanna ran to the ferry to retrieve Nick in time to pull his tools out of the burning building. The family will never forget this hair-raising experience.

Even those who had finalized their deals with Hydro had deep feelings when they saw torches put to the homes they had struggled so hard to build and maintain during the preceding hard-scrabble years. Asaph Domke wrote this letter to cousin, Herb Domke, who was away at college:

Makarewicz and Weston children in bucket of land-clearing cat, circa 1967. (Weston family photo)

Water beginning to fill cleared reservoir. View looking south near Weston access off Highway 23, circa 1969. (Weston family photo)

November 8, 1965

This week all the buildings on your farm got burned to the ground by the Hydro. This gives me a funny feeling when I think that our home is doomed to the same fate. Our buildings will receive the same treatment probably by next spring.

(So much for the bulldozing rule!) In fact, the Asaph Domkes' frame house was sold by BC Hydro and salvaged for its lumber. Their farm buildings were burned. Their original log cabin was preserved as part of the park that was established there.

COMPENSATING THOSE DISPLACED

Hydro's original policy first published in 1964 in its "Property Owners' Guide," page 3, stated that "each purchase of land will require *special negotiations* with the individual property owner," that the purchase price offer would be "as fair and generous as possible." It "will be based on a *generous* interpretation of the appraised value of your land. It is our policy to try to obtain land *not at the lowest possible price but at a fair price*. In most instances, it will include *an extra allowance to compensate for disturbance and moving expenses*." However, through some twisted reasoning, by 1965 Hydro added that it would be "unfair to the majority of property owners if bargaining were permitted." (Emphasis added.) (See *Columbia News Letter*, April 28, 1965, p. 2.)

UNJUST COMPENSATION FOR THOSE DISPLACED

In reality, not permitting landowners to bargain put everyone but Hydro at a disadvantage. Landowners could not possibly receive a fair settlement if not allowed to make a case for the worth of their property and negotiate. Factors seemingly ignored by Hydro included the reality that the market values of the land had fallen to nothing as the Columbia River project had made the land unsaleable. Thus, local market values became irrelevant when attempting to arrive at a fair price. One gauge of land value was the fact that according to the *Vancouver Sun* (February 11, 1966) Hydro was paying up to $1,500 per acre for land clearing contracts in the area. Landowners, who had done the backbreaking land clearing over the years had a right to expect similar compensation for their cleared land, but did not. For example, Asaph Domke received only $27,500 for 80 acres of land, about half of which was cleared. In addition, Domkes had two dwellings, cow barn, horse barn, chicken coop and a couple of garages. Their property was also landscaped with lawns, gardens, swimming pool and decorative rockwork.

Landowners complained to each other about the offers they were receiving from Hydro. Attempts by some to find lawyers to fight Hydro found that legal firms of any size were already tied in some manner to Hydro or some other B.C. government entity that would result in a conflict of interest. Thus, each landowner found himself to be an individual up against an overwhelming coalition of government and legal powers. The message circulated through the community that Hydro wanted a few individuals to contest their low appraisals in the courts. Hydro's scheme was to obtain a settlement lower still than was the original offer. Such punishment would get the message across that citizens could not win against the government.

An incident that took place in a Nakusp tavern suggests that the low compensation offered to Twelve Milers may have been due to low opinions of them held by BC Hydro officialdom. Conversations at the bar included a stranger who identified himself as a BC Hydro agent. When asked his business, the agent replied, "I'm going up to Revelstoke to buy out those hillbillies south of town." The one who had inquired responded, "Oh, you must know my father-in-law (name withheld); he is negotiating with BC Hydro right now." Apparently embarrassed by his derogatory characterization of those living in the south valley, the BC Hydro agent had nothing more to say on the topic. Readers can judge for themselves whether or not the Twelve Milers described in the foregoing chapters, were deserving of such disdain.

The experience of the Makarewicz family bore out the reality that there would be no justice for the displaced of Twelve Mile. Theirs was a viable, working farm with fairly new, modern buildings. Hydro's offer was clearly below its true value, but Hydro stuck to its policy of not bargaining. The case was finally heard in court with Hydro prevailing. It paid Makarewiczes about 80 percent of the appraisal value by a qualified, objective third party. The appraisal no doubt would have been higher if not for the devaluation caused by the disruption of the Project.

Common sense justice required that the displaced people be relocated to a site similar to that which they had previously occupied, plus moving expenses and some compensation for the disruption of their lives. However, this was not to be. Some found it difficult to locate a home (even without land) of the size and quality they had left, with the meager amount they were given. Some of the older folks were not able to search for new homes and asked Hydro to relocate them, per its policy. In some cases, the homes they were moved to were of much lower quality than the ones they left. It is no wonder there still exists an undercurrent of resentment or anger among family and friends of those whose homes were expropriated and under valued.

ABOVE THE HIGH WATER MARK

Some homesites were located above the high-water mark, but although they would not be inundated, westside homes would no longer have ferry access to what remained of the eastside

Ferry house on east side flooded by rising water in reservoir, spring 1969. (Weston family photo)

highway from Revelstoke. The only way out was the rough Celgar logging road on the west side that was suitable only for high-clearance vehicles. Apparently, by the time of the displacement, the BC government was already planning to build modern Highway 23 from Revelstoke to Shelter Bay which would provide access to the west side, but this was not common knowledge to the Twelve Milers at the time, and Hydro apparently was not publicly informing people about this plan. Asaph Domke declared that he would not have sold if he had known the new highway was to be built. He was also surprised to learn that his homestead was to become a provincial park, occupying land high, dry and accessible, and was a highly valued piece of property by Hydro and Parks for which value the Domkes were not fully compensated.

The Weston family was the only one that stayed in Twelve Mile. It wasn't an easy decision, but in order to maintain their current quality of living, Gordon and Sophie felt they had no option. They had their own hydroelectric power plant, a shingle mill and beautiful gardens, most of which were above the high water mark. Hydro purchased the lower portion of their property and the Westons went about moving and rebuilding their newly-built home on higher ground. A big problem was that they were located on the west side of the river cut off from the road to town. They used the old Celgar logging road to get to town. Even after Highway 23 was built, they had to maintain a mile-long driveway over the old logging road to access the new highway that was eventually built above them. They used a radiophone for communication, and had to be creative in getting their children to school in Revelstoke.

THE END OF THE RAILWAY, HIGHWAY AND FERRY

The railway was also a victim of the Project. Not only were many miles of railbed to be inundated, its post of Arrowhead would also be destroyed. A rail line that nearly became an alternate route[*] across the nation would be obliterated.

Frank Christian, who served as one of the engineers on the Arrowhead run during its last 10 years, recalls that the maintenance of the line ceased after its abandonment became known. The track became soft and uneven. The condition of the 50-foot-long bridge over the Akolkolex River at Wigwam became so tenuous the speed limit was reduced from the usual 15 MPH to 5 MPH. One of the train crews refused to ride across the bridge. Instead, the fireman and brakeman walked across and waited on the other side. The engineer set the diesel's throttle just enough for the train to creep forward, then dropped off the engine and let it cross the bridge unmanned. The fireman on the other side hopped aboard and stopped it once the train cleared the bridge. Then the engineer walked across and rejoined the train.

Barry Camozzi remembers October 2, 1968 when he and the crew made its last commercial run to Arrowhead before the tracks were taken up. "When we got to Twelve Mile we found car loads of poles on the tracks. We just pushed them onto the siding and kept right on going to Arrowhead." The crew on that last run were: Ken Cameron, Engineer; Armando Lazaratto, Conductor; Barry Camozzi, Head Brakeman.

After the reservoir was cleared and the water began rising, temporary ferry landings were established until the day the ferry closed.

REMNANTS STILL VISIBLE

In the spring of 1969, the Upper Arrow Reservoir began filling. This was the beginning of annual seesaw water levels, with limited and undependable water recreation between Revelstoke and Shelter Bay. At Twelve Mile some of the cement pilings from the ferry towers are still visible, along with portions of the ferry wharfs. A few charred chimney bricks and scrolled metal from desks from the old school that was burned in 1968 have escaped souvenir seekers. Random pieces of metal from farm implements and fences peek out of the sand, washed in by the now slow-flowing river. During low water, the sandy beaches host parties, ATV-ing and four-wheeling. The Asaph and Oscar Domke farms were developed into Blanket Creek Provincial Park, a favourite spot for campers from near and far. One of their hayfields (that was originally Nufree Huckle's), was scooped out to form the park's swimming lagoon fed by Blanket Creek. Asaph and Kellina's homestead log cabin that was preserved by Parks as a heritage home, finally collapsed under heavy snows during the winter of 1997. Some of Asaph's elaborate rock walls and swimming pool still remain, but the stone arch over their driveway was knocked down by some careless, partying kids. The terrain has been changed considerably in the Blanket Creek area. The gravel below the old highway between the creek and homesteads was scooped

---

[*] The Arrowhead and Revelstoke line was once planned and surveyed to link up with the Arrowhead and Kootenay Railway forming an alternative CPR route via the Kettle Valley line east through Lethbridge to Swift Current.

out for paving Highway 23 above and in exchange, the Public Works Department paved the campground roads for Parks.

OPPORTUNITIES TO RETURN

After the new reservoir's high-water line was established, Hydro began surveying plots of land for resale along the reservoir. Former property owners were given first chance to purchase any of the land, not necessarily what had been theirs. B.C. Hydro & Power Authority issued a bulletin dated 1 September 1982, *Details of Hydro Properties on Arrow Reservoir Available for Sale to Eligible Former Arrow Lakes Owners*, in which Charles W. Watson stated:

> You are eligible to apply to purchase a property if you were an owner of property acquired by B.C. Hydro for the Arrow (sic) Project, and you did not retain reservoir frontage, and you have not since acquired a property from Hydro under this program. Former waterfront owners are eligible to purchase property with or without reservoir frontage and former owners of non-waterfront property are eligible to purchase property that does not have reservoir frontage. Lists are available for both categories.

> . . .

> Please apply at the Hydro Nakusp office for further information. P.O. Box 428, Nakusp, B.C. V0G 1R0, Attention Mr. Earl Moffat, Telephone: 265-3626.

To Mr. Moffat's credit, he attempted to get the above word out to as many former residents as possible, and treated everyone in a kindly manner.

BUY LOW, SELL HIGH

Now that Hydro owns the land, it seems to have come to realize its high value. What it had bought at dirt-cheap prices now sells for much more. One Twelve Mile family that received $50 an acre for their land, bought back a few of their own acres for $1,000 an acre. Another family purchased back part of their farm, now overgrown, for 30 times more than the amount they had received. Theirs are not isolated cases. Many such stories abound throughout the valley.

MOVING ON

About 15 Twelve Mile families discovered that sometimes life moves them out of their comfort zone. The entire upheaval was bittersweet to most. For some it meant no more pesky mosquitoes; no more shoveling snow; no more waiting for the ferry; no more cold winters. Change always comes with a price. Except for the homesteads preserved as Blanket Creek Provincial Park, and Weston's, now Mulvehill Creek Wilderness Retreat, there remains no tangible means for the folks to feel connected to their Twelve Mile roots. Those once uprooted from their homelands overseas, never dreamed they would again be displaced in their new land of freedom.

SOURCES

Atkins, B. R., Affleck, E. L. and Forde, G. B. *Columbia River Chronicles*. Vancouver: The Alexander Nicolls Press, 1977.

B.C. Hydro and Power Authority. *Columbia Newsletter*.

British Columbia Hydro & Power Authority. *Columbia Treaty Projects Property Owners' Guide*. Vancouver: British Columbia Hydro and Power Authority, 1964.

Broadfoot, B. Ten Lost Years 1929-1939: *Memories of Canadians Who Survived the Depression*. Toronto: McClelland & Stewart, 1997.

Clemson, Donovan. "Refugees from Arrow Dam." *The Western Producer* 27 January 1966.

Domke, Asaph. Letter to Herb Domke. 8 November, 1965.

Guest, Dennis. "Family Allowance," *The Canadian Encyclopedia*© Historical Foundation of Canada, available 5/13/2007: http://www.thecanadianencyclopedia.com.

Morton, Val. *Dam Lies*. Canada: self published by author Morton, 2006.

Parent, Milton. *Caulkboot Riverdance (Working the Columbia. Canada s Wildest Log Drive)*. Nakusp, B.C.: Arrow Lakes Historical Society, 2006.

_____. *Circle of Silver*, Vol. 4. Nakusp, B.C.: Arrow Lakes Historical Society, 2001.

_____. *Silent Shores & Sunken Ships*. Nakusp, B.C.: Arrow Lakes Historical Society, 1997.

Revelstoke Herald. Revelstoke Museum Archives. Revelstoke, B.C.

Revelstoke Museum Archives. Revelstoke, B.C.

Revelstoke Review Archives. Revelstoke, B.C.

School District No. 19, Revelstoke, B.C. Archives.

Struthers, J. *No Fault of Their Own: Unemployment and the Canadian Welfare State, 1914-1941*. Toronto: University of Toronto Press, 1983.

Tate, Ken, and Janice Tate, eds. *Good Old Days on the Farm*. Berne, Indiana: House of White Birches, 1996.

Thompson, Joey. "This Land is My Land." *The Province* 18 May 1997.

Waterfield, Donald. *Land Grab, Oliver Buerge versus the Authority*. Toronto/Vancouver: Clarke, Irwin & Company Limited, 1973.

NOTES

NAMES

Families who emigrated to Canada found it necessary to translate the spelling of their surnames into English. For this reason, some of the names have been spelled differently over the years. Oral history included names of people who could not be located and thus their names may be spelled incorrectly. Some families shortened their names. Some changed their names slightly to avoid confusion with another family with the same name.

Astrahantseff was changed to Astra

Dedosenco aka Dedoosenko

Hulyd was changed to Hold by some family members

Kozek was changed from Kozak

Kupchenko may have been Kupchanko

Petrashuk aka Pytrashuk

Ullman may have been Almen or Ulman

Akolkolex River was known as Isaac and Icey Creek

Blanket Creek was known as Gold Creek

Drimmie Creek was known as Twelve Mile Creek and Kaduhr Creek

Echo Lake was known as Twelve Mile Lake and Orchid Lake

Sutherland Falls was known as Gold Creek Falls

ACKNOWLEDGMENTS

Many generously shared time and information to make this book come alive. Special thanks to Toni Johnston and Olympe Astra, who were initial partners in the idea to record Twelve Mile's history.

Walter Kozek, Dorothy Banks Pegues, Sharry Kelly Reynolds and Beverly Weston contributed many invaluable documents.

The following shared pictoral histories and information: Olympe Astra, Dorothy Pegues, Rhonda Bittner, Irma Kaercher, Emma Wood, Nellie Auger, Gloria and Ron Dedosenco, Helen Smith, Rose Camozzi, Sharon Folden, Judy Percy, Rob Deverall, Ted DeVolder, Eugen Domke, Evelyn Riegert, Ben Domke, Herb Domke, Cathy English, Ken English, James Floyd, Barry Camozzi, Russell Gowanlock, Gordon and Karen Gowanlock, Mary Meehan, Peggy Corbett, Ivan Graham, Sam and Betty Olynk, Pete Ozero, Danny Gawiuk, Margaret Jones, Bruce Kaduhr, Lena Kaduhr, Elleanor Klassen, Millie Combatly, Olga Bernard, Lil Robison, Eric Kramer, Donna Lamontagne, Dorothy Lindsay, Phyllis Luschnat, Helga Pennell, Gail Hendrickson, Sheila Makarewicz, Robert Maraun, Judy Walenstein, Diane Visser, Merle Michels, Ken Millar, Lois Masur, Evelyn Garbutt, Alyce Renaud, Terry Burkitt, Helen Toebosch, Pearl Myers, Della Johnson, Florence Johnson, William McLeod, Marla Manson, Mary Lietz, Ann Forlin, Eric Norris, Don Lindley, Claudia Cole, Susy Podzun, Fred and Hans Podzun, Rose Olson, Lorne and Lorna Selden, Tiny Rauchert, Emily Recknell, Genny Wilson, Carolyn Nutton, Bobbie Chabot, Leo Rohde, Karen Vigue, Daryl Tucker, Barbara Flock, Issy Leveille, Minnie and Fred Dowdy, Charleen Zacker, Jerry Story, Valerie Townsend, Val Fitzgerald, Rick Vigue, Sandra Cowley, Wendy Walker, Diane Lang, Harold Catherwood, Doug Mackey, Evelyn Rusenstrom and John Mamchuk.

Revelstoke Times Review generously provided access to newspaper archives and copy services.

Revelstoke Museum provided access to its archives.

Milton Parent and Arrow Lakes Historical Society shared historical documents and information.

Revelstoke School District No. 19 shared archival documents.

Rosemarie Parent and Evelyn Domke Riegert contributed countless editing hours.

Coralee Brown and her writing class provided much helpful input along the way.

Although my husband, Bill, never lived in Twelve Mile, he visited there several times and always held an affinity for that part of the Columbia Valley. He generously shared his writing talents and historical knowledge to fine-tune these chapters. He has also relieved me of my household duties allowing me time to finish this undertaking.

My brother, Eugen, has been my much-needed and appreciated photo and computer consultant and constant support.

I am deeply indebted to Flint Johnston, my technical consultant friends, Karen Hay, Wayne Isaeff and Livieu Imbir, and my son Matthew, who bailed me out of many hair-pulling sessions and mentored me along the high-tech pathway!

Thanks to each of you!

ABOUT THE AUTHOR

Ada Domke Jarvis was raised in a log cabin on her family's homestead in Twelve Mile. She left home after grade nine to attend boarding school because school bus service was not provided for the Twelve Milers. After finishing high school and business college, she was employed in the business world for 15 years. She returned to college and earned a Bachelor of Science degree in occupational therapy from Loma Linda University.

Since retiring from occupational therapy in 2001, she has had time to pursue her interests in art and writing. Although Ada lives in Loma Linda, California with her husband, Bill, and their two sons, she and her family spend several months of each year at their vacation home in Revelstoke, B.C.

Ada has also authored two editions of *Huckleberries for All*, available through Grizzly Books in Revelstoke, B.C.